Analysis in Human Resource Training and Organization Development

ANALYSIS
in Human Resource Training
and Organization Development

GORDON E. MILLS,
R. WAYNE PACE, AND
BRENT D. PETERSON

Addison-Wesley Publishing Company, Inc.
Reading, Massachusetts   Menlo Park, California   New York
Don Mills, Ontario   Wokingham, England   Amsterdam
Bonn   Sydney   Singapore   Tokyo   Madrid   San Juan

Library of Congress Cataloging-in-Publication Data
Mills, Gordon E.,
    Analysis in human resource training and organization
development / Gordon E. Mills, R. Wayne Pace,
and Brent D. Peterson.
        p.   cm.
    Bibliography: p.
    Includes index.
    ISBN 0-201-09224-7
    1. Employees, Training of.   2. Organizational
change.   I. Pace, R. Wayne.   II. Peterson, Brent D.
III. Title.
HF5549.5.T7M55   1988   658.3'124 — dc19   88-14046

Figure on p. 161 courtesy of Pitney Bowes Inc.

Sponsoring editor, Scott Shershow
Production coordinator, Lynne Reed
Cover design by Copenhaver Cumpston
Text design by Joyce C. Weston
Set in 10½/13 point Palatino by Compset, Inc., Beverly, MA

ISBN 0-201-09224-7
ABCDEFGHIJ-HA-89
First printing, February 1989

CONTENTS

FIGURES AND TABLES

PREFACE

Writing a book can be both an individual and a group experience, and it is especially interesting for a group of authors with diverse learning and teaching styles. This book is a melding not only of authors' styles but also of the content of many fields and disciplines.

Analysis was written to meet a gap in the literature of human resource and organization development focusing specifically on the early stage of information and data gathering on which solid solutions and interventions are based. It was prepared to help generate data bases from which rational and proactive decisions can be made.

Analysis was written for the teacher, student, and practitioner in all disciplines and in all organizations involved in the process of documenting concerns. The skills of problem solving learned here transfer well to analyzing personal issues and can be useful throughout one's life.

Analysis contains a model of the process of analysis that provides a systematic way of looking at and organizing materials. It contains specific details about how to use methods and analytical tools, and it includes sample copies of inventories, questionnaires, forms, and other instruments. Instructions on scoring and interpreting the information are provided.

Analysis is grounded in principles and theory, but it is practical and applied. The procedures are drawn from real life, while most of the instruments have been tested in the classroom and laboratory and used in organizations.

Analysis was created out of our need for a text to prepare professionals to understand and use analytical methods to diagnose gaps in how individuals and systems perform and function. Our students in human resource development at Brigham Young University in Provo, Utah, and Laie, Hawaii, comprising a cross-section of scholars from Pacific Rim countries, mainland U.S.A., South America, Scandinavia, Europe, Great Britain, and Africa, have used the materials with consistent and gratifying success.

Analysis can be used in diverse disciplines and by those who do analysis in organizations of all kinds. Students at all levels in the university should find the content, methods, and style suitable. The same is true for professionals coming from a variety of work settings.

This book has not been produced without a significant commitment of time, and we wish to acknowledge and thank our families, friends, colleagues, administrators, and students for making this possible. Without the encouragement of loved ones and associates, the struggle truly might not be worth the costs. Without the challenges posed by inquiring minds in the classroom and curious faculty in the hallways, the changes and modifications might never have occurred. Without the trips to ASTD conferences, we might not have had important messages and visited quite so long about such issues as analysis. Without the HRD Professors Network, we might not have seen the vision, and we might have faltered and fallen too soon.

And for some, without Hawaii, we might have missed the beach, the sun, and the inspiration.

Gordon E. Mills, Spanish Fork, Utah
R. Wayne Pace, Laie, Hawaii, and Orem, Utah
Brent D. Peterson, Orem, Utah

Analysis in Human Resource Training and Organization Development

1. Becoming Analytical: An Introduction

Few scholars or practitioners disagree on the importance of analysis in laying the foundation for making changes in human resource attitudes, information, and skills, and for changing the functioning of the organization. Although there appears to be a fairly high degree of consensus on the importance of analysis, how to become analytical seems to be more of a mystery.

Value

Knowing how to conduct analyses of several different types provides the human resource development professional with a broad range of tools and increases the strength with which the entire training and development program converges on its goals. Too often the reasons why one should design a program to change human resources and organizational functioning are quite offhand, and even more often are a bit obscure. Being able to identify clearly *who* or *what* ought to be upgraded, and *what kinds* of changes should be made to accomplish the goals of the organization and the people in it, gives confidence to both the management of the organization and the human resource training and development staff.

This introduction describes the analytical function and suggests how thinking analytically can facilitate behaving in an analytical way. A model of analysis is explained, and five sources of information derived from an analysis in human resource training and organization development are identified.

1

Objectives

At the conclusion of this chapter, you will be able to do the following:

- Define the concept of analysis and cite three values of conducting an analysis.
- Explain why symbolic or mental practice helps one acquire the skills involved in doing an analysis.
- Diagram, define, and explain the main features of each of the five points or stages in a model of analysis.
- List five sources of information usually available for making an analysis in human resource training and organization development.

Thinking Analytically

Effective analysis is vital to the selection of appropriate interventions for bringing about change in people or organizations. Too often, it seems, training and development decisions are made on the basis of what someone else did, or what happens to be in vogue at the time, or what an executive heard about at a conference. On the other hand, what we do should be tied to where we are going. Analysis, at least as we are presenting the concept here, represents a way of thinking about human resources and organizations that enables and empowers analysts to recognize, document, and justify making decisions about what ought to be taking place in human resource training and organization development.

The analytical function has become more sophisticated over the years, with the creation of interesting and effective analytical tools, instruments, and methods, as well as some models of the entire process. Since becoming analytical is such an important part of what most people are trying to do in their lives anyway, to bring together all of the materials on analysis seems to be a worthwhile goal. Thus this book does more than just describe how to do a needs analysis or a task analysis. It does more than look at performance problems. This book helps you *become analytical*, especially at work, but also at home and at play.

The methods of analysis are very important. Without a way to do analysis, you may have a tough time becoming analytical.

However, *thinking analytically* and *feeling analytically,* as well as *doing analytically,* all provide the foundation for *being analytical.* Paraphrasing Harless (1974), "an ounce of analysis may be worth a pound of intervention."

How we think about something — our perceptual set — has a powerful effect on how we feel and what we do. Orne (1962), for example, reports that just telling people that "this is an experiment" may have an interesting effect on what they do. He notes that if you go up to a stranger and say something like "Lie down," the stranger usually just laughs or gets out of there as fast as possible. On the other hand, if you preface your request with the statement "This is an experiment" and then say "Lie down," more often than not the person does as asked, as long as there are other environmental cues that support the request.

Obviously, the person who is told that "this is an experiment" must have some idea as to what an experiment involves and what the proper behavior for someone participating in an experiment is before he or she will do what you ask. The statement, by itself, is usually not enough, but it triggers an "associative network" of ideas that do influence behavior.

Those who study language recognize that the symbolic nature of thought processes enables thoughts to occur anytime, anyplace, and in any setting; thought processes can be applied to whatever a person is doing. Thoughts can be generalized more readily than actions. Thoughts are also stopped less easily than actions. For example, you may have heard the story of the king who was promised that he could have any wish he wanted as long as he never *thought* of the left eye of a camel. It goes without saying that the king did not get his wish; however, he might have met the conditions easily if they had involved not looking at the left eye of a camel.

Thought sequences are simply harder to control voluntarily than *action sequences.* You may learn to operate a machine, type on a keyboard, shoot baskets, dance, or swim, and with relative ease you can also avoid *doing* any or all of these things. On the other hand, it is not as easy to stop *thinking* about something once you have learned what is involved in a process. For example, motor learning experiments (Hovland 1951) have demonstrated that symbolic or mental rehearsal facilitates actual performance of the motor skills. It appears that mentally rehearsing actions instead of just going through physical actions, produces a form of "muscle memory" that allows you to perform the task better.

Mental Models = Ways of Thinking

A mental model is simply a way of thinking about things. Using the example above, to produce the muscle memory of a physical or motor activity, the imaginative processes or the way the mind goes through the steps needs to be the same as the way the muscles would go through the steps. The mental pattern is the same as the physical pattern, allowing the mind to produce a trace or memory in the muscles.

When a mental activity or pattern is very similar to a physical activity or pattern, we refer to them as being analogous. When the mental pattern has little similarity to the real world or that which is actually to be done or is being done, we refer to them as being dissimilar or nonanalogous. In either case, the mental activity or pattern is called a *model*.

Model of Analysis

A mental model helps facilitate the way a person thinks about something (Hawes 1975, 126–143); it also, as pointed out above, helps establish a memory of the way things should be done. The more accurate the model, the better will be the way a person thinks about something. A model of analysis can increase both the quality of our thinking about analysis and the way we conduct analyses.

The important issue is that the model represent as accurately as possible the actual process we are trying to think about. In this case, we are attempting to model the process of analysis; thus we shall present a *model of analysis,* not just a model of some aspect of analysis, such as a model of performance, or a model of a task, or a model of individual perceptions, or a model of organizational functioning, or a model of files procedures. With such a model, we shall have a systematic way of thinking about analysis and how to conduct an analysis.

The rest of this introduction will be devoted to defining the concept of analysis and explaining and portraying a model of analysis.

Definition of Analysis

Analysis is defined as the act and process of separating any material or abstract entity into its constituent elements, which involves determining its essential features and their relations to one another. An analysis provides a description of how something or someone is functioning or behaving or performing. From the analysis, one should be able to recognize strengths and weaknesses in what is happening and, eventually, to take corrective actions that will upgrade the person and/or the organization.

Analysis is grounded in the philosophy of problem solving. Problem solving is widely understood as the process of recognizing differences between what is occurring and what we would like to have occur, and devising ways to narrow the gap between the two (Patton and Giffin 1973, 141). We often talk about the gap between what we have and what we would like as a deficiency.

Analysis involves all of the activities associated with recognizing the existence of a problem (differences between what is happening and what we would like to have happen) and its causes and consequences, and classifying the problem in terms of what kinds of interventions might reasonably be used to narrow the gap.

The five stages in a model of analysis may be listed as follows:

Stage 1: Point of Concern
Stage 2: Point of Documentation
Stage 3: Point of Preference
Stage 4: Point of Comparison
Stage 5: Point of Determination

We shall briefly characterize each of these stages here and provide more detailed explanations throughout the book.

Stage 1: Point of Concern

Most organizational activity has some historical roots. A drop in productivity represents, for example, a movement in time from one level of production to another, lower one. Most of the time it is difficult for a newcomer to understand an organization as well as a person with a longer history in it understands it. Information about what has happened in the past may be highly revealing about what precipitated a change.

Analysis is frequently provoked by a sense that something seems wrong, that what has been done historically is now producing consequences that appear different and undesirable. If what has been happening in the past seems to have positive results, it is unlikely that much analysis will occur, even simple and informal analysis, much less complex, in-depth, and detailed analysis.

In the process of living and working in an organization, there almost always occurs some point of concern that triggers interest in analysis, in identifying a problem and its sources, causes, and effects. Most of the time, the point of concern is subtle; things just seem to feel a bit different from how they have felt in the past. In any case, the first stage in analysis is the feeling that there is something about which we are concerned.

Stage 2: Point of Documentation

Once a concern has been sensed, the next stage is to provide some documentation for the concern. This phase is often the most critical activity in the entire process; it often calls upon and involves not only HRD staff but also outside consultants. People interested in analysis must document their concerns if they are to be believed and have a basis for proceeding to subsequent stages.

Documentation involves gathering information about what is happening now in the organization, as well as what may have happened in the past. Most analyses focus on one or more of the five sources of information:

1. *Files* or existing documents possessed by the organization.
2. *Task* or the job itself and how it is supposed to be done.
3. *Needs* or perceptions of organization members and how they feel about their work and the organization.
4. *Performance* or how members of the organization actually carry out their duties, task, and assignments.
5. *Organization* or objectives, resources, allocations, and the total socioeconomic-technological environment within which the organization exists.

A files analysis focuses on the organization's policies, plans, organization charts, and position descriptions; employee grievance, absenteeism, and accident reports; records of meetings and program evaluation studies; attitude surveys and budget reports. The files are examined for indications of gaps and circumstances that appear to interfere with optimal task performance.

A task analysis involves the methods of instructional and job design, and examines what activities constitute the task, how they are to be performed, and what skills, knowledge, and attitudes one must have to perform the tasks. Clinical observations are also used to verify how tasks are done while employees are working on the job.

A needs analysis (focusing on individual employees' perceptions) is probably the most widely used approach. Employees complete questionnaires and participate in interviews, both individual and group, to report how they feel about what needs to be done to narrow the gap.

A performance analysis (focusing on the reactions of third-party observers, such as supervisors) consists of evaluating the quality of employee performance, mostly through third-party judgments and appraisals. A wide variety of employee performance procedures and methods are available for use in conducting a performance analysis.

An organizational systems analysis develops in a way similar to a needs analysis, since survey questionnaires, direct observations, and interviews are probably the most common ways of gathering data about the organization as a whole (Schein 1969, 98). A systems analysis tends to focus on systems-wide variables, such as climate, leadership, cooperation, group decision making, role relationships, and productivity.

Once data have been gathered that provide some documentation of the concern felt in stage 1, we must turn our attention to the next stage.

Stage 3: Point of Preference

The third stage in analysis involves the development of a "normative prescription" (Lawrence and Lorsch 1969, 19) indicating what kinds of behaviors and organizational functioning are preferred. Preferences do not always represent those that may be best for the employees and the organization, but they do represent the guidelines that will be used to determine whether anyone feels there is a problem worth doing something about.

Preferences should be turned into guidelines against which the documentation can later be compared. The purpose of the guidelines is to help locate differences between a situation in which there are no problems and the situation being analyzed. The preferred, ideal situation, principles, or notions help direct the analyst's thinking about what kind of performance, behavior, or organizational practices ought to be expected.

Stage 4: Point of Comparison

This stage involves coming to grips with the definition of a problem and arriving at a statement of the problem or problems. The point of comparison attempts to determine whether the documented concerns represent human resource and organization practices that deviate in any significant way from the preferences and guidelines established as the best fit for developing organization and employee goals. The documentation of concern has provided a description of how things are functioning, while the preferences set the goals for change.

The point-of-comparison stage is where we attempt to determine which concerns should be attacked in order to develop the human resources and the organization so as to achieve the goals. If both the documentation of concerns and the preferences are clear, differences may be easy to recognize as definitely detrimental to the organization; if there is some ambiguity or uncertainty, critical differences may be more difficult to identify and clearly describe, making problem identification a more challenging task.

Stage 5: Point of Determination

The fifth stage in the analytical process involves determining what kind of problem or gap exists in the organization. A truism suggests that the types of problems or gaps identified tend to correlate with the types of documentation used. It is a little bit like owning a great hammer: if your only tool is the hammer, everything looks like a nail. To reduce the hammer-nail syndrome, we like to use triangulation, or the cross-checking of gap areas by using several different methods. If you have information from a variety of instruments and techniques, chances are that you will reveal real problems and gaps rather than idiosyncratic or peculiar ones tied to a single analytical method.

Three types of gaps tend to occur: (1) *performance gaps*, deficiencies in the way employees carry out or execute their assignments and duties; (2) *management gaps*, deficiencies in the way in which people are managed and motivated in the organization; and (3) *organization gaps*, deficiencies in the way an organization is conceived and designed.

Each of these three types of gaps has its own methods and techniques for reducing, minimizing, or eliminating the differences. Performance gaps are usually reduced through the methods of training and development. Management gaps are usually resolved through changes in management practices. Organization gaps are usually alleviated through the procedures of organization development. The careful classification of gaps and problems confronting the organization can lead to more powerful methods and strategies for solving problems.

The model of the analytical process just described is portrayed in figure 1.1.

Figure 1.1 Model of Analysis

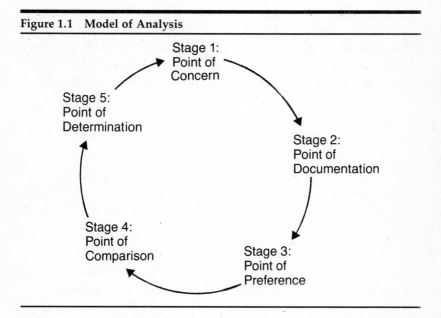

Summary

Analysis was defined as the act and process of separating any material or entity into its constituent elements, and determining its essential features and their relations to one another. Analysis provides the tools and methods for identifying clearly who or what ought to be improved and what kinds of changes ought to occur. It was pointed out that the process of becoming analytical is facilitated by using a model to think analytically. Because of the symbolic nature of the thought processes, thoughts are generalized more readily than actions and they are stopped less easily. Thus, if you can begin to think in a way consistent with the model of analysis, your thoughts will aid you in behaving more analytically. A model of the process of analysis involving five stages was presented: Stage 1, Point of Concern; Stage 2, Point of Determination; Stage 3, Point of Preference; Stage 4, Point of Comparison; and Stage 5, Point of Determination.

Remainder of Book

The remainder of this book is an explanation and demonstration of how each step in the model of analysis is implemented and actually conducted. Specific instructions are given for understanding and using a wide range of analytical methods, instruments, tools, and techniques associated with a variety of approaches to analysis and basic types of analysis.

Activity

Thinking analytically is grounded in problem solving. Consider an area where you are not doing as well as you would like to and want to do better. List this concern.

Concern: _____

Step 1: As you look at the concern, state what you are now doing, and what you would like to be doing, on this issue.

CURRENTLY DOING

1. _____

2. _____

3. _____

SHOULD BE DOING

1. _____

2. _____

3. _____

Step 2: As you look at the differences between statements on the left and right, see if you can quantify the difference between the two performances. This statement is the gap or deficiency.

Step 3: Classify the consequences of the gap or deficiency you have noted in step two. Usually, these will appear as a loss or a benefit not realized.

Step 4: List some possible steps you could take to correct this situation.

Step 5: Begin the process of implementing the change by developing a plan. In the plan, set time lines for the changes to occur, list the support you will need from all people to make the change, and list any material or resources that would be helpful to carry it out.

Time Line: _____

_____

Cooperation of others: _____

_____

Resources: _____

_____

Step 6: After implementation, evaluate the impact of the change.

References

Harless, J. H. 1974. *An Ounce of Analysis*. McClean, Va.: Harless Performance Guide.

Hawes, Leonard C. 1975. "Models: Their Structure, Substances, and Types." In *Pragmatics of Analoging*. Reading, Mass.: Addison-Wesley.

Hovland, C. I. 1951. "Human Learning and Retention." In S. S. Stevens (ed.), *Handbook of Experimental Psychology*. New York: John Wiley.

Lawrence, Paul R. and Jay W. Lorsch. 1969. *Developing Organizations: Diagnosis and Action*. Reading, Mass.: Addison-Wesley.

Orne, M. 1962. "On the Social Psychology of the Psychological Experiment: With Particular Reference to Demand Characteristics and Their Implications," *American Psychologist*, 17: 776–783.

Patton, Bobby R. and Kim Giffin. 1973. *Problem-Solving Group Interaction*. New York: Harper & Row.

Schein, Edgar H. 1969. *Process Consultation: Its Role in Organization Development*. Menlo Park, Calif.: Addison-Wesley.

2. Stage 1: Recognizing a Point of Concern

A human resource problem represents a person who is not doing as well as someone feels the person should be. An organizational problem represents an organization that is not doing as well as someone thinks it should be. A need to make an analysis is usually provoked by a "trigger point" centered in the feeling of someone that things are not going too well. We often refer to these concerns as a "hurt," relying on a physiological or medical analogy. A hurt is one of those points of concern that impel us to take some type of analytical action.

Value

When things are not going as you feel they should, and you have a sluggish feeling that progress and success are a bit further away today than yesterday, you can react with lethargy and hope that things will get better by themselves. You can also try to help by focusing your senses on potential sources of difficulty and concentrating on understanding what is bothering you. If you are sensitive to the differences between what you have got and where you ought to be, you have the basic conditions that lead to becoming analytical.

Chapter Organization

This chapter deals with the first stage in the analytical process—point of concern. The concept of concern is defined, how to recognize concerns of two different orders is described, and sources of concern are identified and explained. A distinction is made between symptoms and consequences as indicators of concerns. Some suggestions for preventing concerns from developing are offered. Finally, a plan is proposed for how to organize your resources to respond to concerns and to move to the documentation stage.

Objectives

At the conclusion of this chapter, you will be able to do the following:

- Explain what is meant by a "concern."
- Distinguish between "reactive" and "proactive" approaches to recognition of concerns.
- List nine sources of concerns in organizations.
- Distinguish between "symptoms" and "consequences" as indicators of concerns.
- Outline a plan for organizing your resources to respond to critical concerns and to move to the documentation stage in the analysis process.

Definition of a Concern

When you think of a "concern," particularly in the context of analysis, your mind should focus quickly on something that affects a person's welfare or happiness. Often a concern is recognized as a "worry," or an activity that seems to provoke a degree of anxiety. In other instances, a concern is reflected in a nagging desire or urge to do something better, to achieve more than is currently being done. A concern, thus, is a disquieting interest, engagement, or involvement in some aspect of one's environment that provokes a caring about what is happening.

In some ways, a concern is simply the way you feel about the situation or circumstances you are experiencing or observing. A concern is often associated with some frustration associated with the way our goals are being accomplished. More often than not, the term *concern* connotes or implies a negative feeling, although the direction of the concern, most of the time, is toward doing something better. If you have a concern, it usually means that you want to do better, to improve the way things are being done, but you are experiencing some degree of frustration in doing it.

Reactive Versus Proactive Approach

Two general approaches to thinking about concerns are common: reactive and proactive. A reactive point of view is one that looks at the way human resources or the organization are currently functioning and defines a problem after-the-fact. That is, a problem is defined as anything that deviates from the usual way of doing things. If the person or the organization seems to be going along just fine, no problem exists; as soon as the person or organization shows signs of functioning differently from before, a problem may be developing.

A proactive approach to problem definition is one in which the analyst attempts to recognize deviations from the potential that could be achieved. A problem is conceived as the difference between what we are doing now and what we could or ought to be doing. What is happening now may not be adequate for a proactive analyst, even though what is happening now may meet minimal requirements. The idea of "what ought to be happening" is one of projecting into the future and picturing something better than what we have now. Analysis, from a proactive point of view, is an effort to visualize better ways of doing things. A problem is the difference between the better way and the way something is being done now.

A reactive point of view leads a person to wait until a deviation from the usual way of operating occurs before a problem is defined. A proactive point of view leads a person to create a picture of the future that is better than what is happening and to define a problem as the difference between what the vision of the future could mean and what is happening now.

Figure 2.1 portrays the difference between a reactive problem definition and a proactive problem definition. The line of performance where no concern exists (baseline) is the point from which we view deviations in both cases. However, the proactive point of view projects a line above the "no concern" baseline and suggests

Figure 2.1   Problem Definition from Two Different Perspectives

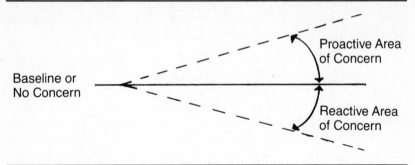

that we have a problem if we are not already accomplishing things or doing things better than what is occurring at the baseline. The reactive point of view takes the "no concern" baseline as a satisfactory state of affairs or even a desirable state of affairs and looks for deviations that dip below the baseline.

Innovative, creative human resource and organization development analysts attempt to locate problems that involve projections of the future and how the resolution of those problems lead employees and the company to do better. Nevertheless, reactive problem analysis often provides information of great value to the development of human resources and the organization. Succeeding chapters that deal with the documentation of concerns present methods, techniques, procedures, and instruments that can be used in both proactive and reactive problem documentation. The method of documentation may be more or less useful depending on the mind-set of the analyst who is attempting to define the problem and the manager or executive who needs to understand the kinds of problems that exist in organizations.

Sources of Concern

In an abstract way, a concern is the perception of some difference between what we are doing or what is happening and the way we would like to be doing something or have things done. Concerns tend to exist in people's minds: that an employee comes to work at 9:30 A.M. is not necessarily the basis for concern; the concern depends on whether the time the employee arrives is consistent with what we would like to have happen. I may have a concern, but my boss may not. The sources of concern lie in our expectations of what is acceptable, preferred, and desirable. A concern, in that case, finds its source in how we think about ourselves, our jobs, and what we would like to accomplish.

To have a concern means that we recognize a difference between what we are doing and what we ought to be doing. If you like to have things continue as they are, you should have few concerns, unless it appears to you that things are beginning to change and you would like them to stay the same. The principle is the same: a deviation from what you would like is occurring. Either a change is occurring when you do not want it, or a change is not occurring when you think it should. In both instances, you have the basis for a concern. If things are consistent with what you would like, you should have no concerns.

In a general sense, anything can be of concern. Some people become "paranoid" (they think that everybody is trying to change things to their detriment) because they are overconcerned about things that may not be important. Although it is somewhat difficult to decide what is important and what is unimportant for any particular person, the constant preoccupation with things that a large proportion of other employees feels are unimportant may be a sign that one's concerns are unfounded. On the other hand, just because five thousand other people are not concerned does not indicate that the concern is illegitimate. Most of the time, a concern should be considered reasonable and appropriate if it moves employees and the organization toward doing better than they are at the moment.

Concerns are tied closely to one's concept of "doing better." Let us look at what we mean by doing better. In its most obvious sense, doing better suggests that a person performs at a level that exceeds what he or she did on that same task at an earlier time. If I do better on the company softball team, that means that I have improved my statistics in some respect. If I do better at batting, that implies that I have hit the ball more often, or more accurately, or with greater distance, or in a more artistic manner. If I have a concern, I, at least, recognize where I can do better.

In its less obvious sense, doing better implies being able to recognize, visualize, and describe what type of activity, performance, behavior, or change would be an improvement. That is, before I can actually do better, I need to have some vision of what "better" looks like. If I were to change, would my actions represent a performance or activity that moves me in a positive way beyond what I am doing now to something that is better?

Recognizing a concern means recognizing those goals and objectives that help us do better. What are some of the terms that represent positive goals and objectives associated with acts of doing better? In general, when we talk about things like *reducing confusion*, we are thinking of a goal that may lead us to do better. In other words, confusion is not a particularly desirable condition, and if we can reduce confusion, we have done better. The amount of confusion that we can reduce determines how much better we can do. We are on the way to doing better when we *improve the rate* at which we complete a task, or *reduce the number of errors* involved in performing a job. We may also do better by *providing a larger number of positive responses* to someone. We also do better when we make things more convenient or accessible, when we make something more enjoyable to do or easier to do, or when we arrange for things to be done more smoothly.

Other terms that refer to personal concern are: inattentive, indecisive, cluttered, messy, reluctant, out of place, unclean, worn out, boring, stubborn, loud, uncooperative, inconsiderate, not working, uncomfortable, lack of privacy, disrespect, and confining.

In organizations, a number of events signal changing conditions that may raise concerns. If you recognize these conditions, you may be sensitive to concerns:

- A climate in the organization that has shifted away from one that encourages productivity and doing better.
- A managerial philosophy that discourages open communication.
- Organization ground rules, norms, and power structure that stifle creativity and independence.
- A department that does not seem to be appropriately organized.
- Colleagues and other employees who seem to lack motivation.
- Groups within the company that are devoting too much time and energy to inappropriate competition.
- Crude, unsophisticated, and somewhat ineffective long-range planning in the organization.

Developing a sensitivity to personal and organizational concerns requires a constant effort to examine ways of doing things better.

Summary

In this chapter we have defined and characterized the idea of *recognizing a point of concern* as the basis for moving to the documentation stage in the process of analysis.

Activity

List another concern or area where you are not doing as well as you would like. This is something you want to do better than you are doing now.

Concern: _____

Follow steps 1 and 2 of the problem-solving approach listed in the activity section of chapter 1 (contrast what you are doing with the preferred way and classify where the differences or gaps are).

Look at step 3 of the process (consequences of the gap) and determine what outcomes may occur if you are reactive rather than proactive in responding to the concern.

REACTIVE	PROACTIVE
1. _____	1. _____
2. _____	2. _____
3. _____	3. _____
4. _____	4. _____

During this comparison, you may see that dealing with the process of planning and taking corrective action for change (step 4) for the reactive concerns is usually crisis driven. Proactive usually allows for more time to ponder and look at alternatives when planning the intervention.

3. Stage 2: Documenting A Concern

Many times people in an organization feel that something is wrong or that the organization is not meeting the employees' or stakeholders' expectations. At other times it may be an individual employee or the corporation itself that seems to be "hurting." This hurt is what motivates people or organizations to do research to document what is causing the concern and determine what might be done to correct the situation. Thus the documentation process includes the methods used to gather information upon which effective decisions are based to correct the situation and allow those involved to do better.

This chapter focuses on a variety of ideas that are based on the philosophy of documentation and the concerns that are present when information is collected for decision-making purposes.

Value

Of the five stages of the analysis process represented in chapter 1, documentation is the most important because it represents the working data base from which the other stages work. Without accurate documentation, the analysis process fails.

The compelling issue behind documentation is accuracy. The emphasis in this stage of analysis is on collecting accurate data. Too often the entire documentation process is based on one or two interviews and a few assumptions. For example, an interview with a disgruntled subordinate, who is mad at the boss, may present the impression that the boss is causing a great deal of trouble.

By interviewing all the employees of this boss, a revised impression is very likely and may indicate that the boss is doing well. In contrast, the real problem might be the first disgruntled employee interviewed. To complete an effective analysis, accurate information must be obtained. This requires using as many sources and different documentation approaches as possible. Accurate documentation is the foundation of strong analysis. Inaccurate documentation is the beginning of a series of problems that can lead to more difficulties than the original concern.

Objectives

At the conclusion of this chapter, you will be able to do the following:

• Define documentation and state its value in analysis.
• List seven key documentation considerations to make when doing the documentation process.
• Define and differentiate between validity and reliability.
• List some basic questions to ask when evaluating data-gathering instruments.
• Discuss the value of using both objective and subjective methods to gather information during documentation.

Definition of Documentation

Documentation is the process of gathering information about what is happening now in the organization, as well as what may have happened in the past regarding the specific concern being analyzed. To document a concern accurately, a variety of methods and procedures is used. Each documentation situation is different, and using a variety of procedures to provide the proper information will always be more helpful than that generated from just one source. It is recommended that you use two or more of the following procedures when documenting a concern:

1. Files Analysis. This procedure focuses on collecting data about the organization's policies, plans, organization charts, position descriptions; employee grievance, absenteeism, and acci-

dent reports; records of meetings and program evaluation studies; attitude surveys and budget reports. The idea behind a files analysis is to look for indications that reveal information that help document a concern.

2. Task Analysis. This procedure involves the methods of instructional and job design, and examines what activities constitute the task, how they are to be performed, and what skills, knowledge, and attitudes one must have to perform the tasks. Again, this approach is used to help isolate data regarding a specific concern.

3. Performance Analysis. This procedure consists of evaluating the quality of employee performance, mostly through third-party judgments and appraisals.

4. Needs Analysis. This procedure focuses on employees' completing questionnaires and participating in interviews, both individual and group, to report how they feel about what needs to be done regarding a concern. This is probably the most widely used documentation approach.

5. Organizational Systems Analysis. This procedure tends to focus on systemswide variables, such as climate, leadership, cooperation, group decision making, role relationships, and productivity. It is similar to needs analysis in that it, too, uses questionnaires and interviews in documenting concerns.

In sum, documentation is the gathering of information about what is now happening and what has happened in the organization using a variety of documentation approaches.

Seven Key Documentation Considerations

While there is a variety of ways to document concerns, any of those used should pass through a review process and be evaluated using seven key documentation considerations. These are listed below:

1. Eliminate Personal Bias

Starting with a preconceived notion of what you will find has its perils. While this is more easily said than done, it is none the less imperative. All of us tend to carry a great many perceptions and feelings regarding the organization and its problems. These perceptions can cause us to miss the actual concern or problem and narrow our focus to issues that are symptomatic rather than causal in nature. An example might be illustrative.

Organizational Associates was hired to analyze a company based on the perceptions of the owner. The owner had pondered his organization on many occasions and determined he knew exactly what was wrong. The owner's intent was clear: hire a consultant and have him or her point out to his employees what was wrong with them. Unlike the owner, the consultant had no bias and began the documentation procedure. At the conclusion of the documentation, the concern identified was not that of the owner; rather, it centered in problems associated with his leadership style. While this finding was troublesome to the owner, it nonetheless provided accurate information on the concern that was causing the "hurt" for this particular company. Had the bias been accepted and acted upon, the problem would likely have been missed.

A caution is offered. There is a tendency, when analysts try to operate free of a bias, to function too objectively and unenthusiastically. Consequently, many of the important issues of subjectivity are squelched in the process. Temper the need to remove all bias with the suggestion of Fred N. Kerlinger (1983, vii–viii) in the preface to his book *Foundations of Behavioral Research:*

> It may seem strange in a book on research that I talk about interest, enthusiasm, and passionate commitment. Shouldn't we be objective? Yes, of course. But more important is to somehow catch the essential quality of the excitement of discovery that comes from research well done. What I am trying to say is that strong subjective involvement is a powerful motivator for acquiring an objective approach to the study of phenomena. I would encourage students to discuss, argue, debate, and even fight about research. Take a stand. Be opinionated. Later, try to soften the opinionation into intelligent conviction and controlled emotional commitment.

Often that commitment to rigorous documentation is motivated by the concern we carry in our perception of the problem. Forcing ourselves to be as bias-free as possible is sound advice; however, we should complement our approach with intelligent consideration of the issue.

2. *Keep Accurate Records*

Accurately record all data, regardless of the approach used in documentation. This is as important and imperative as remaining objective. If you are interviewing an employee, for example, it is crucial to quote the employee correctly and to record all needed bits of data he or she presents. Inaccurate data or unrecorded data can lead to many wrong conclusions regarding a concern. Accuracy goes far beyond the interview; accuracy is needed in all aspects of documentation. Using a questionnaire, a card sort technique, a nominal group process, or a files analysis requires rigorous attention to detail. Double-check the data and make certain you have recorded all pertinent information properly. Excluding critical information causes as many problems as inaccurately recording the data.

3. *Verify Sources of Information*

Verifying the sources from which you received or gathered the data is crucial to the documentation process. For example, if you are conducting interviews in a bank and want to obtain customer reaction to a bank policy, make certain that you interview only customers. Often, to get the documentation stage finished, we ask anyone who comes into the bank what they feel. Verify and make certain that the sources of the data are those that meet the standard you have set.

When reviewing records during files analysis, it is important to cite the source document properly and attribute the information to the respective individual. Data are meaningful only if we understand correctly who said what, when, and where. Often the analyst forgets to document these matters properly, and when reviewing the data later is unable to provide the proper attributions. In sum, verify, keep track of, and certify the authenticity of the analysis participants.

4. *Always Use a Variety of Documentation Methods*

In the classic story "The Parable of the Blind Men and the Elephant," John Godfrey Saxe (1968) describes six blind men who individually documented their perceptions of what an elephant is through touching different parts of the beast; each offered an observation that was correct in part. Through this single documentation, each blind man classified what an elephant is. The elephant was described as a fan (ear), rope (tail), snake (trunk), tree (leg), wall (side), and spear (tusk). In a like sense, one documentation tool may well create a single perspective. While not blind, an analyst can still make a similar mistake when he or she narrows the alternatives for documenting the concern. If you want to establish an accurate point of view, use a variety of viewpoints (methods) to gain this added dimension.

A questionnaire is a very good method for obtaining information regarding attitudinal data on a specific subject. However, questionnaires rarely gives respondents an opportunity to say what they really feel. Frequently, respondents indicate the questionnaire was fine but that it did not allow them to talk about their true feelings because they were forced to answer questions on a scale, through a true or false statement, or multiple choices. Indictments like this seem to indicate that more and better data could be obtained by using both a questionnaire and an interview.

The more analysis work you do, the more you will become aware of the importance of selecting appropriate documentation approaches. The people in a specific organization might respond better to a card sort than a questionnaire or to a critical incident approach than an interview. On the other hand, the use of all four of these approaches will probably work better than any single approach. We are constantly reminded of a group of illiterate custodial staff employees who could not read our questionnaire but were very able to respond to our interviews. In sum, always use as many approaches as possible and your documentation data will always be more accurate.

5. Confirm, Check, and Recheck All Facts

Although this activity is a key part of the second consideration listed above — keeping accurate records — it is reiterated here. Excellent data have a high premium; the increased cost comes from detailing dates, facts, places, and any other specifics relating to the data being collected. If you misplace dates and places, the data can become less than meaningful very quickly. This is particularly important if data are collected at more than one time or in more than one location.

6. Formalize Procedures and Methods That Others Can Follow and Duplicate

There is a tendency when doing documentation to make it a "one-time approach." When doing research, formalize the procedures and methods used so that others can use your approach in the future or follow-up studies. This is extremely important. In detailing your approach, complete at least these two steps:

• Write a complete description, as if you were writing a journal. Begin with the very first thing you did in your study and include a description of every step in your documentation process until you have definitively described everything you did. This should be written in such detail that a person who has never seen your approach can complete a documentation similar to yours.
• After you have finished your description, attach a copy of all instruments and interview guides that you included in your study. The reason for this is to help others who wish to replicate your study or need to do a follow-up.

7. Be Flexible and Adaptable

Doing these types of analyses is a bit different from doing scholarly experimental research. When collecting data or doing documentation in organizations, there are many variables that are difficult to anticipate. Consequently, control as many variables as you can and use a number of approaches. This will allow you to make more accurate inferences and predictions from your documentation, and subsequently make fewer mistakes.

Adapting to change will be essential; the dynamics of many organizations necessitate that you respond to new and varied situations. Do not be locked into a procedure at the expense of collecting helpful data.

The Question of Reliability and Validity

When making a decision on the methods to use in documentation, consider two additional dimensions: (1) is the method you use going to provide reliable information, and (2) how valid will it be?

These two questions are central to both experimental research and documentation efforts. In brief, reliability deals with how accurate the instrument is in making the measurement. Validity looks to the end results of measurement and deals with the issue, Are we really measuring what we think we are measuring (Leedy 1983)?

It is critical to select instruments that are reliable (consistent, predictable, and accurate). In addition, they must produce valid information (measure what it claims to measure).

When selecting instruments, it is recommended that you look for instruments that have reliability information accompanying them. The reason for this suggestion is the issue of time. Too often you are asked to do an analysis where little or no time line has been given to do the field testing required to produce a highly reliable instrument. If you must develop your own instrument without this time benefit, you must be willing to accept the fact that it might not be measuring in the way you anticipated.

The question of validity is much more difficult to deal with than the question of reliability. A valid questionnaire measures what we want to measure. It does what we expect. If we are trying to determine if the employees in an organization have a high degree of trust toward each other, we select a valid trust-measuring questionnaire. Again, if you create your own instrument, be careful about the types of generalizations you make from the data you collect in your documentation. Your questionnaire may not measure what you think it does. This will be the issue you must think through.

When evaluating instruments, look for the data representing both the reliability and validity measures. Determine from these measures if they are consistent and accurate, or if the instrument truly measures what it claims to measure.

Objective and Subjective Documentation Approaches

When doing analysis, it is important to remember that all approaches to collecting data can and should be used. We suggest in the next seven chapters of the book a variety of approaches for collecting data. Most of these approaches tend to be of the objective variety. Chapter 10, however, deals with the concept of interpretive analysis, which by its nature is a very subjective approach. The analyst uses stories, accounts, or metaphors to document deficiencies, adding a dimension that is absent in other methods. We are saying that the analyst is asked to make sense of an organization or its employees using all the means available. As an analyst, do not be so concerned with objectivity, reliability, and validity that you avoid occasionally using illuminating subjective methods.

Preview of Documentation Chapters

As you continue to read, you will note that chapters 4–10 look at methods used to document concerns. Look at the titles of each of these chapters; notice they all deal with documentation. Chapters 4–9 deal with the objective methods, while chapter 10 describes the subjective method of interpretive analysis. These chapters are the core of the book. While they do fill a large segment of the book, they only represent the second stage of the model of analysis. Using them to achieve this purpose is the basic intent.

Summary

Documentation was defined as the gathering of information about what is happening now in the organization, as well as what may have happened in the past regarding the specific concern being analyzed. Seven key documentation considerations were discussed as they related to making your documentation work effectively and accurately. The question of reliability and validity was discussed with the general recommendation that an analyst should generally select data-collection questionnaires that have been found to be reliable and valid. The final suggestion of this chapter was to select a variety of documentation approaches that are both objective and valid while not overlooking the potential of the more subjective methods. Above all, select approaches that will yield the best data for making an accurate analysis.

Activity

Answer the following questions and do the activity listed below:
1. What is the definition of documentation?

_____

2. How does one accurately document a concern?

_____

3. What is the value of multiple methods of documenting issues of concern?

_____

4. Documentation is a very common activity and is represented in many places in our society. Go to a grocery store and observe the checkout procedure of the grocery clerk. Make a record of your observations.

_____

_____

5. Now take your observations and compare them to the seven documentation considerations. What did you find? How well did the grocery clerk's procedures represent the considerations listed?

_____

References

Kerlinger, F. N. 1983. *Foundations of Behavior Research.* New York: Holt, Rinehart & Winston.

Leedy, Paul D. 1983. *Practical Research Planning and Design,* 3d edition. New York: Macmillan.

Saxe, John Godfrey. 1968. "The Parable of the Blind Men and the Elephant." In *Communications: The Transfer of Meaning,* by Don Fabun. Beverly Hills, Calif.: Glencoe Press, pp. 13–14.

4. Methods of Documentation: Using Files

Files are where sources of information are located. The library, books, employment records, laws, rules, memos, documents, histories, contracts, annual reports, and data bases are all files. Files analysis involves learning how to use these sources of information to document points of concern in human resource training and management development.

Value

Fritz Roethlisberger, during his late sixties, wrote an autobiographical account of his work in the field of organizational behavior at the Harvard Business School. In the opening page, he stated: "For some of us there comes a time when we feel the urge to review our past in order to see where we have been" (Roethlisberger 1977, 1). The past, as noted by Roethlisberger, becomes a rich source of information to use when evaluating what led to a present concern in a company. Such corporations as Citicorp, AT&T, and Consolidated Edison are using their own histories to understand how they got where they are and are using this information to guide them in future planning (Smith and Steadman 1981).

Any concern that is evaluated has a historical perspective, and records and files within the organization provide the context for any meaningful consideration of the concern.

Chapter Organization

This chapter describes the process of using files analysis. Two major classes of files are defined: (1) internal records located in the organization, and (2) external data bases that provide a broader perspective on the issues of concern. The last part of the chapter describes how to manage information obtained from files analysis.

Objectives

At the conclusion of the chapter, you will be able to do the following:

- Make a list of internal files, which are sources of information, and correctly describe types of information each can provide to establish the point of concern.
- Make a list of external files, which are sources of information, and correctly describe types of information each can provide to complete the documentation process.
- Given some examples of data from files, state the correct procedures to use to record and manage the information during the files analysis process.
- In a files analysis practice activity, achieve a mean score of seven on the feedback form provided.

Definition of Files

Files are containers of records; therefore, files analysis is often referred to as records analysis. Technically, a record is a copy of any event or happening that has occurred in the past. The records can be written documents, pictures, drawings, audio- or videotapes, scraps of paper, and/or chemical traces.

Not all records are immediately available for analysis, such as some personal files, financial files, or classified files. The rights of privacy occasionally preclude a review of certain records in closed files. Files, then, contain the records of the information needed for the documentation desired.

Overview of Files Analysis Procedures

Two major classes of files, internal and external, are used during this process. The internal files evaluated most frequently are located in the personnel department, the corporate communications department, or the industrial relations department. The major effort of documentation occurs using internal records. The external files are essentially used following the internal search to provide broader meaning and perspectives.

Conducting files analysis involves six steps:

1. Stating the point of concern to be documented
2. Identifying probable internal and external sources
3. Classifying information available on those records
4. Determining a method of analysis
5. Creating a form to record the data
6. Systematically listing the data on the form

Developing a statement for the point of concern (step 1) was defined in chapter 2. Precise statements of the point of concern help direct the entire documentation process.

The work in files analysis begins at step 2, by systematically identifying as many internal and external sources as possible which may be useful to document the concern — for example, identifying what files are available in the human resource information system.

In step 3, the files are physically examined to determine all the types of information that are included on the records. A list is made of the type of information each record contains. For example, if the employee application file contained information on education level, skills, and biographical information, this is listed. No evaluation of the record occurs at this time; rather, the files are reviewed to classify the types of information included in them.

The information analysis procedure is formalized in step 4. Some of the questions asked when beginning this process are the following: "Is a descriptive narrative emphasizing historical or thematic data going to be helpful?" "Are the data more suited to a numerically based analysis?" "Will a combination of both analyses need to be used?" The answers to these questions guide the files analysis. This decision is made prior to data gathering and requires a great deal of thought; once it is made, then the method of observing, recording, and evaluating the information is outlined.

Forms frequently are developed (step 5) to record the data, and, in the long run, are usually more efficient than just making notes. The forms developed are influenced by the type of information desired and can be tailored to the data analysis needed. For example, when using numerical methods, construct a form where rapid coding using numbers occurs so the data can be effectively processed by a computer program. On the other hand, if a descriptive approach is used, the form should be constructed to make note taking more effective. Note cards, which may be sorted and shuffled, frequently are used so the analyst can organize and manage the data effectively to determine what patterns and trends are evident.

With the recording form or multiple forms developed, a rapid and accurate recording of information is performed (step 6) and the data are listed.

Table 4.1 on page 34 displays this process. The balance of the chapter describes the use of this model in files analysis.

Internal Sources

Internal sources are the files available in the organization being analyzed. Five basic types of internal files are described to provide a beginning point for the analysis: (1) human resource information systems, (2) labor relations documents, (3) benefits documents or services, (4) corporate and legal affairs, and (5) financial and payroll records.

Note that this is only the beginning; while you are becoming familiar with these files in a company, other files will become apparent. These files are described below, along with some typical types of information that may be included in them.

Human Resource Information Systems

A human resource information system, or personnel records, is the file where the records of each employee are maintained. Some of the records included in this file are employee application forms, performance evaluations, letters of commendation, personnel

---

Table 4.1   Procedure for Conducting Files Analysis

Step 1: State the point of concern.
Step 2: Identify potential sources.

INTERNAL	EXTERNAL
1. Human resource information systems 2. Labor relations documents 3. Benefits documents or services 4. Corporate and legal affairs 5. Financial and payroll records	1. Professional associations 2. Industry-related groups 3. Government bureaus, departments, and agencies 4. Periodical literature

Step 3: List the types of information on each record available from the files.
Step 4: Determine the method of analysis.

DESCRIPTIVE	NUMERICAL

1. Historical
   a. Chronological
   b. Topical
   c. Structural
2. Thematic
   a. Themes
   b. Trends
	1. Nominal: mode, percentage values, or chi-square
	2. Ordinal: mode, percentage, chi square, median, percentile rank, or rank correlation
	3. Interval: mode, mean, standard deviation t-test, F-test, analysis of variance, product moment correlation

Step 5: Develop data-gathering forms.
Step 6: Record data.

---

change notices, and, in some cases, compensation information (Cherrington 1987, 126–128).

Each organization has a unique set of forms and policies that govern how these records can be used. Initially, request a sample of every document that is listed in the file from the personnel director or individual charged with managing these records. List each file and write down the type of information included in the record. Study the sample records to determine how the information in them can be used in the documentation phase. Ask for periodic updates of these records to keep current.

Employee Application Form   An application form usually contains information about the employee's educational level and skills, and some biographical information. Once the employee is hired, more detailed information may be included.

Performance Evaluations   Performance evaluation forms have additional information that may be helpful in the documentation process. Annual reviews are common in many firms, and some organizations perform them more often. Programs such as career and executive development, forecasting employment needs, and strategic and long-range planning may require that individuals with potential for promotion be identified. Laws of privacy may complicate the use of some of these records.

Letters of Commendation   Outstanding efforts inside and outside the organization by certain employees may be recognized from time to time and associates or supervisors may write a manager a letter of commendation to be included in such an employee's file. These become helpful data when personnel planning or compensation issues are a matter of concern.

Personnel Change Notices   Information such as transfers, terminations, promotions or upgrading of job duties is located in this file. Where points of concern deal with such issues as employee turnover, this record becomes a rich source of information.

Compensation   In some cases, payroll matters are included in employee files. Data regarding base pay, raises, bonuses, commissions, and other considerations are helpful in documenting concerns in needs analysis where employees feel they are not paid fair wages for work done.

Labor Relations Documents

Files that relate to employment practices and policies of an organization are meaningful when documenting concerns on employee needs. Some of the files to become acquainted with include the following:

• Policy and procedures for hiring and dismissing
• Grievances
• Labor contracts

These files frequently are located in the personnel office of the organization.

Policies and Procedures for Hiring and Dismissing   Hiring and firing practices are usually well defined for the firm because of the legal ramifications contained in many of the labor laws. Legal counsel often is retained to develop these policies and procedures to make sure they conform to the law. Therefore, these statements are a good file to review when the point of concern relates to employee grievances or needs.

Grievances   Grievances represent the complaints and concerns employees have about such issues as work, promotions, treatment, or work conditions. These grievances can be evaluated with respect to time, frequency, intensity, locations, levels of employment, or costs. In most cases, the number of grievances will increase when job satisfaction declines or morale is low.

Labor Contracts   Labor contracts govern many operations and typically are administered by the union. Labor relations personnel and union leaders use this document to reference all grievances, disputes, or disciplinary matters. The contract, therefore, is a file that directly impacts on the needs of employees.

Benefits Documents or Services

Benefits require as much as 40 percent of the payroll budget for an organization and provide health care and accident programs for employees. Three types of benefits (Cherrington 1987) are usually considered by a firm:

1. Optional benefits, such as health and accident insurance, life insurance, and holidays or vacations
2. Required benefits, such as workers' compensation, unemployment, and social security
3. Pay regulations, such as retirement, pension plans, or pay deductions

Optional Benefits   Programs such as major medical and hospitalization, dental, psychiatric, and vision care are typical services provided in health care benefits. Some group life insurance policies are available in this package. Since many of these benefits are optional, employees often participate in the premiums paid. Vacation and holiday pay are considered a benefit because the employee is paid for work not performed.

Required Benefits   The mandatory benefits include workers' compensation, unemployment, and Social Security. Concerns of employees relating to this type of protection can become evident in needs analysis.

Pay Regulations   Often the organization with its pension plan and the employee with his or her savings plan will both participate in a financial plan for retirement. Individual retirement accounts (IRAs) and 401(k) or Keogh plans are common tools the employee has to supplement what will come through Social Security. Becoming aware of these options often is necessary to understand some of the concerns that will be evaluated through analysis. Other activities, such as payroll deductions, are protected by law to insure and protect the employee.

Corporate and Legal Affairs

Many of the files described above are administered by formal departments in the organization, such as personnel, labor relations, or human resources. Management of those files is their entire or primary mission. Accessing those files will be coordinated through specialists in those respective areas. When using files in the corporate and legal affairs area, administrative people are involved who have multiple responsibilities rather than the narrower range of duties found with the more specialized staff. Therefore, locating the individual who controls these records for permission to use them is more difficult. A number of phone calls may be required to identify and eventually obtain permission to use them. The records included in this area are corporate policies and procedures, organizational charts, corporate history, and the legal and formal documents of ownership.

Corporate Policies and Procedures   Policy documents list the company's philosophy, guidelines, controls, and directives to admin-

ister the affairs of business. Typical places to find these statements
are recruiting brochures, annual reports, and other marketing documents. Additional data are found in company handbooks or
managerial guides. These records are helpful in needs analysis.

Organizational Chart   A line organizational chart displaying the
line and staff positions in the firm is one of the key records the
analyst should locate. It provides the base point for understanding
some of the relational issues that govern the organization.

Corporate History   The history of a corporation is an important resource, because it can become "a way of thinking about the company, a way of comprehending why the present is as it is and what
may be possible for the future" (Smith and Steadman 1981, 70).
Well-written commissioned histories are becoming a vital resource
to many such as Delta Air Lines, Arco, Sun Oil Company, Wells
Fargo, Manufacturers Hanover Trust Company, AT&T, and Citicorp. Smith and Steadman (1981) have portrayed history as a diagnostic tool — a means of expanding manager's experiences, a
way of anticipating and coping with change, a means of helping
other companies that face similar problems, and a way of helping
unveil the heritage, culture, and traditions that made the firm
what it is today.
      Histories may not be as formal and expansive as Wells Far-
go's, which has a corporate history department as well as a mu-
seum (Anderson 1981). In most cases, there will be none. This
does not suggest, however, that there is no corporate memory;
that memory is in the minds of the men and women who have
made and developed the firm to the point where it is today. You
will have to interview them to obtain the information and in the
process create the file. History and the corporate memory will be
needed in all phases of analysis, and this is especially true of the
needs, performance, and systems approaches.

Legal and Ownership Documents

Legal records may not be readily available, for they include such
documents as the articles of incorporation, stock offerings, bonds,
contracts, and leases. If a matter of concern were to arise where

the management could see that some of these records would be helpful during an analysis, they would share, in part, what was germane to that issue. In many cases, it is not that these documents are secret; rather, they are private, and that appears to override the issue of access.

Financial and Payroll

Privacy may be extended to the financial matters of the firm. Some of the records have limited access to protect the integrity of the financial concerns of the firm. Therefore, a rule of thumb for accessing information is "Find out all you can from other sources, and then ask for specific information." Some of those other sources are public, such as the year end report that is sent to the stockholders and perhaps a prospectus that describes that offering. General information relating to profits and losses, budgeting, and capital expenditures normally is available here. Another source for financial information is a union contract, because job classification and compensation are detailed in this document. In a like manner, public institutions are required to make compensation issues a matter of record. With the "other sources" information in hand, study the concern of the analysis again and determine what additional information is going to be needed to provide meaningful data. In asking for financial information, be as specific as possible and demonstrate how the information will be used, and it will likely be given.

External Sources

Meanings are relational, and for internal data to have a perspective, it is often important to compare your organization to other like organizations within the business sector. For example, for turnover, absenteeism, or cost per unit to have meaning, they can be compared with other organizations in like situations. This is the situation in which external sources of information are most helpful to analysis. Four external sources are often used to obtain meaningful data: (1) professional associations; (2) industry-related groups; (3) government bureaus, departments, and agencies; and (4) periodical literature.

Professional Associations

Professionals and academicians who have interests in specific areas within industry join together and form an association. The association is more than something to join; it can act as a congressional lobbying agent, provide professional development opportunities, communicate the latest and most successful practices within the industry, recognize outstanding achievement, provide networking opportunities, and provide regional and national conferences so members can share ideas. The American Management Association (AMA), American Society for Training and Development (ASTD), and American Society for Personnel Administration (ASPA) are all examples of groups that are interested in human resource and management development. The AMA, for example, indicates a membership of over eighty thousand; the ASTD is near twenty-five thousand. Each organization focuses on different issues. The ASPA, for example, consists primarily of personnel and industrial relations executives in both the public and private sector and has an effective lobby effort in Congress. The ASTD attracts individuals who are concerned specifically with training and management development activities. Its membership includes training professionals in business, education, and government, and commercial vendors of training materials.

Information that is central to issues of human resource development may be gathered by these associations for distribution to their members. For example, the AMA conducts surveys of managerial and professional occupations, and publishes various reports on the salaries of top managers, middle managers, and supervisors. The ASPA collects wage information from its members and publishes a report showing salary levels analyzed by position, geographic region, experiences, and education. Wage surveys also are reported in various periodicals (Cherrington 1987). This information can in turn be compared to the data gathered internally and provide perspective for its meaning.

Industry-Related Groups

Many professional associations encourage members to identify the industrial group where they practice their profession. For example, ASTD includes groups such as computer and data processing, petroleum and natural gas, banking, retail, manufacturing-industrial, state and local government trainers, hospitals and health, insurance, and utilities. These groups, while members in the larger organization, are further identified with members who deal with common problems within the practice area. Membership lists are available for each of these practice areas. At the national conventions, these practice areas have special meetings to consider topics that are specific to them and provide for networking opportunities. By going to the membership directory of such associations as the ASPA and the ASTD, names can be located of directors and co-directors for each of the numerous industrial groups available.

Government Bureaus, Departments, and Agencies

Federal, state, and local governments often provide leadership in publishing information and norms for industry. In addition, these agencies are charged with the responsibility of administering the laws created by Congress. For example, the secretary of the Department of Labor is charged with the responsibility of promoting the welfare of American workers. Within the Department of Labor, an assistant secretary of occupational safety and health oversees the Occupational Safety and Health Administration, the Office of Safety Standards, the Office of Health Standards, the Office of Training, Education, Consultation and Federal Agency Programs, Office of Technical Support, and the Office of Field Coordination and Experimental Programs. Each of these offices has information and files that may help document an area of concern. The commissioner of labor statistics supervises the efforts of the Bureau of Labor Statistics, which collects and publishes information about the labor market. These statistics are published monthly and include the following:

- Establishment Series, which lists employment, hours, and earnings data
- Insured Unemployment Series, which lists labor turnover and unemployment payments
- Current Population Survey, which determines the number of persons employed, unemployed, or not in the labor force

These publications can be obtained from the Government Printing Office, and also are printed in many periodicals, such as the

Monthly Labor Review. The Bureau of Labor Statistics also publishes periodic projections for the employment and economic outlook for the coming decade from their current data bases.

Periodical Literature

There are numerous periodicals that are specific to the areas of human resource and management development. Each of these publications contains information that can be used to document concerns. When looking for publications that contain articles reporting original research, the following may be helpful: *Academy of Management Journal, Academy of Management Review, Industrial & Labor Relations Review, Journal of Business, Journal of Business Research, Journal of Industrial Relations, Journal of Management, Occupational Psychology, Organizational Behavior and Human Performance, Personnel Psychology,* and *Sociology of Work and Occupations.*

Journals that relate to broader issues of concern in the field include *American Journal of Small Business, Business, Business Management, Employee Benefits Journal, Forbes, Fortune, Harvard Business Review, Human Behavior, Human Resource Management, Human Resource Planning, Human Systems Management, Monthly Labor Review, Nation's Business, Organizational Behavior Teaching Review, Personnel, Personnel Administrator, Personnel Journal, Training,* and *Training and Development Journal.*

Abstracts and articles are available in *Business Periodicals, Index to Social Sciences and Humanities, Management Abstracts, Personnel Management Abstracts, Reader's Guide to Periodical Literature,* and *Wall Street Journal Index.*

Much has been written that will help establish a perspective on the point of concern being evaluated. For someone new in the field, this scholarly approach is encouraged in order to broaden the capacity to see implications involved in the issues being studied. A good program of professional development that includes reading from these or other publications is encouraged.

Management of Information Gathered from Files

Knowing where to look is certainly important in documentation; managing what is found is where the payoff is realized. Therefore, learning how to record and manage data from files is critical. Table

4.1 listed six steps: (1) state the point of concern, (2) identify potential sources, (3) list the types of information on each record available from the files, (4) determine the method of analysis, (5) develop data-gathering forms, and (6) record data. Thus far, steps 1 and 2 have been explored in detail, and step 3 has been referred to when describing typical types of information included in each file. An expanded look at each of the remaining three steps is warranted.

Determining the Method of Analysis

Two major methods of analysis, descriptive and numerical, are represented in figure 4.1. Determining which will be most effective for documenting the concern should occur prior to data gathering. In many cases, both methods are utilized and needed to properly document the concern. To make a proper judgment on which analysis to use, consider first how information in the files is typically classified from a narrative and numerical point of view.

Narrative

Information in many of the files described above is recorded as narratives rather than numbers. Reading the documents with a purpose to determine what can be used is essential. Abstracting

---

Figure 4.1 Data Classification of Employee File

FILE INFORMATION	DATA CLASSIFICATION
1. Name of employee	nominal
2. Name of spouse	nominal
3. Number of dependents	interval
4. Prior employment	nominal
5. Current place of employment in firm	nominal
6. Months and years of employment	interval
7. Ranking during annual performance review	ordinal
8. Hourly pay rate	interval
9. Health and accident coverages	nominal
10. Group life insurance coverage (dollars)	interval
11. Independent life insurance coverage (dollars)	interval
12. Date last promoted (days, months, years)	interval
13. Participation in 401(k) (dollars)	interval

and utilizing the information where narratives are involved is not simple, but can be done. Statements that may be useful include quotes, concepts, facts, opinions, or decisions. Taking excellent notes, properly citing source attribution, and developing a management system to enable rapid recording and effective use are important.

Descriptive analysis, using a historical perspective, is similar to writing a term paper; the rigor of good research and careful analysis, using narrative data from the files to emphasize respective points, is required. Three approaches are used to describe the data: (1) chronological, (2) topical, and (3) structural.

Chronological   Placing the information in a time series of first to last represents the chronological approach to reporting narrative data. This allows the analyst to recognize when events occur in the organization.

Topical   Information may be more meaningful if it is described by topics. If turnover, absenteeism, lateness, or injuries were the concern, treating the topics individually in discussion has merit. Each may have historical elements, which may be reported, but the major analysis may best occur topically.

Structural   A line organizational chart represents structural elements in a company. Completing and reporting an analysis may follow organizational lines. Reporting by department, work group, production, and so on is a logical approach to both analysis and reporting what has occurred.

Thematic analysis also focuses on the narrative. For example, to record data, the analyst actually lists the narrative statements in the file. These statements are then organized into common themes. For example, if an analyst were looking at former employees' exit interviews in a personnel file, each reason for leaving the firm is listed. Eventually, repetition of ideas in the documents begins to appear; the analyst marks the number of times each idea is observed and continues to record all new or not previously mentioned reasons. The summary of the data is made by listing the frequency of specific statements. Common statements are grouped by themes and described as trends or probability statements of why turnover may have occurred. Statements rather than numbers are recorded for this analysis. Interpretation comes from evaluating the themes that appear in the files.

Numerical

Numerical data are traditionally identified by their characteristics, which in turn classify the data type. Three types are common to files analysis: (1) nominal, (2) ordinal, and (3) interval.

Nominal   Nominal in Latin means name — a name that describes individuals or things. Characteristics unique to nominal data thus include independent, stands alone, and has no relationship to other classes. Many of the data gathered in files analysis are nominal. Race, gender, work classification, job, benefits, prior employment, tasks, activities, role, group, social status, and power are all names of independent groups or categories. When describing the data, list the frequency or percentage of each classification. In some cases, a chi-square is used to determine if there is an interdependence between a class of individuals (e.g., gender) and the way they respond to specific questions. These are the limits of how this information can be reported.

Ordinal   Ordinal data are relational and are characterized by size and length. Such terms as larger-smaller, more-less, and greatest-least are used to describe the relationships. The distance between ratings, as measured on a scale, is not known or necessarily equal. Only the relationship between respondents is defined by a measure such as rank order. For example, data gathered from performance files where employees have been ranked, or classification where ranks have been used to describe jobs, work conditions, safety, health, and difficulty, are ordinal data. Ordinal data can be described using modes, percentages, chi-square, median, percentile rank, or rank correlation.

Interval   Equal distance, as measured on a scale, between the intervals characterize these data. Information that includes numbers, scales of equal distance, and graded semantic distance, such as a Likert scale, are examples of these data. Many financial records, statistics, and frequencies of occurrence are common to this classification. Interval data can be described by the mode, mean, standard deviation, t-test, F-test, and product moment correlation. Both descriptive and inferential statistics are used to manage the data. Differences between mean performances or achievements can be determined for respective groups.

These three classifications are well suited to analysis using simple statistics that most readers can determine. Observations, representing data from the files, have to be converted to numbers for analysis. Consider, for example, figure 4.1, which may represent a personnel file being reviewed. The data are first classified by characteristics and then recorded using a number to represent each observation.

In the example, names of both employee and spouse may not be useful; however, knowing how many employees have a spouse might be. In this case, a yes = 1 and no = 0 is used to represent the information. If the location of the last job held before hiring was important, in state = 1, out of state = 2, local = 3 might be used. The nominal information is changed into a number for computer analysis to represent the classification. If a computer program is not used, simply record the number of times each observation is noted.

In the example, line 7 represents ordinal data. To change the rating to a number, 1st = 1, 2nd = 2, 3rd = 3, and so on, can be used. Computer analysis or simple frequency counting can occur.

Several interval types of data are listed in the file. Since dollars and time have fixed intervals where $2 is twice as much as $1, or 60 seconds is twice as much as 30 seconds, data are recorded as listed in the file. For example, if group life insurance for the spouse was $50,000, this number is listed. The number of dependents would similarly be recorded.

Determining the method of analysis prior to gathering the data is helpful, because it influences how the data will eventually be reported. A descriptive use of the information may require more notes and extended quotes, whereas an approach governed by a rich use of statistical evaluation encourages the use of data converted into numbers for processing. The types of analyses are limited by what data are available. For example, descriptive statistics for the noninterval data of nominal and ordinal are limited —

a mode is possible for the first and mode and median for the ordinal. Percentages, chi-square with the addition of some percentile, and rank correlation for the ordinal round out the analytical
possibilities. Going beyond these measures requires interval data.
Thematic data require notes and statements from the files to complete the analysis. Knowing what types of statements are needed
to document the data is the first step. Classifying the type of data
available is the second. From this information, the method of analysis is determined.

Developing Data-Gathering Forms

The form created to record the data reflects the need of the analyst
to rapidly and systematically record the information from the files.
A second factor that will influence the development is the method
used to gather the data. Three basic tools or methods are possible:
(1) note cards, (2) computer, and (3) copy machine.

Note Cards

Note cards made of card stock are effective in this process. The
same effect can be achieved by using twenty-pound paper cut into
3×5's for bibliographical information and 4×6's or 5×7's for
more substantive note taking. Establish what should be on the
form, and then copy it on the paper and cut to the desired size.
With biographical information, the following should be listed: author's name, title of publication, publisher, date of publication,
and page numbers. Identify a place on the card where it can be
numbered, and provide a place where additional information,
such as a main or subheading to organize your information, can
be recorded. The key concern is to list all the information needed
the first time the file is reviewed so that extended delays caused
by going back to the original source can be avoided. With note
taking, prepare the information in a neat manner so that it can be
read and reviewed quickly when used later. Limiting one idea to
a card often allows for greater flexibility when managing the information later.

 Where data are recorded as numbers rather than in a narrative, develop a form with a note card such as represented in figure
4.2. A code booklet is developed to place the established number
values (e.g., in state = 1, out of state = 2, local = 3, or hourly =

Figure 4.2   Data-Gathering Form for Employee File

# FILE INFORMATION	DATA CLASSIFICATION
_____ I.D. no. of subject:	_____
_____ 1. Number of dependents:	1 2 3 4 5 6 7 8 9 10 11 12
_____ 2. Prior employment:	in state __ out of state __ local __
_____ 3. Employment in firm:	hourly __ salaried __ mgt. __
_____ 4. Months and years of employment:	months __ years __
_____ 5. Ranking during annual performance review:	ranked __
_____ 6. Hourly pay rate:	__
_____ 7. Health/accident:	major med. __ dental __ vision __
_____ 8. Group life insurance coverage (dollars):	__
_____ 9. Independent life insurance coverage (dollars):	__
_____ 10. Date last promoted (days, months, years):	__
_____ 11. Participation in 401(k) (dollars):	__

1, salaried = 2, mgt. = 3, for each item on the note card. When recording the data, the number assigned is placed in the left column under the number for each item.

Computer

Two ways are suggested to use a computer in files analysis: (1) Rather than use the card represented in figure 4.1, place the information from the employee record directly into the computer and eliminate one step by going immediately to the encoding phase. When recording the information in the computer, a file is created for the data, and if the number of dependents was 5, the number 5 is to be typed in the file; if a prior employment was local, a 3 is placed in the computer. Using personal computers and data management programs, the analyst can speed up the process. For example, a software program like *WordPerfect* (1987) can be used to code information, which in turn can be transposed, so data management programs such as SPSS (1983) or SAS (1985) on the mainframe computer are possible. Another alternative is to use a personal computer program such as *CRISP* (Bostrom and Stegner 1986), which will manage the data on the personal computer for data analysis. (2) A second approach to using the computer is typing the notes directly into the computer. The notes can be managed as a note card. Some advantages are possible when using this approach because of the sorting and merging capabilities.

Copy Machines

Copy machines are excellent tools for extracting parts of records and information. Copyright laws will apply to much of the information from external publications and records being accessed. Internal files should be relatively free of these constraints. One caution is added when using this information: always place all the critical information needed to reidentify the source document on the copy made. For example, when copying articles from a publication, place the same data on the copy as you would in a complete bibliographical entry. This makes source attribution possible and saves valuable time in not having to sift through endless primary documents to complete your written report.

Recording and Coding Data for Use

The last phase of files analysis is placing the information on a card, developed form, computer, or photocopy so that it can be processed using the appropriate evaluation procedures. The question of how to evaluate the information should have been answered earlier. Follow that procedure.

Develop a system for saving and filing the information obtained. If cards are used, find a container that can not only protect them but be updated easily. When photocopies are used, have a filing system that can be organized in a similar fashion. Creating a system that allows for quick updating as well as easy accessing is the goal to achieve.

Summary

Files have been defined as an event in time that may be accessed during the analysis process. Internal documents that represented those events were described, such as the human resource information systems on employees and benefits packages, and labor relations records, corporate records, or financial records. External files were described as essential to give the concern a perspective and included information from associations, industry related organizations, government, and periodical literature. Managing the data included the issues of note cards, computers and copy machines. The procedure for evaluating these data were listed and reviewed.

Files analysis is part of every documentation activity and gives all issues perspective and meaning. The tools described here are used frequently and allow for a more exhaustive review.

Activity

Scenario: Your top managers have been complaining that their salaries are much lower than those of other professionals of equal experience, education, and position in competitive companies. You have told them you will look into their concerns. How would you go about evaluating this issue?

1. In one sentence, state the point of concern.

_____

2. List the internal and external files you would use to document this point of concern.

   INTERNAL _____   EXTERNAL _____

3. Develop a form you would use to record the type of data gathered from the files to substantiate what is currently happening in your organization and those of the competitors.

Scenario: Several complaints have been forwarded to you about safety conditions at your factory. You have an appointment with a labor union leader in two days to review this issue. In preparation for this meeting, you are determined to document this issue. How would you proceed?

1. In one sentence, state the point of concern.

_____

2. List the internal and external files you would use to document this point of concern.

   Internal

   External

3. How does your safety record compare with other regional companies? How does the safety record compare with data of the past five years? Has safety been a reactive or proactive concern within the firm? What type of information will you need to meet with the union representative?

References

Anderson, H. P. 1981. "The Corporate History Department: The Wells Fargo Model." *The Public Historian*, 25–30.

Bostrom, Alan, and Bruce Stegner. 1986. *CRISP, Crunch Software Interactive Statistical Package*. San Francisco.

Cherrington, D. J. 1987. *Personnel Management: The Management of Human Resources*. Dubuque, Iowa: Brown.

Roethlisberger, F. J. 1977. *The Exclusive Phenomena*. Cambridge, Mass.: Harvard University Press.

SAS User's Guide: Statistics. Version 5 Edition. 1985. Cary, N.C.: SAS Institute.

Smith, G. D., and L. E. Steadman. 1981. "The Value of Corporate History." *Harvard Business Review* 59 (November/December): 69–76.

SPSS X User's Guide. 1983. New York: McGraw-Hill.

WordPerfect. Version 4.2 Edition. 1987. Orem, Utah: WordPerfect Corporation.

———. "Prefatory Note," 1987. *Business Periodicals Index* 29.

5. Methods of Documentation: Analyzing Tasks

Each method of analysis is designed to look at different issues. For example, a systems analysis can document issues within the organization, performance analysis looks at how individuals are doing their work, and task analysis lists the detail that describes specific behaviors within the jobs people do. Each form of analysis is important to the documentation effort.

Of all the documentation procedures studied, task analysis will be the most microscopic because of the attention given in order to detail each behavior that is part of the job. Through this form of analysis, each job is classified in terms of the tasks that are performed, and each of those tasks is evaluated until a definitive list of subtasks is produced. Through this exhaustive effort, the list of duties and tasks necessary to perform a job is produced. In many cases, this attention to detail is necessary to pinpoint the concern being evaluated.

Value

The profitability of an organization or operation is determined by many separate factors, some of which will be discussed here. Among them is the productivity of the workers, since this is one area where small increases make a difference. For example, in coal strip mining, if operators of the large shovels dig just one more scoop per hour, these additional twenty-four scoops per day over a year's time translate into millions of dollars. This type of additional productivity, throughout the work world, is frequently achieved through task analysis. Detailing the sequence of behaviors and determining where workers can be more efficient, and helping them become so, make a firm more profitable.

This example should not suggest that the heart of task analysis is time and motion studies. Task analysis is broader and will be described as a combination of methods used to determine how behaviors are observed and recorded to document the duties that workers perform.

Chapter Organization

This chapter describes work behavior, methods of recording these observations of behavior in task analysis, identifying and using subject matter experts in the documentation phases, and how to use work measurement methods in evaluating tasks.

Objectives

At the conclusion of this chapter, you will be able to do the following:

- List the key elements that are used to describe work behavior.
- List five methods that are used to record behavior during task analysis.
- Describe an effective process to use when working with subject matter experts in performing a task analysis.
- Describe three methods that are used when employing the work measurement methods of task analysis.
- In a practice task analysis activity, achieve a mean score of seven on the feedback form provided.

Preparing to Conduct a Task Analysis

Learning how to observe others is essential to being most effective in this phase of documentation. This may sound strange to individuals who have been watching others all their lives and have learned to use this information to determine how they will act and respond within their social network at work and in nonwork settings. Observation has taught them to identify approaches that work and do not work, and approaches that reward and punish. These same observational skills will be helpful in doing a task analysis and defining worker behavior.

Worker behavior will be defined as each observable act, with its required knowledge and skill, that is used to produce a result correctly or accomplish a task within a specific job. When observing this behavior, look for the following characteristics: a definite beginning and ending point; the necessary interaction with equipment, media, and/or other people; the subsequent measurable results; and the decision making, perceptions, and or physical activities that made the act possible (Mallory 1987). Therefore, to monitor each of these characteristics effectively, development of these observational tendencies is essential.

Observing and classifying worker behavior is the first phase, recording it is the second. The complexity of what we observe is not easily clothed in language. The most descriptive method to record this information is the use of the action verb. The verb is the tool in our language that allows the analyst to classify the acts of others. Yes, he or she also will need to rely on nouns, adjectives, and adverbs, but the action will be labeled by the verb. Take a simple task of describing how to open a book: *place* the book in one hand, *lift* your second hand and *place* it on the edge of the book, *select* the approximate place where you would like to begin reading, *open* the book and *find* the exact place, *read* as desired. Each underlined word classifies the action taken that can be recorded to describe the behavior appropriately. Essentially, the action-verb noun combinations are used (place book, lift hand, select place) in recording what is observed.

Methods of Observing and Recording Tasks

Five methods are described to conduct a task analysis:

1. Job-duty-task method
2. Stimulus-response method
3. Time-motion study
4. Workplace layout
5. Human factors studies

All differ but accomplish the similar result of providing a definition of worker behavior.

Job-Duty-Task Method

A task analysis is an audit and inventory of the knowledge, skills, critical interactions, perceptions, and aspirations that are essential to producing a specific result. In looking at the job-duty-task method, the result is considered the outcome of the work, while the duty or task describes what must be done in order to produce the result. (Davis, I. 1973) The task analysis therefore must isolate all those overt acts that characterize the who, what, when, where, why, and how of the job.

Conceptually, looking at the task analysis is like diagraming the authority structure in an organization. The job (chief executive officer, for example) represents the first descriptive level; the second level (senior-level management) represents the specific set of duties assigned to the job; at the third level (middle managers), all the tasks associated with each duty are added; and at the fourth level (supervisors), tasks are further defined by the task elements that eventually represent the individual acts of behavior, or the smallest individual unit of analysis (the worker).

In conducting the analysis, listing the job title and the respective duties is relatively easy. The systematic effort of looking at each of those duties and describing the tasks is where the work really begins. As described earlier, listing the tasks is only one part of the analysis because the knowledge and skills required to perform each of these tasks need to be defined at the same time. A form, such as the one represented in figure 5.1, can illustrate how this occurs. Five levels are listed: (1) job title, (2) a specific duties, (3) respective tasks under each duty, (4) subtasks, and (5) skills or acts with their respective knowledge that must be evident to produce the result.

The form in figure 5.1 is used to guide the task analysis. For example, if the task analyst were looking at his or her own role, the information in figure 5.2 would be placed on the form.

All the duties of the task analyst are not included, as noted below in figure 5.2; rather, the list represents the beginning of the process. The task analysis, using the job-duty-task method, rec-

Figure 5.1   Task Analysis

Job title: _____   Specific duty: _____

TASKS	SUBTASKS	KNOWLEDGE AND SKILLS REQUIRED
1. _____	1. _____	_____
		_____
	2. _____	_____
		_____
	3. _____	_____
		_____
2. _____	1. _____	_____
		_____
	2. _____	_____
		_____
	3. _____	_____
		_____
3. _____	1. _____	_____
		_____
	2. _____	_____
		_____

Figure 5.2   Task Analysis Example

Job title: HRD Professional   Specific duty: Task Analysis

TASKS	SUBTASKS	KNOWLEDGE AND SKILLS REQUIRED
1. List tasks	1. Observe behavior	List four characteristics of behavior
		Classify behavior
	2. Select verb	Knowledge of action verbs
		Grammatical skills
	3. Record behavior	State so understood by others
		Recorded neatly
2. List subtasks	1. Observe behavior	List all remaining acts
		Classify behavior
	2. Select verb	
		State correctly
	3. Record behavior	Grammatical skill
		Neat and understood by others
3. List knowledge	1. State what must be known	Classify all information
	2. Determine complexity of skill	Determine if skill represents a series of acts that must be learned in a sequence.

ords the worker behaviors and skills and knowledge required to perform the job.

Stimulus Response Method

The stimulus-response (S-R) method of task analysis is a behavioristic approach that takes its roots from the work of B. F. Skinner (1953, 1974). Skinner was concerned with how cues could elicit certain responses in a person and how these patterns of cue-responses can be modified to control behavior. Deterline (1968) used these guidelines to describe and develop his approach to task analysis by listing, through the notations of "cue" or "stimulus" and "action" or "response," the behaviors that were critical to performing a task. Through noting what prompts the individual (listing the cue they are seeing or reacting to), then by stating the subsequent action taken (recording the response made), the details within the job are defined. Figure 5.3, using the same basic information listed in figure 5.2, shows how this method works.

As apparent, the cue or stimulus (information needed) led to the subsequent action or response taken; the need motivated the response made. In this type of example, defining precisely what the cue is that produces the response is difficult, because the task is conceptual rather than technical. A conceptual task occurs in the mind and provides very few overt behavioral cues to link to the actions or responses taken. This may be more apparent if a tech-

---

Figure 5.3   Cue-Response Example

CUE OR STIMULUS	ACTION OR RESPONSE
1. Need a title to describe job and responsibilities	List the job title
2. Need a classification and title for first duty	Classify it and title the specific duty
3. Need an action verb and noun to label first duty	List the first task
4. Need an action verb and noun to label first subtask	List the first subtask
5. Need to know what is required to perform this subtask	Study and list the knowledge one needs to perform activity

nical task is defined in a second example and one can see how the
S-R method is used to describe the technical skill of drilling a hole
in a blank piece of steel (Zemke and Kramlinger, 1982, 40). In this
example, a blank is a short piece of steel that needs a hole drilled
in a specific place. The blank must meet certain specifications, or
it is not drilled and is rejected.

In comparing the two examples, the technical (figure 5.4) has
more precision; this precision is possible because of the nature of
the task. With conceptual tasks (figure 5.2), the task analyst performed the task using the powers of reasoning and the symbols
of language. This statement does not suggest that performing
technical skills does not require thinking; rather, it suggests that
precision associated with recording technical skills, which are a
sequence of events in a series, are usually overt, can be observed,
and, therefore, can be recorded with more exactness. Contrast this
to a conceptual process, where the reasoning is covert and relies
upon symbol manipulations that occur in the mind; subsequently
recording the details of conceptual tasks will not be as precise.

Using the stimulus-response method for task analysis is more
suitable for describing repetitive technical tasks as suggested in
the example of drilling the hole in the piece of steel. Note that the
S-R method does not list the knowledge required to perform the
task; rather, it sequences and orders the acts of behavior used to
produce the results, and this is its prime benefit in task analysis.

Time-Motion Study

One of the most delightful introductions to the use of time and
motion study is the book *Cheaper by the Dozen*, about a family with
twelve children. Rearing a dozen children is a marvelous feat in

Figure 5.4   Task Analysis for Drilling a Hole

CUE OR STIMULUS	ACTION OR RESPONSE
1. Need blank to drill	Reach into bin and secure blank
2a. Blank in hand	Inspect blank
2b. Inspect blank — reject	Put in reject barrel (go to cue 1)
2c. Inspect blank — accept	Move blank to bed of drill
3. Blank at bed of drill press	Secure blank in jig

and of itself, but doing so as industrial engineers, who were early pioneers in time and motion study, gives this book added meaning. As stated in the foreword of the book; "Lillian and Frank Gilbreth were industrial engineers. They were among the first in the scientific management field and the very first in motion study. From 1910 to 1924, their firm of Gilbreth, Inc., was employed as 'efficiency expert' by many of the major industrial plants in the United States, Britain, and Germany" (Gilbreth and Carey [1948] 1984).

Some of the interesting time and motion tasks described in the book include "buttoning a shirt and vest," "shaving," "taking out tonsils," and "getting the family together." For example, buttoning a vest from the bottom up, instead of the top down, saved four seconds (three seconds versus seven seconds); using two brushes to lather when shaving cut seventeen seconds off of shaving time. Gilbreth showed that he could save forty-seven seconds while using two razors rather than one, but then he lost two minutes when he had to apply bandages (Gilbreth and Carey [1948] 1984, 2).

Time and motion study is similar to both the job-duty-task and stimulus-response methods described above in that behaviors are observed and recorded by individual acts. In the time and motion method, the time to complete each of these acts is also recorded. Through analyzing the acts of several persons performing the task and recording the exact time taken to complete the subtasks within each task, norms are established for each phase of the tasks associated with each job. More important, using this form of analysis helps determine the types of motions that top performers use and compare the efficiency of those acts with the motions used by low performers. Initially, film was used to study the motions of persons performing the task. By examining a frame-by-frame record of the performance, the time to perform each act could be recorded and wasted motion could be identified. The data from the film became the task analysis and provided the documentation to determine what was the most effective procedure for performing routine tasks. Today, videotape has replaced film and makes it possible to provide immediate feedback to performers; no delays are required for developing the film and the analysis can occur promptly.

Zemke and Kramlinger (1982, 30) note five reasons for con-

ducting a task analysis using time and motion study: (1) to measure productivity, (2) to develop performance incentive systems,
(3) to determine product/manufacturing costs, (4) to estimate costs
and procedures for projected new products, and (5) to develop
work load and crew assignments.

Measuring Productivity   Developing norms or standards of performance is essential to measuring productivity of the persons performing a task. Many firms use a minimum level of units per hour
or per shift to make decisions on whether to retain new hires. New
hires who have been trained have a trial period of time to come
up to a specific standard. When that performance level is not obtained, employment is terminated. The standard becomes the
point measuring the productivity.

Develop Performance Incentive Systems   Where attempts to reward
top performers who exceed a base level of performance are made,
bonuses are often paid. In many firms, the cost of producing a
unit above a set standard is relatively inexpensive, because the
overhead and fixed costs associated with production do not increase after the standard has been achieved. Thus each unit above
the standard is produced at a substantial savings to the firm. Since
the firm benefits from this increased productivity, it is willing to
provide incentives to the workers to exceed the standard level of
performance. The incentive usually is negotiated to set the incentive rationale and schedules, particularly if a union is involved.
Some negotiated incentive systems require that safety standards
be maintained to avoid compromising safety for speed. Again,
time and motion study helps provide the baseline levels from
which these decisions are often made.

Determine Product/Manufacturing Costs   The total process of costing
is influenced by time and motion issues. As the fixed and variable
costs for developing the components of the product line are calculated, the cost per unit produced can be determined. For example, a contractor will use a cost-per-square-foot figure to
estimate what expenditures are at various stages within the construction project. From these data, cost overruns or savings can
be updated and time lines evaluated to project whether the development will come in on budget.

Estimate Costs and Procedures for Projected New Products   As noted above, the same data bases for determining and tracking costs are used in estimates for projecting new product development. Data bases can be used to project budgets, design production lines, and provide information about inventory and shipping.

Develop Work Load and Crew Assignments   Many firms use data bases to produce the schedules required to meet production needs. For example, a fast-food restaurant may need the capacity to respond to fluctuations in demands on a daily, weekly, and seasonal basis. If the restaurant firm knows what these fluctuations may be and how many units per work hour it takes to provide these services, a computer program may produce a work roster and schedule for personnel needs based on the fluctuations. Again, the key to this process is having time and motion information.

The first stage in gathering information using a time and motion study is complete documentation of all the acts that are involved in the task being evaluated. Documentation frequently is done by videotaping the repetitive act and analyzing the motions and time taken to perform each one. When a videotape or film camera is not available, a clipboard and stopwatch are used for recording the acts. The task of recording these acts is accomplished by observing each hand and what is done. If the feet also are involved in a task, such as operating a large tractor, the foot acts are noted also. Videotape or film cameras are especially useful, because acts occurring with the right and left hand and the right and left foot (if involved) and eye patterns, can be studied frame by frame and recorded. The simple task of tying a square knot may be helpful, as an example, to illustrate the first phase in the time and motion process (see figure 5.5).

With the detail listed, evaluating the efficiency of each person performing the task is possible. For example, note through observation that top performers hold the rope between the thumb and the finger when making both the first and the second twist when tying the knot. The thumb and finger movement may be omitted by the lower performers. Without the detailed list of individual acts, that activity may have been overlooked. Therefore, one approach to work efficiency/work improvement studies is to use a detailed list of behaviors to monitor the activity.

Figure 5.5   Task Analysis for Tying a Square Knot

LEFT HAND ACTIVITIES

RIGHT HAND ACTIVITIES

1. Place end of rope in hand with a three-inch length sticking out.
2. Bring rope ends together and place the left-hand rope under the right-hand rope.
3. Pick up tail of rope that is pointing to the right and twist it over, then under, the tail of the rope pointing to the left.
4. Pull the rope until you have a three-inch tail again.
5. Turn the tail of the rope toward the tail in the other hand.
6. Put the tail in the left hand over tail in the right hand.
7. Hold both ends of the rope in the left hand between thumb and pointer finger.

1. Place end of rope in hand with a three-inch length sticking out.
2. Bring rope ends together and place the right-hand rope on top of the left-hand rope.
3. Hold both ends of the rope in the right hand between thumb and pointer finger.
4. Turn the tail of the rope toward the tail in the other hand.
5. Take rope end and place under the left-hand rope.
6. Pick up tail of rope that is pointing to left and twist it over and under the rope pointing to the right and pull rope to make the knot.

The second phase of time and motion study is to establish the standard. Therefore, after the task is learned, determine how long one repetition of tying the knot takes. Because the sequence of events as shown in figure 5.5 is relatively short, timing each separate act may be difficult. By removing the notations of right hand and left hand and reducing the task to three major subtasks rather than all the acts, timing may be easier (see figure 5.6). For example:

Figure 5.6   Time Study for Tying Square Knots

	1	2	3	4	5	6	AVERAGE
1. Pick up rope with end in each hand.	—	—	—	—	—	—	——
2. Tail of right over left and twist.	—	—	—	—	—	—	——
3. Tail of left over right and pull.	—	—	—	—	—	—	——
Total							——

Videotape or observe the task and time for each subtask to determine what the average is for the group trained, such as a group of Boy or Girl Scouts. Each scout is timed tying the knot six times, and the average time for completing the task is determined for each of the three subtasks and the total for tying the knot. A group average is determined, which becomes the standard. A scout might determine if he or she were above, at, or below the standard of the group when performing the task. Offering an incentive, such as a small piece of candy, may be all that is required to bring performance above this level.

The example of tying a knot and a population of scouts may not be the normal task analysis a consultant completes. However, the process, rather than the subject, is what is important. In short, the process involves a systematic evaluation of the individual acts associated with the task and a set of established norms or standards that are associated with the process. These industrial engineering tools have value in the documentation process of task analysis. Again, not all tasks are adaptable to this approach, but time and motion study is most suitable for analyzing repetitive motor skills that must be performed in a series to achieve the best results.

Workplace Layout

Industrial engineers also analyze tasks by studying the workplace layout. Not much will be said here other than to indicate that this method of analysis looks at how work can be organized into tasks, and how the output of these tasks can be organized into a work flow to operationalize the total time required to produce the product line. Workplace layout broadens the analysis to a systems perspective, rather than an individual task or duty. This analysis will be discussed further in chapter nine.

Human Factors Studies

Another method used by scientific engineers is the study of human factors. Interest in looking at productivity from a human performance perspective began in the late 1950s and was motivated by changes that were occurring in the workplace.

Historically, at the turn of the century, the nation moved to an industrial society and began the process of mass production. Scientific management had its beginnings during this period of time, which began an effort to study the nature of work in industry. One of the driving forces for organizing work became the focus on task analysis, which was a key element in this process. Through these analyses, specialization was introduced to the work setting as a means of increasing productivity. Specialization required a person to do a limited number of tasks with the assumption that if someone had only one task to do, he or she could do it very well. The results of this analysis were correct, and the specialist, rather than the generalists, increased the production effort. This approach influenced management approaches to organizing and assigning work through the first fifty years of the twentieth century. As the nation moved into the postindustrial era, new approaches were sought to study the issues of how work was assigned and if specialization created the optimal output. Issues of job enlargement, rotation, and enrichment were introduced. Automation, new technologies, and computers were additional elements that required a redefinition of work, roles, and purposes of people in the work system. Studies began to show that the work world, which had been characterized by specialization and task-duty relationships, was no longer producing as other systems, such as those in Japan or the sociotechnical systems in England, which were being introduced.

A shift in how to study productivity occurred. Rather than study just the tasks associated with doing a job and working more efficiently, the human factors that caused employees to feel satisfied and/or dissatisfied with their work and how this impacted on productivity were reviewed. Human factors studies were initiated in conjunction with the information provided in the task analysis. Studies by Herzberg (Herzberg, Mausner, and Snyderman 1959) led him to develop a two-factor theory, where a motivational and hygiene continuum were introduced. Emery (1964, 1976) extended the awareness of intrinsic and extrinsic characteristics of the job. Job enrichment and job characteristics theory (Griffin 1978) are additional examples of this approach. Again, since a human factors approach to task analysis is broader than the perspective we would like to deal with in this chapter, more is not included here. These issues will be discussed in greater detail as we look at needs analysis in chapters 6 and 7.

The point to be made is that task analysis often is studied in conjunction with needs and systems analysis, because most documentation efforts ought to respond to broader issues, such as needs of the individual and how he or she fits into the larger organization called the system. The intent of mentioning workplace layout and human factors studies within this chapter was to note the close tie they have with task analysis during the documentation phase or stage.

Five data-gathering approaches to task analysis have been described, each of which achieves different purposes in documenting and recording worker behavior. The balance of the chapter now looks at how to use a subject matter expert to gather this information.

Using a Subject Matter Expert

The subject matter expert (SME) is a professional in the area where the task analysis is conducted. Trade, professional, and skilled labor are examples of individuals who qualify as SME's. Doing a task analysis with the SME can be a joint effort, or the analyst can prepare him or her with the forms necessary to provide the information to complete the analysis.

In a joint effort, the analyst interviews the SME while he or she is performing the task. After observing the SME for a period of time to establish the series of events, the analyst begins asking the SME the what, when, where, why, and how of what he or she just did. For example, "What did you just do?", "Does this always occur just after the preceding step?", "Why did you decide to do that?", "What equipment does this require?", "What do you need to know to perform this task?", and "How does this relate to other steps you have done?" The process of inquiry helps detail the tasks that are involved and determine the knowledge and skills necessary to complete the task analysis. Once the analyst has formalized this list into a job-duty-task form as described in figure 5.1 or some of the other suggested forms included above, the list is shared with other SME's to have them verify this listing procedure. This second set of opinions usually rounds out the task analysis.

A second approach in working with SME's is to provide them with some forms, such as the one described in figure 5.7, and have them fill in the details that are sought.

Figure 5.7   Task Analysis Using SME

Job title: _____   Specific duty: _____

TASKS	SUBTASKS	KNOWLEDGE AND SKILLS REQUIRED
1. _____	1. _____	_____
		_____
	2. _____	_____
		_____
	3. _____	_____
		_____
2. _____	1. _____	_____
		_____
	2. _____	_____
		_____
	3. _____	_____
		_____
3. _____	1. _____	_____
		_____
	2. _____	_____
		_____
	3. _____	_____
		_____

The SME, in turn, completes this form. Review by other SME's occurs, and that feedback is added to the form to represent the task analysis.

Some suggestions that may be helpful in working with an SME follow:

• Define his or her role.
• Define what is meant by a duty, task, subtask, and acts.
• Introduce him or her to the task recording form.
• Show him or her an example of a completed form.
• Work through an example of one task together by listing the duty, task, subtasks, and knowledge and skills required.
• Realize this is a hard task that you have given him or her, and be available for assistance to make sure the job is completed.
• Submit the SME's task analysis to other SME's to review.
• Reconcile differences.

Be prepared to probe when working with the SME to add the required detail to complete the task activities. In many cases, the SME has done the task so many times that he or she will omit the detail required to evaluate the issue. The SME may just do it automatically without really thinking about each independent action he or she takes.

Work Measurement Methods of Task Analysis

Three work measurement methods are often used to supplement the task analysis procedure: (1) work sampling, (2) standard data, and (3) flow charts (Griffin 1978). Although these methods may be used in performance appraisal, they are listed here to augment the discussion of approaches used to document task analysis.

Work Sampling   Work sampling is a method of expanding a task analysis made by recording the amount of time expended in respective tasks included within the job. For example, with a secretarial job, there are a number of tasks involved in the duties performed on a regular basis. Random visits are used to observe the secretary and note how much time is spent typing, answering the phone, greeting visitors, and so forth. Through a reasonable number of observations, a holistic view of the job is obtained and the portion of time spent in doing respective tasks is assessed. A second approach to gathering work sampling information is to use a daily log. In the log, the day parts are broken down into minute segments (5, 10, 15, 20, or 30). These are kept by the secretary or person performing the task. At the end of the week, the log is analyzed to determine what tasks are being performed and the portion of time spent in each. An example of a daily log divided into 30-minute segments is listed in figure 5.8.

Standard Data   This work measurement method is used to project costs and development of new products that are similar in nature and design to the tasks currently being used in producing a product. The initial step in this method is to use the data base of information currently available on existing similar tasks. From this

---

Figure 5.8   Daily Log

Name _____   Title _____
Beginning date _____   Ending date _____

Record your activities in a half-hour sequence to identify the task you are working on during the day. Keep this record for a five-day period.

TIME   DAY _____   ACTIVITY INVOLVED IN DURING THIS TIME

_____ :00 to _____ :30   _____
_____ :00 to _____ :30   _____
_____ :00 to _____ :30   _____
_____ :00 to _____ :30   _____
_____ :00 to _____ :30   _____
_____ :00 to _____ :30   _____
_____ :00 to _____ :30   _____
_____ :00 to _____ :30   _____

---

base, projections of the requirements of setup time, essential activities of production, and expected outputs in terms of units produced can be established. Again, this analysis moves more toward systems analysis issues, but it is mentioned here because of the focus on tasks and subtask data bases as a function of projecting costs and resource issues. For example, a traditional move of a piece of equipment in a mining operation has a "tear-down," "move," "setup," and "testing" set of tasks to move the machinery from one location to the next. Although the conditions differ, the standard data method helps predict what will be required in terms of resources to produce the change. Whether it be a move of equipment, or the development of a like product, the data base provides some discrete information that can be generalized to the new situation. A task data base is often used to guide this planning effort.

Flow Charts   The last approach mentioned in this chapter is the use of flow charts to determine tasks associated with producing a product. Through the use of a diagram, the key activities associated with the process are listed. Some authors, such as Merrill (1976), have chosen to use an algorithm to produce the task analysis. Each task that is analyzed has a beginning and end, and the steps in between are diagramed using questions that can be answered yes or no. For each answer, a recommended action or additional question is provided. As you proceed through the diagram and respond to the questions and/or actions recommended, you complete the task. This process is shown in figure 5.9.

As you can see, the step-by-step approach to completing the task of conducting a practice session was provided through the use of an algorithm. Additional algorithms might be provided for each of the substeps within the process to deal completely with the issues suggested in figure 5.8. The point to be made is that algorithms are effective methods of charting the series of steps associated with completing a task, and many SME's respond well to using an algorithm approach to record this process.

Note that the specific knowledge required to perform each of the tasks is not defined, nor is the time required to complete the steps listed. All algorithms do is present the series of events and list the alternative actions to take if a subtask cannot be performed. The approach is systematic and direct and is suited for defining processes, procedures, and conceptual issues, such as directing a practice session in training, balancing a personal checkbook, or diagnosing maintenance problems.

Summary

This chapter has described task analysis as a method of detailing the respective tasks that are associated with completing a set of duties within a job. Task analysis is somewhat narrow in that it relates only to the specific job an individual performs. Work behavior was described as having four characteristics: (1) a definite beginning and ending point, (2) the necessary interaction with equipment, media, and/or other people, (3) the subsequent measurable results, and (4) the decision making, perceptions, and/or physical activities that made the act possible (Mallory 1987). Five methods of recording these observations of behavior in task analysis were described with a notation as to when each might be more effective in documenting the concern. Identifying and using subject matter experts in the documentation phase was discussed and suggestions made on how to make the SME more effective.

Figure 5.9   Preplanning for Practice Activity

Given: Performance does not meet the standard.

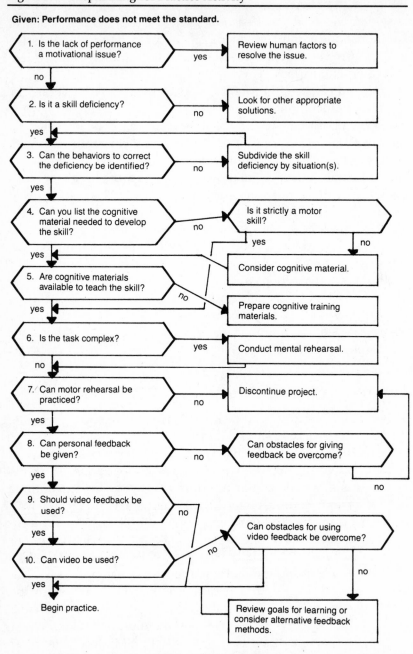

The last section described how to use work measurement methods in evaluating tasks.

Activity

Identify a recreational activity you like to participate in during your free time (swimming, basketball, skiing, tennis, checkers, playing cards, etc.).

Activity: _____

As you ponder this activity, think of one specific task (sequence of events) that is involved in this activity (jumping, throwing, falling, serving, dealing, shuffling).

Task: _____

List one specific skill that is necessary to be effective in performing this task.

Skill: _____

List the best action verb you can to describe what you are doing when you perform this skill (breathing, following through, cutting, stroking, lifting).

Action verb: _____

List two subtasks that are necessary to do this task. Describe these tasks with action verbs.

Subtask 1: _____

Subtask 2: _____

List what knowledge is necessary to enable you to perform each of these subtasks.

Knowledge, subtask 1: _____

Knowledge, subtask 2: _____

List what skills are necessary to perform each subtask.

Skill, subtask 1: _____

Skill, subtask 2: _____

References

Davies, I. 1973. *Competency Based Learning: Technology, Management Design.* New York: McGraw-Hill.

Deterline, W. A. 1968. *Instructional Technology Workshop.* Palo Alto, Calif.: Programmed Teaching.

Emery, F. E. 1964. *Report on the Hunsfoss Project.* London: Tavistock Documents Series.

———. 1976. *Rutures We Are In.* Leiden: Martinus Nijhoff.

Gilbreth, Frank B., and Ernestine G.Carey. [1948] 1984. *Cheaper by the Dozen.* New York: Bantam.

Griffin, R. W. 1978. *Task Design an Integrative Approach.* Glenview, Ill.: Scott, Foresman.

Hertzberg, F., B. Mausner, and B. Snyderman. 1959. *The Motivation to Work.* New York: Wiley.

Mallory, W. J. 1987. "Technical Skills," In *Training and Development Handbook, 3d edition,* edited by R. L. Craig. New York: McGraw-Hill.

Merrill, P. F. 1976. "Task Analysis: An Information Processing Approach." *NSPI Journal* 15, no. 2: 7–11.

Skinner, B. F. 1953. *Science and Human Behavior.* New York: Macmillan.

———. 1974. *About Behaviorism.* New York: Knopf.

Zemke, R., and T. Kramlinger. 1982. *Figuring Things Out: A Trainer's Guide to Needs and Task Analysis.* Reading, Mass.: Addison-Wesley.

6. Methods of Documentation: Performance Analysis

Chapter 5 described how to study the elements of worker behavior associated with the job an individual was asked to do. This chapter describes the steps in documenting performance and focuses on how to measure worker behavior in terms of outcomes of accomplishments or achievements.

Value

Sports have become a key part of our society, and many people adopt a team as a fan and use the sports page to follow its progress throughout the season. A box score usually reveals the statistics of a team's performance and then provides the bottom-line result, the score, which is an indication of who won and who lost the contest. Studying the statistics of the box score becomes an important part of the game for true fans, because they indicate what influenced or produced the bottom line or the score. The same assumption is associated with the documentation process when performance analysis is used; the analyst is looking for ways to develop a box score of results of human performance in the workplace which will help determine what caused, or produced, the bottom line or profitability of the firm. In industry, unless the firm remains profitable, the real metaphor of winning or losing has a true-lifelike meaning.

Chapter Organization

Effective analysis of performance in the workplace is not as easy
as counting the number of yards, goals, baskets, hits, or putts.
Achievements frequently are not as precise as these indicators
used in sports. The challenge is to make performance measures of
a job, like those in sports, and define achievement in terms of
number of sales, number of units produced, number of rejects,
number of repeat sales, number of satisfied customers. This is not
always done and therefore complicates the documentation process
of performance. This chapter seeks to present information that
points to the importance of precision in measurement, which sim-
plifies the real objective of documenting performance. In doing
this, the following will be discussed: how to differentiate between
evaluation of behavior and evaluation of achievement; and how to
gather data using comparative procedures, absolute standards,
management by objectives, indexes, and behavior frequency
counts.

Objectives

- Differentiate between evaluations made of behavior and achievement, and describe why achievement rather than behavior
  should be used to document performance issues.
- List four comparative methods used for assessing performance.
- List three absolute standards which are used to measure
  performance.
  a. Name three qualitative methods.
  b. Name two quantitative methods.
- List four steps associated with management by objectives, and
  describe how the employee helps define objective measures used
  in the performance process.
- List three indexes used to measure performance.
- List three approaches used to provide behavior frequency
  counts.
- In a practice activity, where you use one of the data-gathering
  procedures described in the chapter, achieve a mean score of
  seven on the feedback form provided.

Evaluation of Behavior Versus Achievement

A common problem in evaluating performance stems from failing to recognize what is being measured. Confusion comes from a long exposure of measuring performance with written tests. Tests administered in schools and industry (e.g., mathematics, mechanical aptitude) help establish cutoff scores for grades and advancement of students or for the selection of employees (Gilbert 1978). In most cases, academic tests measure behavior rather than achievement. For example, are multiple choice tests an accurate measure of what is learned? What the test measures is the behavior of selecting the best answer, which is given credit, and may not really monitor the achievement that is called learning. Knowing which is the best answer may or may not mean that learning has occurred. A person may be very good at taking a test and capitalize on this skill because it represents the behavior measured by the exam. The example shown in table 6.1 demonstrates this issue.

Measure A is a performance measure of achievement as represented in the number of shots made, sales completed, and cases solved correctly. Measure B is a performance measure of behavior

Table 6.1   Comparisons of Behavior and Achievement in Measuring Performance

TASKS	ACHIEVEMENT	SCORES FOR 1	SCORES FOR 2	BEHAVIOR	SCORES FOR 1	SCORES FOR 2
1. Basketball	Foul shots made	9	2	Correct procedures for shooting followed	85%	100%
2. Phone calls on book sales	Number of sales made per 100 sales calls	77	18	Rating on sales techniques used on scale 1 10	10	7
3. Case studies in business policy	Number of case studies solved correctly	7	4	Score on test to measure knowledge of business policy	78%	95%

as represented in demonstrating the procedures to use in shooting baskets, using sales techniques, and answering questions on business policy. Measure A monitors outcomes while measure B evaluates the process that is typically used to help individuals achieve. Note that both are performance measures.

The distinction to be made here is that performance scores can be classified as either achievement or behavior measures. When considering performance analysis to document a concern, identify which approach will provide the best description of the performance. In one sense, the box score metaphor more correctly represents performance of achievement rather than behavior. Comingling performance measures (achievement and behavior) or failing to distinguish between them makes interpretation difficult, at best, and in many cases it produces inaccurate statements of the concern being studied.

Using Comparative Procedures to Gather Data

Performance is a relative issue and has meaning as it is compared to other performances on the same task. Ranking is the most frequent method used to provide this comparison and includes the following four approaches: (1) straight, (2) alternative, (3) paired, and (4) forced distribution (Cummings and Schwab 1973). Each of these are described below.

Straight

With the straight ranking procedure, performers are ranked from best, number one, to the individual who is least effective on this measure. The basis for ranking may range from a subjective judgment, if the measures are not precise, to an objective one where the scores are exact. For example, scores such as the achievement measures described above can provide the bases for ranking and make it quite easy to order the scores to produce the rankings. A "box score," such as of number of sales contracts signed, provides information for ranking salespeople (see table 6.2).

Alternative

The alternative ranking procedure is slightly more complex than the straight one in that it uses a process of elimination to narrow

Table 6.2 New Contract Sales or Renewals for Month

SALES-PERSON	NEW CONTRACTS	RANK	RENEWED CONTRACTS	RANK	TOTAL CONTRACTS	RANK
A	27	3	12	4	39	4
B	38	2	58	1	96	1
C	18	4	41	2	59	3
D	72	1	18	3	90	2

the choices made when ranking (see table 6.3). For example, if eight mechanics are to be ranked, identify the most effective and the least effective person and assign the rankings of one and eight respectively. Repeat the procedure with the six remaining persons on the list by determining which of these are most and least effective, and assign them the rankings of second and seventh. Continue the process of narrowing the number of people to be ranked by assigning the third and sixth, and finally the fourth and fifth rankings to the remaining two persons on the list. This method works well when the measures are not precise and the analyst has to rely on a more subjective consideration of the individuals being evaluated.

Table 6.3 Alternative Ranking of Mechanics

MECHANICS	RANK	MECHANICS	RANK	MECHANICS	RANK	MECHANICS	RANK
A	___	A	___	A	ME* 3		
B	LE* 8						
C	___	C	LE* 7				
D	___	D	___	D	___	D	LE* 5
E	___	E	___	E	___	E	ME* 4
F	ME* 1						
G	___	G	___	G	LE* 6		
H	___	H	ME* 2				

*Most effective or least effective

Paired

In paired comparisons, rather than omit and narrow the number on the list, as described in the alternative method, expand the list to include all probable pairs of comparisons possible. For example, if four secretaries are in a word-processing center, six probable pairs could be made as contrasted with the two of the alternative approach. The paired listing, as shown in table 6.4, allows individual comparisons to occur. With these probabilities listed, underscore or circle the best person within the comparison. Ranking occurs by assigning the top rating to the person most frequently chosen (1st = C, 2nd = A, 3rd = B, and 4th = D). The argument favoring this method is that all possible combinations are evaluated against each other and thus better represent the true ranking.

Forced Distribution

The three ranking methods described above create an even distribution by sequentially ordering the performers through the evaluations given. With these methods, there is a first and a last, and a relational order is produced. With the forced distribution approach, performers are grouped, rather than sequentially ordered. Through forced distribution, the evaluator is required to assign a certain portion of individuals to various categories that suggest a range in performance. For example, if the categories are "low," "below average," "average," "above average," and "high," and the portions are respectively "10 percent," "20 percent", "40 percent", "20 percent", and "10 percent" for each category, the forced distribution illustrated in table 6.5 occurs.

Table 6.4   Paired Comparison of Cashiers in Store

CASHIER	COMPARISON		COMPARISON		COMPARISON		TIMES CHOSEN	RANK
A	_A_	B	A	_C_	_A_	D	2	2
B			B	_C_	B	D	1	3
C					_C_	D	3	1
D							0	4

Note: Cashier underlined is most effective of pair.

EMPLOYEES BEING EVALUATED	LOW	BELOW AVERAGE	AVERAGE	ABOVE AVERAGE	HIGH
40	4	8	16	8	4
20	2	4	8	4	2

Table 6.5   Forced Distribution System for Appraising Employees

This method forces the evaluator to differentiate between the performances of the employees, much like the ranking methods described above, but accounts for a grouping to occur within the ranges described by the categories.

Using comparative procedures has four limitations, as stated in the following questions: (1) Are the individual factors chosen to describe the performance representative of the total performance (generalizable)? (2) Are the ratings given by more than one rater going to be the same (interjudge reliability)? (3) Are the rankings of different groups or departments the same (comparable)? (4) Are the results, as they are individualized, helpful or dysfunctional to those evaluated (purposive)? Ponder these limitations when interpreting ranked or forced distribution information, because the rating does not accurately reflect the range represented in performance of individuals; that range may be so slight that calling one most or least effective may not be productive. The analyst must know the limits of the range and be prepared to justify those differences in order to communicate effectively with those evaluated, or interpret this information during the documentation process.

Absolute Standards for Gathering Data

Absolute standards, contained in either written qualitative or quantitative performance measures, evaluate individuals on several factors rather than the single global dimensions reported in the comparative methods above. These standards are statements that describe what is expected of the employee in terms of behavior, value, or output.

Qualitative Performance Measures

Qualitative performance measures are written standards used by the evaluator to determine if the individual does or does not meet the performance level that has been set. For example, does the individual use and wear the proper safety equipment and clothing? In this case, the written standard is stated in a question, and the evaluation is an either-or judgment. Two respective methods are used to determine this performance: (1) weighted checklist and (2) forced choice.

Weighted Checklist

Evaluating performance, using a checklist, can be done by the analyst to produce information about the point of concern. The checklist includes all the important tasks that need to be done to produce top quality products. Since some of the tasks are more important than others, a weighting is developed so that behaviors that are most important are given more credit than those of little importance. When the rater evaluates an individual using the checklist, the decision made considers if he or she did or did not do each task on the list.

Developing a weighted checklist is accomplished by generating a comprehensive set of statements about the work behavior necessary to do a specific job. A task analysis is helpful in producing this list (see chapter 5). After the task analysis has been completed, a group of SME's assign each item on the list a value, which represents how important each behavior is to doing the task. Using a seven-point scale, the SME's assign unfavorable values with low scores (1–3) and favorable values with high scores (5–7). A mean score of the ratings is determined, and a scale value for each item is assigned. The purpose of the scale value score is the weighting factor; the most important items have higher values and are the tasks that need to be done.

Consider, as an example, the task of preparing a technical written research report. The initial step is to develop a set of statements as shown in figure 6.1. The list is then given to SME's who assign the values using a scale of 1–7. The mean score for each item becomes the value scale.

If an SME feels that every item on the list is absolutely essen-

---

Figure 6.1   Tasks in Preparing a Research Report

Listed below are twenty tasks that are included in preparing a technical research report. Please assign each one a value using a scale of 1–7, with 1 being unimportant and 7 imperative.

VALUE	TASK
_____	1. Carefully prepared research question
_____	2. Carefully developed theme
_____	3. Completed a detailed outline
_____	4. Cited current literature in field on topic
_____	5. Made good note cards
_____	6. Organized quotes and documents sources well
_____	7. Prepared bibliography correctly
_____	8. Carefully proofread final copy
_____	9. Completed rough draft with enough time to rewrite effectively and correct omissions
_____	10. Printed paper on good-quality paper
_____	11. Margins at top, bottom, and sides were correct
_____	12. Spacing between paragraphs was correct
_____	13. Pagination was correct and placed properly
_____	14. Sources cited were authoritative and appropriate
_____	15. Punctuation was correct
_____	16. Verb-subject agreement was correct
_____	17. Provided good summary and conclusion
_____	18. Provided strong introduction that established the direction for the entire paper

---

tial, then values of 5–7 are given. If an item receives a very low rating (e.g., spacing between paragraphs correct), the item is dropped from the checklist.

The scaled values are important when looking at the analysis because these are the areas where significant differences in the outcomes may lie. If a performer is not doing the things that are of most value, then the concern should be greater than when he or she is omitting the low-scaled or -valued items.

Evaluators use the list, without the value rankings on them, to check if individuals do or do not do each task mentioned on the checklist. The final evaluation is determined by summing the value scores of the items that have been checked.

Forced Choice

Preparation of a forced choice performance analysis instrument begins in the same manner as that of the weighted checklist. Statements are obtained about job performance from persons familiar with the job. Judges then consider each statement using a scale of 0–5, and if the statement represents behaviors that are exclusively those of a very effective employee, a 5 is given. If no difference can be seen with respect to behavior of very effective and very ineffective employees, the statement is given a 0. A score between 0 and 5 represents the gradations of the judgment. When the scores of the judges are summed, a mean score is determined and becomes the discrimination index for each item. For example, if effective employees always turn in work assignments promptly and ineffective ones are always late, this item not only becomes a fine predictor of a good employee, but effectively discriminates between workers who are evaluated. The mean score of this item should approach an index score of 5.

A second index is produced to evaluate how essential the items are and measure the issue of whether they are favorable or unfavorable to job effectiveness. A scale of 0–5 is also used here by the judges, with a 5 meaning the behavior is very essential to the effectiveness of the job and a 0 meaning it is very questionable. For example, how essential is it to have work assignments turned in promptly? Promptness is valued, and so the index is high, or approaches 5. If the behavior was "to maintain a clean and orderly desktop while working," the index may be lower (3.27) because, although it may help and is nice, it may not make all that much difference in doing the job effectively. In short, each of the items on the list receives a rating by judges; one rating discriminates between effective and ineffective workers, and a second represents the perceived value of how it contributes to job effectiveness. Combined, these indexes give a notion of what effective employees do and what is perceived as important in realizing that potential.

Items are then clustered in sets; one item represents an effective employee, and a second represents a less effective one. The rater is forced to select the statement that best describes the employee; thus the term "forced choice." In the cluster sets, items are included that are capable of discriminating between effective and ineffective employees and at the same time determining favorability or unfavorability.

An example of a forced choice instrument that represents two clusters is shown below in table 6.6. Note that two items are compared and are clustered to represent behaviors that discriminate and yet are similar in terms of the favorable index.

The two items in 1 are highly favorable, but only 1A differentiates substantially between successful and unsuccessful employees. Both items in 2 have lower desirability; and only 2A has a high discrimination index.

These indexes, like the value rating in the weighted checklist, are removed when given to the evaluators. The evaluator chooses between the two items in each cluster that best describe the employee. The employee's score consists of the sum of the discrimination indexes of the items checked. High scores represent more desirable performance; low scores indicate less desirable performance (Tolle and Murray 1958).

Quantitative Methods

Both of the methods above use absolute standards and require the evaluator to decide if the statement applies or does not apply to the individual being evaluated. This either/or decision characterizes the qualitative method of analysis. With the two quantitative methods described — (1) conventional rating scales and (2) behaviorally anchored rating scales (BARS), the evaluator is asked to determine the degree to which the statements apply. Unfortu-

Table 6.6   Forced Choice Clusters

CLUSTER ITEMS	DISCRIMINATION INDEX	FAVORABLE INDEX
1a. Promptly turns in work	4.31	4.78
1b. Is confident and at ease in any situation	.91	4.68
2a. Is seldom late and reports to work on time	3.70	3.30
2b. Easily makes friends with others	.95	3.27

nately, conventional rating scales permit a *halo effect* to occur, which may consistently bias evaluations for or against an employee. They also tend to focus on personality characteristics rather than on performance. Nevertheless, conventional rating scales are widely used. Behaviorally anchored rating scales are designed to reduce bias and error while providing useful information for employees during a development program.

Conventional Rating Scales

Two considerations must be met when creating a conventional rating scale: (1) the characteristics to be evaluated must be identified, as occurs in the qualitative approaches, and (2) a scaling format must be selected. To begin, determine what key behaviors represent the performance indicators of the job being studied. The list may be small or large and may represent as many as twenty-five items. The number of items should be governed by the amount of fatigue that develops when a rater uses the form. After eight to ten items, the rater may show signs of tiring and may not provide the accuracy desired. Next, select a scaling format that provides the information desired.

A continuous scaling format uses two bipolar adjectives, such as low and high, and places a line between each of these words.

Low _____ High

The evaluator places a mark on the line to describe his or her rating. It is difficult to analyze the response, because the rater may not be able to find a discrete word or number to assign to the mark to give it a relative meaning. Therefore, discrete scales rather than continuous ones are recommended. Discrete scales use numbers that are placed on the scale to represent the equal intervals between the beginning and ending point of the scale.

Low   1   2   3   4   5   6   7   High

Words can also be placed on the scale at the equal interval points if desired.

1	2	3	4	5	6	7
Low	Below Average	Average	Above Average	High		

The rule of thumb to remember is this: don't exceed nine intervals when looking at the beginning and ending number on the scale. Seven intervals are common. It is best to keep the number of intervals at an odd number so a middle point can be quickly identified for ratings that are neither positive nor negative. Figure 6.2 illustrates a typical conventional rating form for appraising employee performance.

Nine items are evaluated using a discrete scale of five intervals. Although the numbers are placed on the scale, they are really word equivalents that label the intervals (5 = outstanding).

Behaviorally Anchored Rating Scales (BARS)

The steps involved in developing a BARS are similar to the processes used in preparing a weighted checklist and a conventional rating scale. Essentially, the four steps include the following: (1) obtain statements about successful and unsuccessful performance from SME's, (2) sort statements into general categories describing the job behaviors, (3) have judges evaluate the favorableness of each statement to determine a scaled value, and (4) assign the discrete scaling format to the selected incidents.

Figure 6.2   Conventional Rating Scale Form

In the space to the right, select the number that best represents the performance of the employee. A score of 1 = unsatisfactory, 2 = meets minimum, 3 = average, 4 = above average, 5 = outstanding.

PERFORMANCE CATEGORIES	RATING SCALE
1. Accuracy, thoroughness, completeness of work	1 2 3 4 5
2. Presentability of work	1 2 3 4 5
3. Care and maintenance of property and space	1 2 3 4 5
4. Judgment	1 2 3 4 5
5. Communication (oral and written expression)	1 2 3 4 5
6. Leadership	1 2 3 4 5
7. Public relations	1 2 3 4 5
8. Safety of self and others	1 2 3 4 5
9. Productiveness	1 2 3 4 5

Step 1: Obtain Statements

Critical incident is an effective method to gather the statements about successful and unsuccessful performance. As the name suggests, essential tasks that are critical to doing a job well are analyzed with this approach. An extensive discussion of this method is provided by John C. Flanagan (1954), who developed this approach to define the critical tasks associated with a job which made a difference between doing the job effectively and doing it ineffectively.

Consider, as an example, the role of a student and assume the list below represents both high and low performers.

- *Effective Incident*: A student reads and develops a detailed outline of the content included in the reading assignment before coming to class.
- *Ineffective Incident*: A student comes to class and listens without taking notes and waits to do reading just before exam.
- *Effective Incident*: A student actively follows the discussion in class, asks meaningful questions to check understanding, and also adds personal perspectives through thought-provoking comments.
- *Ineffective Incident*: A student sits in class and ponders what might be going on and asks questions that could easily have been answered if reading assignment had been completed.
- *Effective Incident*: A student carefully formalizes the question or theme of a paper, does extended research, and completes a rough draft two weeks prior to deadline so that time to ponder, rewrite, and do additional research can occur, writes and prepares it flawlessly, and hands it in on time.
- *Ineffective Incident*: A student begins the day before a paper is due to develop research question or theme, completes research, writes paper without proofreading, and submits it after deadline.
- *Effective Incident*: A student prepares for a test well in advance, ponders the total scope of the content for the exam, reviews thoroughly, and approaches testing situation calmly.
- *Ineffective Incident*: A student begins studying for an exam by reading the material for the first time the night before the exam,

makes a few notes, crams, rushes to the testing setting, and anxiously writes and answers questions.

The statements represent incidents when the student is considered very effective or very ineffective — the middle ground is usually not included.

In many cases, subject matter experts (SME's) are used to develop the statements by observing top and low performers, determining what makes the critical difference between the two groups' performances. The differences are formalized into statements or illustrations, reconciled with additional SME's review, and included in the list of categories to be used by the rater.

Since many jobs evaluated using this method are not as routine and repetitive as a technical skill, it is more difficult to determine, through observation alone, the critical tasks within a job that make a difference between doing it effectively or ineffectively. Therefore, interviews with those doing the job, such as a foreman and/or those he or she supervises, will be helpful; for example, ask the foreman: "What do you do to be effective in working with others?" "What are those things which distract you and keep you from being as effective as you could be?" "What, if done differently, would make you more effective?" "What are the types of attitudes, values, abilities, knowledge, or skills that seem to be necessary to be successful?" "In a like sense, what types of attitudes, values, inabilities, lack of knowledge or skills, limit your effectiveness?"

Questions, such as those following, to workers supervised by the foreman may add to your list of critical behaviors that a foreman uses to succeed: "What has a foreman done that in your opinion made him or her very effective as a supervisor?" "What has a foreman done that led you to believe that he or she was not up to par?"

Step 2: Sort Statements

The statements, or description of incidents, are then abstracted into a smaller number of behavior categories. The International Communication Association (ICA), Organizational Communication Audit Project, for example, developed eight categories that represented hundreds of statements on highly effective and ineffective communicators which included such items as perception of interpersonal relationships, clarity of role, and adequacy of information (Pace 1983). Kirchner and Dunnette (1957) did the same with sales positions by abstracting and listing thirteen categories, such as communicating important information to sales managers, initiating new sales approaches, and calling on all accounts. Zemke and Kramlinger (1982) looked at the same issue of sales and listed seven categories, such as finding prospects and leads, opening the call, uncovering the need, presenting the solution, closing the sale.

In the example of the student, four major tasks were evident, and the statements were consolidated into these categories: preparing for class, participating in class discussion, writing papers, and taking exams.

Step 3: Sorting to Determine Value

Performers do vary in skill, and a scale helps capture the differences. Using the example of the student, table 6.7 shows the typical sort of statements that represent a range in behavior in class participation.

Step 4: Assign Discrete Scaling Format

The final step, as shown in table 6.8, is to assign the values to the scales that are used in the evaluation.

The evaluator uses the form represented in table 6.8 to evaluate the student on class participation. A BARS form could be

---

Table 6.7   Statement Sort of Class Participation

- Actively follows the discussion in class, asking meaningful questions, and adds thought-provoking comments.
- Actively follows the discussion in class, asking meaningful questions.
- Listens to class discussion.
- Tunes in and out of class discussion and ponders issues outside of discussion topic.
- Ponders what might be going on in class and asks questions that could have been answered easily if reading assignment had occurred.
- Warms a seat in the class but is totally preoccupied by outside interests.
- Comes to class but leaves shortly thereafter for another appointment.

Table 6.8 BARS of Class Participation

ASSIGNED VALUES		STATEMENTS REPRESENTING PERFORMANCE
Excellent	7	Student has read assignment before coming to class, actively follows class discussion, asks meaningful questions, and adds thought-provoking comments.
Good	6	Student has read assignment before coming to class, actively follows class discussion, asks meaningful questions.
Above Norm	5	Actively follows class discussion, takes notes, rarely asks questions.
Average	4	Listens to class discussion.
Below Norm	3	Tunes in and out of class discussion, ponders issues outside of topic discussed, and asks questions that could have been answered easily if reading of class assignment had occurred.
Poor	2	Is present, warms a seat in the class but is totally preoccupied by outside interests.
Very Poor	1	Comes to class but leaves shortly thereafter for another appointment.

established for term papers, case studies, and home work assignments. The ratings would be summed across all categories, which in this case is the score taken from the assigned values placed at the left of the form. BARS require a great deal of work to develop, but the scale is an attractive alternative to conventional ratings, because it provides so much more detail on how the rater saw the performer. Contrast BARS with the conventional scale in figure 6.2 and determine what is meant by judgment or leadership. The BARS method details incidents that describe an excellent rating (7) or a minimum rating (3 or lower). With class participation, the detailed behaviors are identified that help the rater determine whether the student is poor or good.

Management by Objectives

A third method of gathering data during a performance analysis is management by objectives (MBO), which clearly establishes worker goals and provides ways to measure progress toward them. MBO, as it is called, is based on the assumptions that goals can be accomplished better if a person knows what is to be accomplished and progress toward a goal should be measured in terms of the goal to be accomplished. The unstated premise is simply that stated, clear goals are easier to accomplish than unclear, unstated ones (Pace 1983).

Another assumption of MBO is that both the subordinate and the supervisor are to be involved in defining and clarifying the goals to be accomplished. A well-stated goal is as quantitative as possible, with specific figures and dates. The process of involvement continues throughout the period of MBO, with the supervisor and the employee doing what is necessary to accomplish the goals. Periodically, the supervisor and the employee compare the employee's performance against the goals that were set. During the evaluation meeting the level of goal accomplishment is discussed, and the reasons for shortcomings and how performance can be improved are reviewed.

Direct Indexes

Looking at performance through direct indexes was referred to earlier when the metaphor of box scores in sporting news was mentioned; sports statistics are the precise measures that are found in discrete increments such as quality, quantity, and costs (Gilbert 1978, 45–47). Direct index measures describe accomplishments or achievements, such as a stenographer's number of typed letters, a salesperson's number of items sold, or a shipper's number of items shipped. A review of these indexes provides a broader view of other means of describing performance during the analysis process.

Quality

Quality has three types of indexes that can be used in evaluating performance: (1) accuracy, (2) class, and (3) novelty (Gilbert 1978). Each represents a different dimension in describing performance.

Accuracy   Accuracy represents the degree to which an accomplishment matches a model without errors of omission or commission. The model is the standard of excellence that the performers strive to achieve. The performers are measured on how well they can reproduce the behaviors displayed in the model. For example, behavior modeling training uses a videotape to display the correct method to perform the act to be learned. Performance is evaluated by how well the trainee matches (accuracy) the behavior displayed in the video model.

Class   Class defines the relative superiority of the accomplishment beyond mere accuracy. Four factors, as shown in table 6.9, are used to distinguish performances that go beyond the mere accuracy standard.

Value is added to products when craftsmen take personal pride in what they are doing and go beyond the standard required of them. For example, two bookcases are assembled properly and accurately. Similar materials are used, but the first craftsman nails the boards together to assemble the case, while the second uses glue and screws to secure all joints. The added attention to how the materials are assembled makes the second superior — of higher quality — and reflects a higher price. From a technical point of view, both are assembled correctly, yet they are not equal.

A second form of class is referred to as judgment points. The number of points achieved puts performers into a respected class, such as Olympian, world class, champion, runner-up. The ratings acquired by these performers set them apart from those who have not reached this plateau of performance. They are superior, and their ability to go beyond a point makes them unique.

A third form of class distinction is defined in terms of physical

Table 6.9   Performances Measured by Class

CLASSIFICATION	EXAMPLES OF MEASURES
Personal pride	high quality, value added
Judgment points	discrete measures of outside judges
Physical properties	soft, harness, size, strength
Opinion	power, pull popularity

measures, such as softness, hardness, size, or strength. Physical properties are used to classify the performance as superior. For example, when steel exceeds specific hardness and strength, it is given a higher quality rating, and those who can produce this product are considered superior.

A fourth measure that defines class is opinion ratings, which represent such factors as power, pull, influence, popularity, acceptance, and goodness. Opinions are influenced by social, personal, and group skills, and may or may not be tied directly to ability to do a job. For example, a person who is well liked, socially acceptable, and an average worker may have far more influence, power, and pull than the most efficient and capable worker. Therefore, opinion is a different measure from judgment points and should be considered when measuring and classifying performance.

Each of the four measures of class create a means of labeling quality in performance and is influenced by the inherent method used to measure them.

Novelty   Novelty represents the issue of uniqueness that distinguishes it from other performances, and because of this novel dimension it has an added value. Not all jobs allow for novelty, but when they do, the personal touch of creativity that gives luster and a sense of refreshment from the norm is encouraged. For example, a technical report written from a unique perspective may be appreciated.

Quantity

The most common indexes used to measure performance and describe achievement are the quantity increments of rate, timeliness, and volume (Gilbert 1978). Each has a unique dimension to add to the study of measuring performance.

Rate   Rate is the term used, when a measure is both time- and product-sensitive, to describe output. For example, if the product produced was hammers, the rate is the number of hammers per hour or per shift that are finished. Rate is the most common method of evaluating productivity and is critical to most incentive programs in place.

Timeliness   Timeliness is the concept used, when the measure is only time-sensitive, to complete a task or project. For example, if the task was changing the afternoon crew with the evening crew and bringing the production line up to full production capacity, the amount of time to achieve full capacity would be an important measure. Time frames, such as deadlines, schedules, and on-or-before issues, all reflect this measure of performance. Handing in term papers on time is a standard used in academics.

Volume   The last measure of quantity is strictly product-sensitive, when performance is measured in numbers of sales, contracts signed, pages written, or points scored. The outcome is not calculated by time as in rate measures; rather, it is measured in units of achievement.

Each of these three measures defines the quantity issues of performance. Each becomes a standard index for indicating how efficient individuals are in doing the job assigned. Again, the number of units produced, and/or the amount of time it takes to complete the unit, will probably be the most common terms used for assessing performance, with cost-sensitive measures rating a close second.

Costs

Controlling costs is a constant reminder that organizations must fight to remain profitable. In some organizations, this goal may be so well entrenched in the culture that measures of performance using labor, materials, and management costs are very apparent.

Labor   Labor costs represent the amount of money expended to purchase all the necessary human resources, overhead, benefits, wages, insurance, and taxes to produce a product. These costs are amortized over the basic unit developed for the customer; for example, the cost of labor to a mining firm may be measured in terms of cost per ton of mineral mined. Accurately reporting and controlling these labor costs is one of the most meaningful tasks managers face. Documenting this cost during performance analysis is essential to effective analysis.

Materials   Materials costs represent the expenditures for supplies, tools, space, and energy. These costs usually remain somewhat stable during the year and therefore are more predictable when calculating costs. Budgeting for supplies, fixing costs to cover overhead, and establishing maintenance and replacement budgets for equipment also become part of the amortized cost per unit to the customer.

Management   Management represents the administrative cost associated with producing a product. These costs include the supervision, public taxes, and internal allocations that support the development of the product. Management cost should be rather stable during the year.

Evaluating performance using cost measures is critical to maintaining a profitable organization. Human resource directors manage costing information to justify the importance of the HRD function within the firm by targeting these three areas. Decreasing labor and management costs through human resource development helps lower the total costs that are built into the basic unit produced.

Using Behavior Frequency Counts to Gather Data

Chapter 5 described the importance of being able to observe behavior when doing a task analysis. The ability to look for discrete acts of behavior and distinguish how a series of these acts constitutes a task was highlighted. That same skill is required to observe specific behaviors and count how frequently they occur during a specific period of time. To gather data using this method, three tasks are involved: (1) pinpointing or targeting a set of specific behaviors to monitor in the performers, (2) counting the frequency of each of those behaviors during a specific time frame, and (3) charting or recording these behaviors. From these observations, the performance patterns are established.

In the pinpointing phase of analysis, many of the procedures described earlier in this chapter and the preceding one are used. For example, pinpointing occurs in task analysis using both the job-duty-task approach and the stimulus-response method; during the meeting with an SME, specific behaviors and critical sequences that appear to contribute to job performance are listed.

The quantity or rate index is developed by counting the number of times each response occurs during a specific time frame. The count is a time- and product-sensitive measure. Record the number of times a process is completed, the frequency of occurrences observed, or the number of units produced in the time frame.

Charting the observed behavior is sometimes troublesome. It is one thing to count; it is another to note accurately that observation. Much like the time-motion approach, behavior frequency counts can be obtained by videotaping the individuals being monitored. Sitting down in front of a video recorder and being able to stop and start or replay the tape makes charting a relatively simple matter. One rater can record a number of behaviors using this approach. Videotaping, however, sometimes becomes an obtrusive factor, and caution should be used so as not to alter the performance of the individual being observed. Where cameras are common, however, such as security monitoring systems in a bank, the video recording method seems very suitable. On the other hand, an evaluator who is observing the behavior can be as threatening and obtrusive as a camera. Caution, therefore, should be taken to position observers where they can effectively monitor the behaviors without drawing attention to themselves. Recording devices, such as a clipboard or stopwatch, and excessive note taking, can often distract, and care should be taken to minimize the feelings that are naturally generated when one is being evaluated. A small note pad that fits in a hand can be used effectively.

The major problem faced is finding a way to record the count and rapidly return to the role of observer. A number of behaviors may be monitored at the same time, making it easy to miss some behaviors when the observer is preoccupied with marking down an observation. Practice is important and will help establish a method for recording an observation quickly and returning to the act of monitoring.

The number of behaviors that can be monitored depends on the tasks involved. For example, if a card dealer in a casino is being monitored to identify (1) the number of hands dealt, (2) four types of verbal transactions, such as polite, indifferent, rude, and value added, (3) the ratio of winning to losing hands, and (4) the amount of money wagered, the observer might find it easy to keep track of the number of hands played and whether the house won or lost; however, the task of monitoring conversations and money wagered might be monumental. Multiple analysts may need to be assigned as the number of tasks increases so that the process of recording can be precise and accurate. Note that this could all be done by one person with videotape. Videotape may be more economical to use when the behavior being monitored occurs rapidly, and/or when there is a significant number of behaviors to observe.

Behavior frequency counts usually are designed to look at broader issues than those associated with traditional time-motion studies. Performance is recorded in terms of the frequency per time frame selected. Behavior frequency counts are effective in establishing performance levels and to monitor areas where high and low performers differ. They use discrete observational measures that are easy to figure mathematically and, in many cases, to manipulate statistically.

Summary

This chapter has reported five methods that are used to gather data on performance measures. The comparative approach involves three methods of ranking performance and a forced distribution method to differentiate between individual performers. The absolute standards approach, in which observations are made by an authoritative model or judge, consists of the use of the weighted checklist and forced choice methods as qualitative ways of evaluating performance. The quantitative methods of conventional and behaviorally anchored rating scales were also described as measures using an absolute standard. Management by objectives demonstrates how employee-objective measures are used to monitor the progress and output of individuals. Although no instruments were suggested for using direct indexes, the discussion described various labels that could be used to represent indexes of performance. Indexes are associated with a variety of methods used to analyze performance. The last approach to analyzing performance was behavior frequency counts.

The question to answer during the documentation of the point of concern is "What type of data are needed to consider meaningfully the issue under study?" Direct indexes, frequency of behavior, or comparative data may be needed. Knowing what would best document the concern will influence which approach is used. Each approach is unique and can provide additional perspectives that other approaches are incapable of providing. Some approaches are more difficult to develop, such as some of the measures that use qualitative measures. The intent of this chapter was to suggest that multiple approaches may be best suited to provide the data needed. Knowing the value of each method and how to develop an instrument to gather the information should be helpful in accomplishing these documentational goals.

Activity

You are going to evaluate the performance of eight people you work with or know. Begin by listing their names.

1. _____   2. _____

3. _____   4. _____

5. _____   6. _____

7. _____   8. _____

Select an ability, skill, or competency that you feel you would like to evaluate them on using comparative measures. The ability may be their competence in adding numbers, drawing figures, memorizing facts, lifting weight, jumping, throwing, and so on. The important thing is that you feel you know them well enough that you could estimate the skill you decide to use.

Ability: _____

Listed below are four different approaches you will use to evaluate these eight people on how well you think they can perform the respective tasks.

Straight Method
Skill or ability: _____

Rank order the people one through eight to represent their competence on this measure. One is best, eight is least effective.

First _____

Second _____

Third _____

Fourth _____

Fifth _____

Sixth _____

Seventh _____

Eighth _____

Alternative Method

Using the alternative ranking method, evaluate these eight people on a second skill and compare them.

Skill: _____

A _____

B _____

C _____

D _____

E _____

F _____

G _____

H _____

Paired Method

Using the paired method of comparison, evaluate eight people on a third skill.

Skill: _____

A _____

B _____

C _____

D _____

E _____

F _____

G _____

H _____

Forced Choice

Using a forced distribution comparison, evaluate these eight people on a fourth scale. In the distribution, put two in the top group, four in the middle group, and two in the bottom group.

TOP GROUP	MIDDLE GROUP	BOTTOM GROUP
1 _____	1. _____	1. _____
2. _____	2. _____	2. _____
	3. _____	
	4. _____	

Looking at the four comparative evaluations you have done, what have you learned about this group of people?

References

Cummings, L., and D. Schwab. 1973. *Performance in Organizations, Determinants and Appraisal.* Glenview, Ill.: Scott, Foresman.

Flanagan, John C. 1954. "The Critical Incident Technique." *Psychological Bulletin 51:* 327–358.

Gilbert, T. 1978. *Human Competence, Engineering Worthy Performance.* New York: McGraw-Hill.

Kirchner, W. K., and M. D. Dunnette. 1957. "Identifying the Critical Factors in Successful Salesmanship." *Personnel* 34, 54–59.

Pace, R. W. 1983. *Organizational Communication, Foundations for Human Resource Development.* Englewood Cliffs, N.J.: Prentice-Hall.

Tolle, E. R., and W. I. Murray. 1958. "Forced-Choice: An Improvement in Teacher Rating." *Journal of Educational Research* 51: 680–685.

Zemke, R., and T. Kramlinger. 1982. *Figuring Things Out: A Trainer's Guide to Needs and Task Analysis.* Reading, Mass.: Addison-Wesley.

7. Methods of Documentation: Analyzing Needs Using Individual and Survey Methods

In the previous two chapters, task and performance analysis was reviewed. The focus in task analysis was on the job and what skills and knowledge were necessary to accomplish it. The human dimension was introduced in performance analysis, and the focus shifted from the job and to how well individuals were performing that task. Both task and performance analyses use observational methods to gather data; an analyst studies the job, then rates and assesses the performance. The focus in this chapter now shifts from an observational perspective and asks the people actually doing the job how they feel about what they are doing, how they perceive the task, and how they see their role in the workplace. The focus, then, is on employee perceptions and how their feelings impact their productivity and the work they do. Needs analysis, therefore, looks at employee perceptions of those things that are keeping them from making their strongest contribution to the organization.

Two chapters are devoted to how to document perceptions of employees: the first considers methods to gather data from individuals using face-to-face and telephone interviews, written questionnaires, and card sorts; the second describes how group methods are used to assess employee needs.

Value

The best-trained workers who know every skill and understand all that is required may not be performing at the level they are capable of reaching. A concern, like a drop in performance, may have nothing to do with ability, experience, education, or cognitive ability; rather, it may be an issue centered in the goals, aspirations, needs, and motives that the individual brings to the work setting. These factors are all within the human dimension of the worker and therefore are difficult to observe. Because these needs are not overt, an observer may be unable to see and record them, as is common practice in both performance and task analysis. Needs assessment requires the analyst to go directly to the employees and ask them about the issues that are influencing their work. By determining what those needs are and responding to them, the small increments of increased performance will make a large difference over time in how profitable a firm can be. If no action is taken, the converse consequence may be a reality.

Chapter Organization

Gathering data from individuals can be done in a variety of ways: personal interviews, telephone, questionnaires, and card sort. These methods are described as they relate directly to the process of assessing needs to obtain the information necessary to document the point of concern being studied.

Objectives

At the conclusion of this chapter, you will be able to do the following:

- List five steps for effectively conducting personal information gathering interviews.
- Define the use and value of various questioning strategies in gathering information.
- List the procedures, pros, and cons of using a telephone to gather information.
- List the pros and cons of using questionnaires as a data-gathering procedure.
- List the steps and rationale for constructing and field testing a questionnaire.

- List the procedures for using a card sort technique.
- In a practice activity, use an individual needs analysis technique and receive a mean score of 7 on the feedback form provided.

Information-Gathering Interview

An interview is very purposive and designed to accomplish a specific intent. Interviews are used to gather or share information, solve problems, persuade, appraise, screen, counsel, praise, or reprimand (Goyer, Redding, and Rickey 1968). They may be highly structured, such as asking a set of questions on an interview guide, or have limited structure, such as in counseling.

Three organizational elements should be included within the structure of the interview: (1) the opening, (2) the body, and (3) the closing (Pace, Peterson, and Burnett 1979).

Opening

Within the opening, establish rapport and formalize the purpose of the interview. Rapport is built by showing interest in the person and being warm, genuine, and basically cordial. A second aspect of the opening is outlining the reason for the interview and stating what will occur as well as listing the time that will be involved; these are helpful in maintaining a sense of professionalism. When the interviewee knows what to expect and the time it will take, he or she will be more relaxed and will quickly prepare to participate.

Body

The body of the interview has the most structure and is where most of the information is gathered. Questions may be either open or closed and are usually arranged to achieve a specific objective. Four sequencing strategies, as shown in figure 7.1, are frequently used in the questioning process: (1) funnel, (2) inverted funnel, (3) tunnel, and (4) quintamensional (Stewart and Cash 1985).

The funnel sequence is much like the metaphor of its name; the initial questions are broad, like the top of the funnel, but narrow and become more specific, like the funnel, when reaching the end of the series. The converse is true with the inverted funnel sequence; specific questions are followed by broader and more

Figure 7.1   Question Sequence

FUNNEL	INVERTED FUNNEL
How do you feel about your benefits program? What types of health care needs are most important to you? Which of these health care services do you value most? Why is that the case? Is it worth the price you pay for this service? Will other employees continue to pay this price for the health care they receive?	Will other employees continue to pay this price for the health care they receive? Is it worth the price you pay for this service? Why is this the case? Which of these health care services do you value most? What types of health care needs are most important to you? How do you feel about your benefits program?

QUINTAMENSIONAL	TUNNEL
What do you know about your benefits program? What role does the health care program play in your family's life? Do you like your current health care package? Why do you feel that way? How do you feel about your benefits program: very strongly, strongly, uncertain, some concern, absolutely no concern?	How would you rate the following elements of a health care package? Use a five-point scale: 1 indicates excellent, 2 fine, 3 no opinion, 4 inadequate, 5 very poor.

TUNNEL (continued)					
Hospitalization	1	2	3	4	5
Death	1	2	3	4	5
Vision	1	2	3	4	5
Death benefit	1	2	3	4	5

general questions about the topic. The tunnel sequence starts with a specific question and then uses a rating scale to evaluate a set of specific alternatives to see how the interviewee feels about this topic. The quintamensional sequence begins by using the funnel sequence approach of asking a rather broad question, then narrows it down to a specific point, and then states the original question in a way that measures how intensely the interviewee feels about the topic.

In short, the body of the interview is where you will solicit information to help document the concern. The questions center on the issues that need to be clarified. You may need to probe and continue to get more specific, such as represented in the funnel method, look for feeling checks, such as found in the quintamensional approach, or use the direct method, as shown in the tunnel sequence. For the data to be meaningful, the interviewer must use and develop the skill of asking questions, evaluating those responses, and then following up with secondary questions that establish what others mean and feel about the issue.

Close

The close of the interview provides a review and/or summary, describes what follow-up, if any, will occur, and expresses appreciation to the interviewee for his or her involvement (Pace, Peterson, and Burnett 1979). This brings the interview to a smooth conclusion and removes doubts about what will occur now that the interview has been completed. Thanking the person is a professional touch that should always be included.

Five steps that lead to an effective information-gathering interview include (1) preparing, (2) beginning, (3) conducting, (4) concluding, and (5) recording what you have learned.

Preparing

Preparation is vital in a needs analysis interview. The interview purpose is to determine what factors are preventing employees from realizing their potential in the organization. Probing for needs is not always an easy task, because a person's goals, motives, and needs are somewhat private in nature. Because of this delicate humanistic issue, be well prepared in order to succeed. Questions are the heart of the information-gathering process, and preparing and developing the skill of using three types of questions will be helpful: (1) direct, (2) open, and (3) clarifying.

Questions

Direct Questions   Direct questions are designed to require a specific answer. They narrow the range of possible answers that can be given and focus on a particular point in discussion. The types of responses obtained through this questioning approach are short and precise. While direct questions are designed to gather specific information, they can also guide the discussion toward a specific issue; for example, "Do you have time to talk now?", "Did you complete the project?", "Will you be able to work this out with them?" Direct questions get right to the issue, and sometimes this directness will appear threatening and arouse defensiveness; it can actually result in getting less information. Use direct questions with skill and be sensitive to the threat, yet at the same time realize the economy and precision that are is possible through them.

Open Questions   Open questions represent the other side of the coin because they produce a wide range of answers rather than specific ones. They are stated in extended sentences instead of in a few words; open questions are somewhat less threatening than direct ones, and they provide the respondent with an opportunity to give unanticipated information. The word *open* implies a wider range of responses when contrasted with the word *direct*, which implies a narrower perspective. With the open questioning approach, a variety of responses can be obtained, and this increases the control an employee has over the interview. This increase in power minimizes potential defensiveness, allows for more personal points of view, and allows the employee to include comments and topics that are concerns he or she faces. For example, "How do you see this situation?", "What do you feel motivated that response?", and "Why is that so?" are types of open questions. As evidenced in these examples, the directness and ability to predict are exchanged for reasoned and elaborated responses. Increased preparation is required to use open questions because of the loss in power to control the interview and the need to go with the flow of the conversation, which may broaden the issues beyond what has been anticipated. The preparation will include a variety of topics and broad issues in order to understand where the employee is coming from and read the cues provided in the answer. Dealing with this shift in the power to control and managing the expanded number of issues that emerge require added preparation.

Clarifying Questions   Clarifying questions are used to probe for additional detail, reduce uncertainty, and search for a more complete explanation of what has just been said. Clarifying questions are used to promote full information, clear up misunderstandings, seek meaning, and show interest in the response. For example, "You mentioned you had a few problems; could you give me some examples to help me understand?" To really understand a point of view, additional follow-up questions will be required.

All of these questioning approaches will be used in an information-gathering interview. Understanding the power each has to help elicit relevant information about employee needs will make the interview a powerful tool.

Study Those Interviewed

A second area of preparation is to learn as much as possible about the background of those being interviewed and to be able to speak their language. For example, buzz words, technical language, regionalism, or generation gap usage are parts of the culture of the work group that are unique, and preparing to use the work group's language in an interview is important.

Sampling

A third dimension of preparation is determining who should be interviewed. Not everyone can be interviewed, so a sample of individuals who will be representative of the group as a whole may need to be selected. Using the recommendations of others may be helpful, but be aware that those providing the recommendations may have vested interests. Random selection frequently is used to govern the selection process. Random sampling seeks to select respondents from the population in such a way that every person has an equal probability of being selected. Two methods of making this selection are (1) Nth name sampling and (2) tables of random numbers.

Nth Name Sampling   The total list of names of employees is usually available for a needs analysis in an organization. The Nth name method is well suited to select names randomly from this list. Begin by placing a number beside each name on the list. Determine the sample size needed, and divide that number into the total number of names. If 1,000 employees were on the list and the desired sample was 250, then every fourth person (1,000/250) would be selected. Randomly select the first person from the list, and then take every fourth person either side of that name. If the first person's number was 3, then select the Nth person (fourth) clear through the list — 3, 7, 11, 15, 19, 23, 27, 31, and so on — to determine the sample population.

Tables of Random Numbers   Many books on statistics contain a list of random numbers. Follow the instructions provided in the book to select the sample.

Sometimes purposive approaches are used, such as selection of peer leaders. Quotas, defined by some demographic consider- ations, are used and a select but equal number from each respec- tive group is chosen. Note that order and preparation bring precision into the selection process.

Outline

Prepare an interview outline that includes the basic topics to be covered and/or establishes the problem parameters to be evalu- ated. The point of concern will influence the outline and parame- ter constraints to be documented through the needs analysis. Basic questions should be organized by topic to keep the inter- viewer focused and to guide the individuals who are being inter- viewed. Always prepare more questions than what might be needed rather than being caught unprepared.

If the point of concern being analyzed involves published data, records, or other objects, have them available to refer to in the interview. For example, if a person is asked about a report he or she has not seen, or which may have called by another name, the actual report would help this person respond from a more precise position.

Practice

Practice will be an added benefit; actually go through the experi- ence with a colleague and receive some feedback before beginning data gathering. This practice is much like pretesting a question- naire to determine what works and what needs revisions.

Beginning

The skills described above on effectively opening the interview apply here; build rapport and set the agenda. These two elements are critical. In addition, help those interviewed understand why they were selected and how their contribution has added value. As they feel the significance of the interview, they will respond with a sense of importance rather than contempt or disinterest.

Conducting

The body of the interview includes the line of questioning and the parameter of the problem identified during the preparation phase. If a highly structured approach is used to gather the data, move from topic to topic, question to question, in a rigorous manner. Often, a prepared written questionnaire is used to guide the process. Interviews with very little structure move with the themes that emerge within the discussion. These themes may well be the topics targeted for data collection; if so, continue, but be prepared to redirect the discussion to the mission statement or intent represented in the opening of the interview. For example, ask "Could you give me additional information on (the target issue)?" and then pose a question that relates to it. Again, structure has its value and is an issue to ponder in the body of the interview to gather the desired data effectively.

Be prepared to probe by using the clarifying questions described above. Often this clarification can best occur when the employee is asked to provide an example of what he or she means. Examples will become rather instructive and give added meaning that is impossible in a statement. If the employee said, "The supervisor does not like me and is always on my case," follow up by asking, "Could you help me understand by giving me examples of some things your supervisor has done to cause you to feel this way?" The examples provide the basis for the feelings. The premise for asking for examples is that humans are rational and provide support for why they feel as they do. Situations that provoke these feelings are real in the mind of the person, although they may seem insignificant to another.

"Listen" with both the ears and the eyes during an interview, because messages are presented both verbally and nonverbally. Feelings of intensity, bitterness, excitement, gratitude, or anger are better measured at times through nonverbal cues.

The interviewer should be concerned with his or her own nonverbal cues, such as gestures, movements, and tone of voice, because the interviewees are watching with equal interest. To show interest, nod the head frequently and make short comments, such as "I see," or "I can understand that," or even just "uh-hun." These comments are short and do not interrupt the employee's train of thought. Supportive statements, such as "Very good!", and "You deserve a lot of credit for that" convey interest and recognize their achievement. Watch out for nonverbal reactions that convey disagreement, shock, alarm, or disbelief. Because they normally affect the interview adversely, avoid such reactions.

Pacing will be an important aspect of the successful interview. The sequence of questions will influence how fast the interview will appear to be moving. For example, in a highly structured sequence, the pace appears to be more rushed, because questions come one after another in a systematic rhythm. In contrast, the unstructured interview may appear to drag because of the absence of rhythm. Control this rate of the interview by mixing up the structured and spontaneous questions.

Pauses are effective ways to prod a person into expanding the answer, but they should not be allowed to last more than fifteen seconds. If a pause lasts more than a few seconds, the employee may feel uncomfortable. Note, however, that by not immediately following an answer with a question, an expansion of the answer follows because the interviewee feels more is expected. If the pause is a function of not knowing where to go or a mental "blackout," ask the person to tell you more about that experience while regrouping and thinking of another question.

Note taking is an essential skill if open and clarifying questions are used and is usually developed with practice. Care should be taken when recording names, dates, ages, percentages, figures, and major points. Ask for the spelling of the name to ensure accuracy, or to repeat the percentages, figures, dates, or ages. Slow down the pace of the interview to make sure these data are recorded correctly. If need be, say: "That's an important point. Let me get that down." Although it is not necessary, asking the interviewee for permission to take notes is a good practice. Some interviewees will not be as open if notes are taken; if this is the case, assure them that the confidentiality of the information will be observed.

To preserve the accuracy of the notes taken, try and type them up right after, or soon after, the interview. This ensures that the major and/or minor points are not lost or overlooked. Too, sometimes the abbreviations cannot later be deciphered accurately and may be recalled here, while forgotten if done later.

Concluding

The elements within the close of the interview provide a review, outline what actions, if any, will follow the interview, and convey appreciation. This is a good time to reiterate what will be done with the data without promising anything specific. Nonverbal cues, such as standing, shaking hands, and vocal inflections, signaling that the interview is complete can be used to make the transition from the body of the interview to the close. Thanks should be given, and if appropriate, a brief memo sent later to express thanks again.

Recording What You Have Learned

The final stage of the information-gathering process is to evaluate the responses and distill from them themes, needs, and trends that are related to the issue you are trying to document. The process of distillation is somewhat different for interviews that use closed or scaled questioning procedures, which will be described later in the chapter. Thus what is reported below is a method to analyze the notes and reactions to a more open-question strategy for gathering information.

To begin, organize the notes and review them as soon as possible to see that they are complete. The abbreviated notes should be expanded into complete sentences that formalize the ideas represented by the respondent. With these additions made, code each respondent's answers with a number, and where multiple pages of notes are involved, place that number on each page of notes. A photocopy is then made of the notes, and the master is retained. The analysis then begins (Pace 1983, 216).

1. Cut up the photocopy of the responses, sort all the answers, and place them together for each question.
2. Having completed step 1, take those same responses to each question and sort them by some prearranged category, such as

position, years in service, or level of authority, and copy each group's answers per question.

3. Identify themes occurring in the answers of the total respondents for each question.
4. State each theme and excerpt some typical responses from the list, which have been appropriately disguised to protect the anonymity of respondents, to illustrate how you arrived at the theme.
5. Repeat step 3 (identifying themes) with the separate groups.
6. After all responses to all questions have been reviewed for themes, compare and contrast by looking for similarities and differences among and between the themes, and between groups of responses for different categories of employees.
7. Write an analysis of the interview responses to indicate what the needs are.

Knowing how the data will be managed influences how the notes should be recorded. During the process of analysis, knowing what is important, where the information should be placed on the cards, or why it is necessary becomes more apparent. There-

---

Figure 7.2   Interview Guide for Employee Needs Assessment

Name of Employee: _____ I.D. no. _____
Title: _____ Work area: _____

1. What are the major problems you are confronting in doing your job?
2. Will you likely confront these same problems in the future?
3. What information would be helpful to make you more effective in dealing with these problems? (knowledge)
4. What situations come up from time to time which make it difficult for you to be as effective as you desire? (motivational)
5. Are there conditions at work that seem to limit your effectiveness? (conditions to motivation)
6. Are there any aspects of your work where additional training or practice would make you more effective in what you do? (ability or skills)
7. If money were not a problem, what equipment would you obtain to make you more efficient in what you do? (lack of equipment rather than ability)
8. If you were to hire a person to help you, what knowledge, skills, and personality traits would you look for?

---

fore, just as practice is encouraged before the interview occurs, so is analyzing the practice notes.

With the five steps in mind, a sample interview guide is provided to evaluate employee needs as shown in figure 7.2. The focus of the questioning is on: (1) knowledge, (2) skills or ability, and (3) motivation to do the job. Only open questions are included in the guide. Other questioning strategies are displayed in the latter part of the chapter describing additional needs assessment methods. With only open questions included, probing and follow-up are implied.

Probe after each question. Ask for examples of concerns, types of information, conditions, equipment, and so on to clarify the needs. The purpose of the interview is to document the needs. The interview guide becomes the working point to find them.

Gathering Data Using a Phone

The telephone is often used to gather information because it is difficult to reach the person for a personal interview. Both interviews are personal in a one-on-one setting, but have characteristics that are unique to each medium involved.

Pros and Cons

The decision to gather data using a telephone will be prompted by several factors. The phone becomes a good alternative that enables you to reach individuals located in remote regions, get a rapid response, reduce the psychological threat or personal intimidation possible in an interview, or schedule appointments. People seldom avoid answering the phone, their attention is evident, and, they are willing, remarkably so, to disclose the information to a relatively unknown source (Alreck and Settle 1985). The cost per interview is less expensive than a personal one, interviewer bias appears to be lower, between 80 and 90 percent of those contacted will agree to participate, and most respondents are far more candid on the phone (Zemke and Kramlinger 1982).

With the above benefits go some equally compelling liabilities. The phone interview tends to be shorter, lacks show-and-tell dimensions, includes more structure, and requires a special personality that is warm, friendly, and pleasant.

Not all people that need to be interviewed have phones. Phones are primarily at home and work, and reaching individuals at locations other than these is improbable. If the concern that is being documented must have responses from those who are not at home or the office, a phone interview will not work.

The heart of the phone interview is the questions. More direct rather than open questions will be likely, and use of clarifying questions to determine what the respondent's answers mean will be limited. Questions that imply short yes or no responses, don't demand significant pondering, and can be answered without creating a sense of failure if the interviewee answers "wrong" will work best.

Preparing

Preparing for the telephone interview is similar to preparing for the personal interview. The questioning sequence is worked out in explicit detail and field-tested to be certain it works.

A distinct difference between the two interviews occurs during the opening. The interviewer will be an unknown, in most cases, and must build rapport rapidly, set the agenda, and begin immediately to ask for responses. Many of the necessary social graces of the face-to-face interview will be eliminated. Keep the greeting as short and simple as possible, state your business briefly, and ask the first question to engage the respondent and get him or her involved. Refrain from asking for permission and time; just begin.

Conducting

Similarities between the interviews occur during the conducting phase of the process. With the phone, however, many of the cues normally available to determine if the person is suitable as a respondent are not present. Therefore, the first question should be a qualifying one; is he or she really the person who has the information needed? Once the person has been qualified, be confident that once you begin, he or she will rarely stop before you have completed the questioning. Early questions should be simple and nonthreatening. The questions must be written for the ear rather than the eye, and this usually means using simple rather than complex sentences — a subject-verb-predicate construct. With a phone interview, complex sentences are difficult to respond to because they cannot be studied; therefore, avoid them altogether or use them sparingly. An "I don't know" response should be a possible and acceptable response to any question. Probing or asking clarifying questions is possible and encouraged when using the phone. These questions need to be anticipated and written into the questioning sequence. Open questions can also be used, but there are some limitations in doing so: Respondents cannot see you and appreciate the time it takes to make notes about their responses; this usually results in a pause that may give them an opportunity to hang up on you. Pacing is very important when using the phone. Also, it is difficult to give the type of nonverbal cues of interest, concern, and support that work well in a face-to-face interview, and this often gives the respondent a feeling of talking to a wall. Include some un-huh's or other cues that you are still there.

With the phone, interject a few progress cues, since they cannot see where you are in the interview; for example, "You are doing great, I have a few more questions left." These cues are important when more than five minutes have passed and the interview is not completed. The opening statement at the beginning of the interview should be short and thus may not completely set in the respondent's mind the length of the interview or the number of questions; cuing statements give an indication that the interview is concluding.

Closing

The closings of the two interviews are similar; thank the interviewee, and state what additional contact will be made.

Example

A hypothetical situation may be helpful in looking at the use of the phone to gather information for a needs analysis. Suppose there was a mining firm that had over twelve hundred workers living in a large geographic area that covered four counties. The mountains in the terrain created seasonal weather conditions that were severe, and absenteeism and lateness were frequent during four months of the year. Public transportation is not available because of the sparse population. The concern for absenteeism, late-

Figure 7.3 Late and Absentee Issue, Transportation and Transit System Survey

Precall: Phone no. _____ I.D. no. _____

Intro: Hello, is this _____ ? Do you work at XYZ? (If yes, continue; if no, thank the person, go to next call) I am _____, from GBW, and we're looking at transportation concerns of employees at XYZ.

Body:

_____ 1. How many miles is your round trip to work each day?

_____ 2. How many minutes does this round trip take?

_____ 3. In bad weather, how many additional minutes are added to your round trip?

_____ 4. If you drove alone each day, how much would it cost you each week?

_____ 5. Do you currently ride in a car pool? (If no, go to no. 6)

    _____ a. Including yourself, how many are in the car pool?

    _____ b. How much does it cost a week to ride in the car pool?

    _____ c. In bad weather, is the decision to come to work a collective or individual matter? (Use C or I to record)

    _____ d. In bad weather, if the car pool voted not to come to work, would you come by yourself?

    _____ e. If the car pool arrived late to work, would you ask the driver to pay for your lost wages?

    _____ f. Have you had any problems with car pooling? (If yes, "Could you give me an example?" _____)

_____ 6. Would you use a private bus if it were available? (If no, go to no. 7)

    _____ a. How many times a week would you ride the bus?

    _____ b. How much a week would you be willing to pay for this service?

    _____ c. In your opinion, how many additional minutes would this add to your travel time each day?

    _____ d. If no overtime were available for those using the bus, would this make a difference? Explain.

    _____ e. How many miles would you be willing to go to catch the bus?

_____ 7. Driving conditions change during the year; is there any particular time or season you would be more likely to use the service? (fall, winter, spring, or summer)

_____ 8. Does the distance you travel each day cause you to consider seeking employment closer to home?

_____ 9. If offered an equal job closer to home, would you accept it? (If no, go to no. 11)

_____10. How many miles closer would it have to be?

_____11. In summary, what are your feelings about paying a fare to ride a private bus to work? (very positive, positive, neutral, negative, or very negative)

Close: Thank you very much; we appreciate your opinions.

ness, and possible turnover could relate to transportation needs of the employees. To determine the needs on this issue, a phone interview is designed to gather data to document this concern.

Figure 7.3 represents an interview guide for a phone interview to look at possible issues of transportation, lateness, and/or absenteeism. Study figure 7.3; the opening or introduction is direct. The first line contains the qualifying question; if the answer is no, the interview ends. Next, it identifies the caller, the firm conducting the study, and the concern to be evaluated. The guide then moves directly to the body of the interview. The first branching question is number 5, and a "no" response sends the interview directly to question 6. This is another branching question, and if "no" is answered, the interview moves to number 7. The last branching occurs with question 9. Not all the questions are simple sentences. The complex sentence is used to establish a condition or assumption that may be associated with absenteeism or lateness, or a probability issue. In question 5f, the first clarifying question is added, and a second is included in 6d. Question 11 represents a scaled question to look at attitudes toward the bus. Questions 8 and 9 view the problem as it may relate to turnover. The close is quick and to the point, and indicates that no future contact will be made.

In this hypothetical case, the respondents were spread out over a large geographic area, phone numbers were available to reach them, rapid return was possible, and costs were minimized. These issues would have justified the use of the phone interview.

Written Questionnaires

There will be times when neither a phone nor a face-to-face interview will be suitable for a needs analysis. A written questionnaire can be a good alternative approach to use. In this case, create a questionnaire to use as a means for determining those needs. Make this decision if employees are both willing and able to give you correct/truthful answers, if more direct or reliable sources for gathering the data are not possible, and if the questionnaire is created and tailored specifically to meet your needs.

Pros and Cons

As with any information-gathering method, there are definite strengths and liabilities associated with a questionnaire's use. Some strengths might be these:

• The costs are minimal when gathering large amounts of information.
• Mail reaches those unavailable through other methods.
• One individual can reach large numbers at one time and over large geographic areas.
• Questionnaires can be administered to large groups gathered at one location.
• Employees can respond to the questions at their leisure.
• Bias is minimized.
• Tabulations are quick and easy.
• The questions are uniform.
• Most people are familiar with questionnaires to the point where they know how to respond.

    Some liabilities might be these:

• Response rates are usually low when mail is used.
• The analyst may not be certain who responded.
• The number of questions asked is reduced to achieve higher rates of return.
• Personal contact is absent.
• The ability to read is required.
• The sequence (if it is important) of answering questions is not known.
• There is a tendency to want to overinterpret the results because of the absence of probing to see what people really meant.

Preparing

Preparing a survey instrument is similar to the other information-gathering approaches described above. Planning must occur to prepare the questionnaire. The first task is to state the goal. This statement should be limited to twenty-five words and include why and what is wanted, and how the information will be used. If this is impossible, it may mean that the goals are not clear. This raises a real question: "Is the analysis worth doing?" Planning a questionnaire involves study — to know the topic, to create meaningful questions, to see the value and purpose, and to assign interpretive meaning to the findings. It also involves knowing about who will be surveyed — to construct properly worded questions, to avoid offense, and to encourage responses. Planning also helps in working with management — to sell the idea, to get support funding, and to meet their needs.

When writing the questions and looking at the design for the survey, the keep-it-simple-stupid (KISS) principle should apply. A questionnaire that is easy to read, to record responses on, to return, to evaluate, and to report has merit.

To begin, review the goal, objective, or point of concern for the study and keep it posted at all times. This statement is what the data gathering is all about. After writing any question, come back and ask, "How does this help me meet the objective, or goal, or find out more about the point of concern I am trying to document?" This will keep the questionnaire development on track.

Demographics to Include

Demographics represent specific groups of people within the larger group to be surveyed. Groups of interest may be gender, age, work classification, years of service, education, or number of dependents. Demographics are useful when analyzing the data, because a specific group may perform differently from other groups, and if you manage the data, these variables make the group comparisons possible.

Questioning Strategies

Several strategies are possible when writing questions, and these have been discussed in part earlier. Open, direct, and clarifying questions were shown to be especially useful in the oral interview. With a written format, the medium changes and questioning strategies are defined by open, closed, scaled, and mixed format. Technically, the oral questioning strategies are open questions because the respondent selects his or her own set of words to frame the response. In contrast, a closed question does not provide any options other than those stated on the questionnaire. For example, only the listed response can be checked — "Yes," "No," "Select a specific number," "Mark a specific feeling," or a "Place on a scale which one represents your agreement or perception." Closed in this case means choosing nothing more than what is listed. Direct questions do model the closed response, in that the length is somewhat controlled, such as the answers "Yes" or "No," "providing numbers" or "I think that is a good idea." A direct question is considered open; however, because the response can be a variety of answers, the only anticipation is that they will be answered in a short response.

Closed questions can be either/or responses, such as yes or no, agree or disagree, like or dislike, right or wrong. Closed questions can also be scaled so that a range of feeling is represented in the question, such as a Likert format of "strongly agree, agree, neutral, disagree, or strongly disagree." The scaled questions expand the options from either/or to the range provided on the scale. Another scaled approach is to use a semantic differential by taking the either/or response and placing it on a scale such as "right 1 2 3 4 5 6 7 wrong," where a score of 1 would mean absolutely right, 4 a neutral feeling, and 7 an absolutely wrong feeling. Rank order questions are also closed and require the respondent to order information to reflect his or her perceptions of what is "top to bottom."

Note that while the either/or, rank order, or scaled responses are closed, they produce different types of data to analyze. Data from the either/or response produces nominal data, which can be summarized by using percentages or frequencies, such as 20 percent agree while 80 percent disagree, 7 said yes while 29 said no. *Nominal* means "a name" in Latin, and so these data are names of groups or a specific response such as boys, girls, work force, management, or yes/no. Rank order responses produce *ordinal* data, which means that these data are classified in terms of being higher or lower, greater or lesser than other responses. Ordinal data can be reported using not only frequency and percentage scores but also percentile rank, correlation, and chi-square tests. The scaled responses represent *interval* data, which means that there is a standard interval between points on the scale.

Using the example above, the standard interval is stated in numbers (right 1 2 3 4 5 6 7 wrong); interval data allow all the measures of the first two types of data, plus measures of central tendency, such as range, mean, median, and mode, and a number of inferential statistics, such as z- and t-tests, F-tests, and univariate and multivariate analysis of variance.

A mixed strategy of questions includes both open and closed questions, as illustrated below:

1. Rank order your preferences for getting to work.
   _____ car pool
   _____ individual car
   _____ public transportation
2. Do you currently ride in a car pool? ☐yes ☐no
3. Car pools are a very good means of getting to work.
   strongly agree   1   2   3   4   5   strongly disagree
4. Why do you feel this way about car pools? Explain.

The sequence begins with three closed questions: (1) a rank order question on transportation preferences, (2) an either/or question, and (3) a scaled question. The last question is open.

In review, a questioning strategy should be developed to achieve your goal and may include a mixture of open and closed questions. The questions used will influence how the information is managed during the analysis phase. Look at the objective and see what needs to be documented. If frequency of response is all you need, either/or questions will be all that are required. When trying to determine if significant differences do exist between specific groups of workers, scaled data are useful. If interpretive analysis is important, the open question will be needed. Again, knowing what is needed and what should be talked about during analysis helps determine how the questionnaire and questions will be developed. Therefore, study the goal, determine specifically what is wanted, determine the method needed to manage the information to report, and write each specific question.

Field Testing

Field testing the written questionnaire is as important as the practice activity used for both the face-to-face and the telephone interviews. This is where the bugs are worked out before the expenses of printing, mailing, and following up are involved.

A valid field test has to take place on the actual population that the survey is designed to reach. This can be done in three ways: (1) go in person and have a few people complete the survey, and then ask questions, (2) use a focus group, where a small group completes the questionnaire individually and gives feedback as a group, or (3) send the questionnaire to a few people in the mail, have them take it, and give feedback in a phone interview. Note that in each method the respondents are from the specific population, individuals take the survey as it is prepared, and they provide feedback on each question — the wording, what did it mean, how could it have been written better for clarity and understanding; the sequence — was it logical, did it flow, were the instructions proper and adequate. In short, the review is quite taxing but it provides the information needed to rework the questions and sequence to make the questionnaire more effective.

Preparing the Final Form

Prepare the questionnaire so that it meets all the following requirements:

- Make it appealing to the eye and as easy to complete as possible.
- Number items so the respondents are not confused when completing the form.
- Add proper instructions and, where necessary, provide examples of how to respond.
- Group items in a logical topical order.
- Begin with nonthreatening and interesting issues.
- Avoid locating important items at the end of a long questionnaire.
- Make good use of white space.

Another way to help make the questionnaire look professional is to choose paper that is twenty-pound bond with a high rag content; is printed on an off-white, gray or beige paper with black ink; and will fit in #9 or #10 envelopes. Have it typeset, if possible, and include a stamped, self-addressed envelope (Alreck and Settle 1985). All these factors give questionnaires a professional look and increase the response rate potential.

Cover Letter

With the questionnaire ready for use, prepare a cover letter to accompany the survey. The cover letter should explain what the survey is about, who wants to know and why, why the respondent was picked to answer the questions and why they are important, how long it will take, how difficult the questionnaire will be to complete, if he or she will be identified, what benefit he or she will receive, how the information will be used, and when the survey should be completed (Alreck and Settle 1985).

Returns Needed

The question is often raised as to how questionnaires should be sent out, but more important, how many should be returned in order to obtain reliable indications of the needs being documented. Some people do not respond quickly to questionnaires, so follow-up letters or phone calls are required to get the questionnaires returned. With a small population, everyone's questionnaire may be critical. As the population grows larger, a smaller percentage of those surveyed must respond to achieve your goals. Here are some rough guidelines for different-sized populations: under 25, get 23 responses; for 50, get 45 returns; for 100, get 75 returns; for 150, get 110; for 200, get 130; for 250 get 150; for 500, get 210; for 750, get 250; for 1,000, get 275; for 1,500, get 300; for 10,000, get 370; and for 1,000,000, get 380. These figures represent a confidence interval equal to 95 percent, which means that you can be 95 percent confident that the data from the sample represent the feelings of the total population. If time and money are going to be spent to gather information, obtain enough responses to state the respondents concerns accurately.

Reporting the Results

As noted above, reporting the results for a questionnaire differs from that of interviews. For example, managing hundreds of surveys, and preparing them for analysis, requires having a plan so that proper evaluation can occur. Record keeping is, therefore, important — know who has returned the survey (so follow-ups can occur), how many have responded, whether mailing costs and phone calls are within budget, where time lines are on target? The management system developed will make this task easier.

Begin by setting up a time line for doing respective tasks. List the first mailing date, target what date the follow-up phone calls will occur, list when the second mailings for follow-up were sent out, list a cutoff date, and list dates for coding, encoding in the computer, data management, tentative results, complete analysis, writing the report, and presenting it to management. This time line of events will help plot the progress.

With a properly prepared questionnaire, the majority of responses will be back within two weeks. From that point on, start following up to generate the second wave of returns. A phone call or card dropped in the mail may move some to action, but the likelihood is that the respondent will have thrown the questionnaire away and will need to be sent a second one. This will be your second mailing. This is often the most difficult part of the task. As the first wave comes back, take each response, assuming it can be identified, and check the list to note completion. Wrong addresses show up in the returns; check to see if a better address can be found and remail those surveys.

This effort is time consuming; therefore, many analysts initially mail out many more questionnaires than normal to get the minimum back to produce meaningful data. Others gather the data through organized groups within the organization and have the questionnaire administered by supervisors to ensure good returns.

Coding begins as the responses come back. Assign each questionnaire a number to identify it for data analysis. Check the survey and see if it is completed. Some are incomplete and not useful and thus may need to be discarded. Keep track of the number of responses that fit into this category.

Encoding is taking the information and placing it in the computer using your respective analysis program. The responses are be translated into numbers. The meaning of those numbers is kept in a code booklet that represents how each question was assigned a variable name and a number to represent each response. The data are then checked to verify that they are accurate.

Data management usually begins with a frequency distribution printout to look for general response patterns in the data. Each question is reviewed, and the percentage of responses for each question part is assessed. Trends often appear in this review and are validated through additional data management. The next manipulation that occurs is to look at the subgroups or demographic clusters within the population. Crosstabs or chi-squares are often run to see how respective groups responded to specific questions. At this time, a significant chi-square means there is an interdependence between how respective groups responded to the question. In short, subgroup members are responding in a like manner. These data are helpful in a needs analysis because they start to paint a picture of how different groups feel about respective issues. Note that this measure does not tell us that the groups are significantly different; rather, it states that there is an interdependence.

The final runs on the data look at correlations between responses for patterns, and, where interval data are available, they look at measures of central tendency and inferential issues to see if subgroups actually respond differently to respective issues.

Again, determine before beginning what the data management procedures to be used are and what types of evaluations are going to be made. This occurs during the planning phase of the project. As data are teased, additional statistics may be selected to perform different manipulations to test some insights that come.

To write the report and present it, follow the guidelines outlined in chapter 14. Again, the interpretations should be based on what can be said: with nominal data, what percent was in each group; with ordinal data, how did responses correlate; and with interval data, were there differences between groups?

With these points in mind, an example of a needs survey is included in figure 7.4. This particular example assesses the needs of supervisory functions. Note that an explanation of the requirements for each function is included on the back of the survey form. This helps maintain the validity of the assessment.

Figure 7.4   Needs Assessment Questionnaire Reporting the Developmental Needs of First-Line Supervisors

---

Notice to mid-level managers: This form is for you to use in planning and reporting developmental needs of the first-line supervisors who work for you. Before you complete this form, please discuss it with the supervisor whose developmental needs are being assessed. If you have any questions about supervisory functions listed, please read the definitions found on the back side of this form.

Your name: _____   Office: _____   Phone: _____
Supervisors: _____   Office: _____   Phone: _____

In completing the survey, check the number that best applies.

"1" means that there is almost no need for development.
"2" means a level of need that would fall between 1 and 3.
"3" indicates some need for further development.
"4" indicates a level that falls between 3 and 5.
"5" means that the developmental need is very substantial.

SUPERVISORY FUNCTIONS

---

1. Helping individuals work with job-related and personal problems.	1	2	3	4	5
2. Giving information to employees and receiving information from employees.	1	2	3	4	5
3. Understanding labor-management relations.	1	2	3	4	5
4. Providing leadership.	1	2	3	4	5
5. Establishing a safe and healthy work environment.	1	2	3	4	5
6. Acting as a link between workers and upper management.	1	2	3	4	5
7. Training and preparing employees to work.	1	2	3	4	5
8. Placing and utilizing the work force.	1	2	3	4	5
9. Planning, scheduling, and organizing.	1	2	3	4	5
10. Checking on work progress.	1	2	3	4	5
11. Appraising performance.	1	2	3	4	5
12. Getting support and services outside the unit.	1	2	3	4	5
13. Preparing administrative reports and personnel actions.	1	2	3	4	5
14. Understanding and implementing equal employment opportunity policies.	1	2	3	4	5
15. Handling disciplinary and adverse actions.	1	2	3	4	5

BACK SIDE OF FORM

---

1. *Helping individual workers with job-related and personal problems.* Help employees with their work problems; give personal attention to employees who have difficulty adjusting to the job; help employees in improving their job performance; explain employees' mistakes to them; be aware of subordinates' personal welfare; help employees solve personal problems;

Figure 7.4   Needs Assessment Questionnaire Reporting the Developmental Needs of First-Line Supervisors (Continued)

---

listen when employees ask for advice; settle conflicts between employees; refer employees with alcohol, drug, or serious emotional problems to the agency's employee assistance counselor.

2. *Giving information to employees and receiving information from employees.* Keep workers fully informed about things of general interest; hold meetings to discuss work activities, organizational directions and policies, current work schedules, employee suggestions, and general work problems; respond to suggestions to improve production and act on those that have merit; encourage employees to express ideas and opinions on job improvement; encourage employees to do the work in the way they think best; consult with employees on important job matters.

3. *Understanding labor-management relations.* Work within the union agreement; explain employee rights and handle grievances.

4. *Providing leadership.* Find a balance between unilateral decision making and abandoning all influence; take prompt and appropriate action; make it easy for employees to discuss things; establish with employees that the supervisor is in charge of obtaining employee cooperation.

5. *Establishing a safe and healthy work environment.* Ensure that employees are aware of the agency's health services; give clear information regarding established safety practices and ensure that they are carried out on the job.

6. *Acting as a link between workers and upper management.* Clearly explain management to workers and vice versa; define, defend, explain, and clarify organizational goals and policies for employees; pass employees' views on to management; assume responsibility for the work group when it is criticized.

7. *Training and preparing employees to work.* Select and give detailed information to each employee about what is to be done and exactly how it is to be done; explain thoroughly and clearly correct work methods, work sequences, and changes in work; teach and train; develop skills of other workers.

8. *Placing and utilizing the work force.* Assign work according to individual abilities so that employees can work most effectively; fit the right employee to the right job; understand how employees feel about their assignments; match individual interests and abilities with the job; understand employee ambitions and abilities.

9. *Planning, scheduling, and organizing.* Plan work; carefully schedule how daily activities are to be conducted by the work groups; plan individual work assignments; plan in advance, sometimes on a long-range basis; plan the content of meetings; follow through to see that work is done on schedule; set priorities.

continued

Figure 7.4   Needs Assessment Questionnaire Reporting the Developmental Needs of First-Line Supervisors (Continued)

---

10. *Checking on work progress.* Know the daily developments and progress of work; keep abreast of details of each employee's progress; see that orders are carried out; correct and assist employees; make certain that work is up to standard; recognize early when something goes wrong; set deadlines; encourage employees to participate in setting deadlines.
11. *Appraising performance.* Establish standards of job performance; write performance appraisal plans; give employees effective feedback on both good and poor performance; do official performance appraisals; recognize good performance personally; criticize performance constructively, giving response for the criticism; keep employees informed of all aspects of the job situation, including progress.
12. *Getting support and services outside the unit.* Get needed equipment and see that employees have the work materials they require; coordinate with other supervisors when group action is needed to solve a problem; get the full cooperation of other units; send work outputs to other units in ways that will expedite action.
13. *Preparing administrative reports and personnel actions.* Complete paperwork on time; prepare accurate production records, reports, and memoranda for the work group; prepare and maintain individual production and performance records; prepare and maintain position descriptions; fill vacancies.
14. *Understanding and implementing equal employment opportunity policies.* Give employees an equal chance to do well on the job according to their abilities; give employees an equal chance to be considered for promotion; provide opportunity to succeed on the job independent of an employee's race, color, religion, age, sex, national origin, or handicap.
15. *Handling disciplinary and adverse actions.* Implement the adverse action regulations so that the actions are not reversed on appeal; explain to employees their rights.

Card Sort Needs Survey

The final needs assessment procedure described in this chapter is a card sort method. The name of the method defines the activity of the respondent — sorting individual statements listed on 3 × 5 cards. Employees' needs are placed on a card and included in a deck to make it possible to sort quickly and compare one need with any other in the deck.

The card-sort method allows the analyst to evaluate three dimensions: (1) directionality (positive or negative), (2) intensity (strength of the need), and (3) the saliency (importance). Initially, the employee reads and sorts cards into three separate piles: (1) I would really like to have training or information on this subject, (2) makes little difference, (3) I would definately not want to have training or information on this subject.

The first step of sorting evaluates the *directionality* of the employee's needs. The analyst knows what issues the employee would like to have information about (positive), those areas where uncertainty is evident (neutral), and those that are viewed adversely (negative). Once the initial sort is completed, the analyst takes the cards in the middle pile "makes no difference", places a rubber band on them and removes them. The employee then takes the pile of *positive* statements and rank orders them. The rank of one through "N" is placed on each card. This ranking evaluates the *intensity* of the employee's need. Once the ranks have been written down, the respondent then makes a third evaluation of the statement: "How important is this issue." A choice on a scale of 7 - 1 is circled with 7 being very important, 4 neutral, and 1 meaning unimportant. This response measures the *saliency* of that need. If the analyst is interested in the *negative* statements of needs, and wants to know precisely how the employee feels about them, the same process as that used with the favorably stated items is completed. For many analysts, the additional sorting of the negative statements is important because it provides information on needs that have either already been fulfilled or appear troublesome to the employees. Figure 7.5 represents a typical set-up for a 3 × 5 card.

Note that each of your cards has a number; the rank order is placed in the right-hand corner, the problem statement of the need is included, and the scale to list the importance of the need is placed at the bottom or on the reverse side of the card.

Figure 7.5   Card Sort Method Needs Assessment

---

14. (Card number)   (Rank Order # _____)
     Problem solving in the day-to-day operations in the
     work which I do. (Needs statement)

                        How important is this to you?
          Very Important   7   6   5   4   3   2   1   Unimportant

---

It may appear that intensity (the rank order) and saliency (importance) are really the same. This is not always the case. For example, if the need identified were safety training, this may be ranked low in terms of the overall needs, but at the same time be considered very important. Both dimensions are important and provide different information.

To gather data using this method, give each employee a deck of cards. Let's suppose that 30 statements were in the deck. The procedure they follow includes: (1) sort cards into one of three piles, *I would like, makes little difference, I would not like;* (2) remove and place rubber band around *makes little difference* group; (3) rank order *I would like* pile from highest (rank of 1) through least and place this number in right-hand corner of card; (4) list the importance of each item by circling the number which best represents this feeling; (5) place a rubber band around this group of cards. Repeat if desired the *I would not like* group by: (same as 3 above) ranking from least desirable (rank of 30) to most acceptable of this group of statements (use inverse ranking numbers); (same as 4 and 5 above). Those in the *makes little difference* group are not sorted or evaluated on importance and are given a ranking score of the median.

Three scores are then available to the analyst to evaluate the employee needs using this method. Initially, the 30 statements are classified by the frequency each was sorted into the three respective groups. This provides a rough estimate of where the needs cluster in terms of what the employees want. The second measure is found by using the mean ranking score of the employees, and this provides a relative sense of how strong they feel about these issues. The mean score of the importance of the need is also considered, and provides information on how salient they are. From these three measures, the analyst knows which of the needs fall in respective clusters, how strongly the employees feel about them, how important they are, and how he or she might look at them for possible interventions.

Bellman (1975) provided an example using this method in assessing supervisory training needs. While his method differs from that listed above, it provides a similar result. Bellman was interested in supervisors rating forty statements which represent ten areas: (1) motivation, (2) delegation, (3) problems, (4) training, (5) performance, (6) planning, (7) time, (8) ideas, (9) teamwork, and (10) communication. Four statements in each area were written and placed on cards. A question was used to guide the sorting activity: "If you had the answers to ten of these forty questions, which ten would be more helpful to you in doing your job?" Those questions perceived as most helpful to the supervisor are selected, and the needs assessment is made by evaluating those chosen. Two examples of Bellman's questions are : (1) "When faced with a difficult situation, how do I identify the real problem?" (2) "How do I know if the work is going as planned?"

Using needs statements and sorting by preferences or using questions to guide the card sort method are both effective. While more time is required to place the statements on cards, the value of comparing statements to one another and keeping the focus centered on the specific need, is worth it. This approach can be used throughout the organization to document needs and has some novelty that often keeps the respondents on target.

Summary

This chapter has defined needs analysis as identifying people's perceptions of those things that are keeping employees from making the strongest contribution possible to the organization. Needs were defined as a perceptual phenomenon, which means that analysis requires using methods that allow employees to report their perceptions, such as interviews, surveys, and card sort methods.

Two types of interviews, face-to-face and telephone, were described as methods to determine how individuals perceived the work done. Pros and cons for each method were outlined along with such issues as planning and conducting interviews and evaluating the information obtained. Questionnaires were described as an additional method for assessing needs. Planning, developing strategies, and preparing the questionnaire were described. Record keeping and data management, which were unique to the survey, were discussed. The last method outlined was the use of a card sort for defining the needs of employees. The analysis of needs is critical to finding those perceptions of why an individual might not be making the contribution that is possible.

Activity

Make copies of the standard needs questionnaire (figure 7.4) included in the chapter. Administer it to some leaders or supervisors
who are part of your same group.

Collect questionnaires and tally responses for each item. Create a frequency distribution table showing the percentage of responses by respondents to each question.

Write a paragraph indicating what seems to be the most common and important supervisory needs of the group.

References

Alreck, P. L. and R. B. Settle. 1985. *The Survey Research Handbook*. Homewood,
    Ill.: Irwin.

Bellman, G., 1975. "Surveying Your Supervisory Training Needs." *Training
    and Development Journal* 29 (February): 25–33.

Goyer, R. S., W. C. Redding, and J. T. Rickey. 1968. *Interviewing* Principles
    and Techniques. Dubuque, Iowa: Brown.

Pace, R. W. 1983. *Organizational Communication, Foundations for Human Re-
    source Development*. Englewood Cliffs, N.J.: Prentice-Hall.

Pace, R. W., B. D. Peterson, and M. D. Burnett. 1979. *Techniques for Effective
    Communication*. Reading, Mass.: Addison-Wesley.

Zemke, R. and T. Kramlinger. 1982. *Figure Things Out: A Trainer's Guide to
    Needs and Task Analysis*. Reading, Mass.: Addison-Wesley.

8. Methods of Documentation: Analyzing Needs Using Group Processes

Group processes are efficient ways of gathering information about the needs and perceptions of individuals who are performing respective tasks within the organization. Rather than interview one person, a group is used to evaluate these same issues. A group is defined as three or more individuals who have come together with a common purpose and with some degree of organization or structure to accomplish a specific goal. Although no upper limit has been set, the group must remain small enough in number to enable each group member to communicate with relative ease as both a listener and an active contributor of ideas. When the size of the group expands beyond the level of easy giving and receiving of information, the definition of a small group no longer applies. Working with a group, rather than an individual, is different and requires additional skills of managing multiple numbers of ideas, encouraging active participation, and reporting information with respect to group agreement, intensity, and feelings. These dynamics change the data-gathering task.

Value

While individual feelings are articulated in an interview, there is an extra dimension that comes as individual perceptions are added together through a group process. Individuals learn to operate in groups and feel as a group, and expression is sometimes easier when the group, rather than the individual, identifies feelings. The consensus process often solidifies impressions or feelings that have not been verbalized by respective individuals, yet, within the dynamics of the consensus process, perceptions are crystallized and find new meanings that were not possible independently. Ironically, feelings often are hard to verbalize; the feelings are real and within, but the words to clothe them with meaning aren't at our command. Yet, within the group, the symbolization is completed and formalized. Thus groups provide clues and precision that may not be possible one-on-one.

Chapter Organization

This chapter describes group processes that are used to gather information on perceptions about how respective jobs are being performed within the organization. These include interacting groups, nominal groups, focus groups, and consensus groups.

Objectives

At the conclusion of this chapter, the following should be possible:

- List the rules and procedures for using an interacting group to do a needs analysis.
- List the procedures used to gather information using a nominal group to do a needs analysis.
- List the procedures to gather and report data using a focus group to do a needs analysis.
- List the skills and methods to use in a consensus group to do a needs analysis.
- In a practice needs assessment activity using a group, achieve a mean score of 7 on the feedback form provided.

Interacting Group: Brainstorming

Developing new ideas and methods for doing a task is often part of the process of helping individuals become more effective. Brainstorming is a proven interacting group technique for producing new ideas. The key to using this technique successfully is the elimination of critical and judgmental reactions to ideas and suggestions offered by the group. Four basic rules govern brainstorming and allow each individual in the group to contribute facts and experiences that no one else in the group possesses: (1) criticism is ruled out, (2) freewheeling is wanted, (3) quantity is wanted, and (4) combination and improvement are sought (Pace, Peterson, and Burnett 1979).

Criticism Is Ruled Out

Adverse criticism is not allowed during brainstorming, and any judgmental inference or nonverbal action is not tolerated. Create an atmosphere that is supportive and accepting of information that is given. Killer phrases, such as "We've never done it that way," "It won't work," "It is too expensive," "It is too hard to administer," "It needs more study," "Let's be practical," and "It's not good enough," are never permitted during the session. The objective of the group is to generate ideas, not evaluate them.

Freewheeling Is Wanted

The wilder the ideas, the better. Initial responses often trigger ideas that are more moderate and practical. Let the imagination run away and have the excitement of not being limited and constrained; imaginative ideas can always be brought down to earth later in the process. At this point, stimulate one another in the group to be creative and thought provoking, and reach out beyond the limits imposed in the day-to-day practical world.

Quantity Is Wanted

One of the goals of the group is to produce the largest number of ideas possible to resolve the concern. The larger the number of ideas, the higher the probability of finding some usable information. It is easier to pare down a list of ideas than expand a short one. Most likely, the best ideas will be quite far down the list, since the routine ones tend to be offered easily and quickly.

Combination and Improvement Are Sought

With the extended list in front of the group, look at creative ways of combining these ideas and improving them. This constant review of all the ideas to see how they can be expanded, trimmed down, combined, reordered, or restated is a useful method of working some of the reality of the workplace into the ideas suggested.

Procedures to Follow to Use Brainstorming

Invite participants to attend the activity, and identify the time and room where the activity will occur. Act as the facilitator. Introductions of the participants should use some novel approach to break down the formality that usually accompanies this type of meeting. The task should be explained so that all understand what brainstorming is and what it can do to help document the concern represented for study. Post the four rules in a place where all can see them. Appoint a recorder to write down all the ideas. A flip chart can be used to record the ideas as they are generated. You are now ready to begin.

1. Have the recorder write down the question or concern on the flip chart you are going to brainstorm. Tear this piece of paper off and post it next to the four rules so that it will be in front of the group at all times. This is the target issue and should be conspicuous throughout the meeting. Refer to it often as the idea generating slows to help redirect thinking.
2. Begin the first phase of listing as many possible ideas as can be generated, stressing quantity and freewheeling. List the questions as fast as you can take them. If participants get an idea that cannot be written down at that moment, have paper for them to jot it down so it is not lost. Record it later if possible.
3. Keep encouraging and supporting the work effort of listing ideas. Sometimes competition for the number of ideas generated is helpful. If you do this, have two recorders and divide the group so you can create the competition. Remember, during this phase, keep the ideas coming — as many as is humanly possible.
4. When the groups or group seems to be exhausted of ideas, go to the lists and review them. That review may generate a few more. If you have two or more groups, reviewing the lists of each may generate some additional suggestions.
5. Begin the combination and improvement phase of brainstorming. With the lists in full view, turn the task to combining these ideas and list these creative combinations. See how many begin

to fit, or how parts of one idea added to another creates a new perspective.

6. Look one last time at the list, and ask them to see if restating the idea would make it clearer. This step will often refine the language of the idea. In no way can criticism of the idea be suggested because of the language. Watch this issue carefully.

7. The brainstorming session usually ends with this step. How the information is used may or may not be the mission of the group. If the group has been charged to look at implementation, have them divide the list of ideas into three areas: (1) those which can be used immediately, (2) those which are near-future possibilities, and (3) those which will be studied over a longer time period.

The purpose of brainstorming is to help develop new ideas and perspectives about an issue or need of the people performing respective tasks within the organization. It can be used frequently when a group faces a situation requiring creative thinking. Brainstorming leads to better understanding of problems and issues.

Nominal Group Process

A sharp contrast to the high verbal participation in the brainstorming session is the quiet ideation of a nominal group. Ideas are written down on paper with no interaction, rather than the highly spontaneous, interacting sharing manner of brainstorming. The nominal group process (NGP) has a common function or purpose, which meets the definition of a group, and yet all members, even though they are working on the same task, are operating at times as individuals. The term *nominal group*, when referring to the technique, indicates a structured group meeting in which participants alternate among individual participation and group actions.

The NGP has several merits because of the procedure used:

• It balances participation among members because all have to participate and become involved.
• It balances the influence of members throughout the decision-making process, allowing equal participation and consideration

of ideas. It reduces the tendency of high-status, highly expressive individuals of strong personality to dominate discussion.
- It tends to produce a higher average number of unique ideas,
  total ideas, and better-quality ideas.
- It controls the premature evaluation of ideas by group members
  and facilitates open discussion and questioning about controver-
  sial ideas.
- It provides individual time and opportunity to engage in reflection and forces respondents to record feelings.
- It allows participants to share in the opportunity for influencing
  the direction of group decision outcome, encourages minority
  opinions and ideas to be voiced, and imposes a burden on all
  participants to work and produce their share in the task.
- It promotes a solution-minded atmosphere.

The NGP involves four stages: (1) writing ideas silently, (2)
recording ideas on a flip chart, (3) offering clarifying comments on
each idea, and (4) rank ordering or rating the ideas (Pace, Peterson, and Burnett 1979) (Pace 1983).

Writing Ideas Silently

The needs analysis begins by having each member of the group
write down short idea phrases or statements, without any conversation with others, about the point of concern that is being documented. During this five- to ten-minute period, no interruptions
occur and any attempts to work together are discouraged. All participants are involved in jotting down notes that represent their
ideas.

Recording Ideas on a Flip Chart

At the end of the time frame selected, the facilitator asks for one
idea from each member, going around the room, and writes the
idea on a flip chart in a short phrase or statement of three or four
words. The process is continued until all the ideas, which are not
duplications, are listed. This is strictly a recording process, and no
evaluation is made about the merit of the idea at this time. At the
conclusion, the pages of the flip chart are torn off and posted in
the room so they can be seen by all members.

Offering Clarifying Comments on Each Idea

Each idea is represented by only a few words on the paper, and may not be understood by other members of the group. Therefore, a second round begins by looking at each notation and having the members clarify what is meant by the statement, not argue its merits. There is no place for debate. This is to clarify and help others understand what is meant by the statement and provide a brief analysis of how the suggestion is important to the issue involved. As each statement is clarified, each team member should be making notes about his or her judgments of each item, noting the pros and cons and the relative importance seen.

Rank Ordering or Rating the Ideas

Two rounds of rating are involved in this process. The first round begins by having each member select four to eight items from the total list. Each of these items is recorded on a 3 × 5 card; each individual sorts the cards to represent his or her rankings, and places the number of the ranking in the left-hand corner, circles the ranking, and writes the item number in the right-hand corner of the card. The cards are then gathered by the facilitator and shuffled. The ranking number for each card is then posted for each item that receives consideration. Items receiving no consideration are eliminated. This completes round one. A discussion occurs about the ranking, and additional clarification is sought to reduce misinformation. Following the discussion, the final ranking takes place. Rather than cards, a sheet is provided, as shown in figure 8.1, to refine the ranking judgments of the participants. Each

---

Figure 8.1   Final Ranking Form, Nominal Group Process

List item in rank order (Number)	Phrase describing item on flip chart	Relative Importance Unimportant — Very important						
_____	_____	1	2	3	4	5	6	7
_____	_____	1	2	3	4	5	6	7
_____	_____	1	2	3	4	5	6	7
_____	_____	1	2	3	4	5	6	7
_____	_____	1	2	3	4	5	6	7

group member selects from the remaining list the five most important items and records them. At the completion of the ranking, the sheets are collected and the rankings are summed for each item to determine the group's perception of the most important issues. Little is done with the relative importance information unless additional discrimination is desired. If some items have very close mean ranking scores, the ones perceived as more important are ordered above those with an equivalent ranking.

Procedures to Follow

Invite the group to determine the time and place where the activity will occur. Preparations for the NGP are important and include the following:

1. **Prepare the room.** Arrange rectangular tables in U- shape pattern, and put the flip chart at the open end.
2. **Provide supplies.** Print question on top of worksheet for the silent generation of ideas, flip chart, masking tape, pack of 3 × 5 cards, felt-tip pens, paper and pencil, and final rank ordering sheet.

Begin the session with introductions of individuals, and outline the events that are going to occur so they are aware of the activities in which they will be involved. Begin the process.

1. Place the question on the flip chart and introduce the concern. Give each participant a worksheet with the question on top. Set a time limit for generating ideas. Have participants list ideas on the worksheet without discussion.
2. Record all the participants' ideas on the flip chart. Record one idea using a short phrase of three or four words from each person, moving from person to person until all ideas are listed.
3. Clarify the meaning of each idea in the order they are listed on the flip chart. Have each participant make notes on the idea while clarification occurs.
4. Distribute 3 × 5 cards to each participant, and have them select between four and eight ideas that appear most important and write each of these ideas on a separate card. Have each participant sort the cards of the ideas according to their importance. Place the ranking number on the left-hand corner of the card

and the item number from the total list on the right-hand corner of the card. Gather cards from all participants and shuffle.
5. Record each rank number by the items selected from the deck of responses. Items receiving no ranking are eliminated. Open discussion for clarification, not argument, on any of the points remaining on the list.
6. Give out the final ranking form. Members need not change their original votes unless they have a new perspective. Ask them to select five items, record them on the form, and rate the importance of the item.
7. The sum of the rankings across all group members determines the final rankings.

Again, the NGP is a method for using individuals, working within a group environment, to produce ideas and evaluate them in terms of rank and importance in a needs analysis.

Focus Groups

A focus group uses an interactive process to provide data on perceptions and needs of individuals. The dynamics of a group influence the information that is produced during the data-gathering activity. The group must be managed effectively to ensure that total participation occurs.

This method of analysis was originally developed for use in gathering marketing information on new and proposed products to determine what consumers felt about the products and services being provided or suggested. It is also effective in needs analysis to determine the feelings of employees performing a task.

Three steps are involved in the focus group process: (1) preparation and selection of respondents, (2) data collection, and (3) data reduction (Pace, Peterson, and Burnett 1979).

Preparation and Selection of Respondents

Since this is an interactive group, whom you select is important for the process to work most effectively. As few as six and as many as twelve can be selected for the group. Participants with common status and work classifications should be placed together to avoid authority or communication barriers. Hold the meeting so it is easy for them to attend. An adequate room must allow for seating and includes a chalkboard or flip chart to record ideas. In some cases, a tape recorder is also used, in conjunction with the flip chart, to record more of the detail.

A detailed topic outline is prepared to help formalize how the focus group leader will proceed in the discussion. The point of concern is used as the focus point of the outline to ensure complete evaluation.

Data Collection

Introduce participants in a novel way to get them involved in the group. Define the process and how you will proceed. As you begin, let the following points guide your actions:

1. The warm-up is important; you must get the participants ready to participate. Good icebreaker activities to develop a feel for others and get used to working together are helpful.
2. After the warm-up is finished, minimize your involvement to approximately 10 percent of the talking; the group's comments are the important ones. You can be a guiding force, but be a facilitator rather than a discussant.
3. As you take comments from the group, write all of them down on the chalkboard or flip chart. List the exact words, not the topic or an abbreviated statement. Listing precisely what is said increases your credibility, because you may be seen as an extension of management, and softening the language or reiterating it may change the richness of the information produced. This is a needs analysis, and the language and words may include more information than the idea it expresses.
4. You have a topic outline, and these points should be covered, but be somewhat nondirective and let the comments surface naturally and spontaneously. Some interaction is okay to encourage such comments as "Say more about that."
5. As statements are made, look for agreement, intensity of feelings, nonverbal cues, or reactions.
6. You will need to manage the group, and sometimes dampen the verbose and encourage the meek.
7. Avoid such comments as "That's good" or "That's interesting." You are not a judge but a facilitator.

8. Don't fear silences; they often produce responses that otherwise would not be given. You may have to prod to get them started again. Be able to sense when all the data are out.
9. When cross talk begins, let it flow.

These suggestions describe the role of the facilitator. A topical outline is used to guide the course of the activity, but be sensitive to the group dynamic and let the process flow. Keep the group on task, but don't let structure kill the development of the idea-generation process. Being able to read consensus, agreement, and the intensity of feelings along with the nonverbal cues of the participants will be essential.

Data Reduction

Schedule time immediately after the meeting to analyze the data. Do not let anything interfere, because over time, some of the fine points are forgotten.

The task is to find themes represented in the comments that have been written or recorded. Between six and twelve themes will be evident in the comments of most groups. Begin by doing the following:

1. Jot down the main themes that come to mind immediately. Record these and look for patterns.
2. Read over all raw data to let other themes emerge. Add these to the themes list.
3. Take each theme and evaluate the intensity of the group's feelings toward them. Add how strongly they felt about this, how many were in agreement, and whether this was a major concern.
4. Trust your hunches and feelings about the rank order of the concerns. Use language or statements from the responses to represent these feelings.
5. Report your data by including themes, mood/tone/feelings, and a raw data section.

The objective of the focus group is to document the point of concern. Needs that are not apparent on a paper and pencil test will emerge through this type of activity.

Procedure

Invite the group to participate, and tell them what room will be used and the time for the meeting. Preparations for the focus group interview include the following:

1. Prepare a topical outline. This will influence the discussion, but not dominate the structure.
2. Organize the room using a half circle or U-shaped seating arrangement, and place the flip chart at the open end of the U. Have felt-tip pens and masking tape available.
3. Write the task statement on the flip chart and show it at the appropriate time.
4. Select a group of equal status.

Begin the session with introductions of individuals, and outline the events that are going to occur so they are aware of the activities in which they will be involved. Begin the process.

1. Reveal the task or topic of the focus group. Post it in the room so it will always be conspicuous. This is why you are meeting.
2. Begin taking responses and recording them. Look for agreement and intensity checks along the way. Maintain flow of ideas and let cross talk flow. Prod where needed.
3. When a page on the flip chart is full, tear it off and tape it up next to the task statement so that the information is always in view.
4. Conclude the session by having members review the statements to see if any others are evident.
5. Thank participants, and after they have left begin the data crunch to reduce the statements into themes of concern.
6. Prepare a report representing themes and feelings, and a list of the original statements.

Using Consensus Skills in Interacting Groups

Small groups can be classified by different purposes, such as problem solving, idea generation, therapy, education or learning, sensitivity, and social (Hindmarsh and Mills 1981). Within this chapter, group processes have been used to generate ideas and perceptions to document concerns in needs analysis. Small groups can also be classified by the amount of interaction between group members. For example, of the three needs analysis methods defined, brainstorming and focus groups were described as interactive because of the high level of involvement between group members, which was both encouraged and expected. In contrast, NGP was described as a group in name only, with very little group interaction, and was classified as a noninteractive group. If brainstorming had been an individual activity conducted on paper rather than by group discussion, it also would have been noninteractive.

Group interaction is a phenomenon that impacts on data gathering and establishing consensus within the group. For example, having different opinions and feelings is far less risky in NGP than in a focus group. High risk mitigates against taking extreme positions within an interactive group. An option to minimize risk is to minimize interaction. This is not always desirable, although using the NGP has been shown to be effective for this very reason. A second option to minimize risk is to increase the skills of the facilitator to manage consensus within a group; increased effectiveness here minimizes the potential risk members take in an interactive group.

While the basic purpose of needs analysis is to identify what those perceptions and needs are, it is just as compelling to know which are most important and have the highest priority. A skillful facilitator can manage this consensus process and add a significant dimension to the documentation effort.

Facilitating consensus involves two parts: (1) goal focus and (2) managing comments and reactions of group members (Pace, Peterson, and Burnett 1979).

Goal Focus

Consensus occurs when everyone in the group agrees to accept and subscribe to the decision even though he or she may have some reservations. When agreement occurs, it is called unanimity or ability to act with one accord. The first step in facilitating consensus is to make unanimity a goal that has value and importance. Without this desire, much of the effort expended may be fruitless. One approach to achieving this goal is to create the feeling: "We want to find the best collective judgment of the group that all can work on and put the plan into effect." This type of approach enhances group loyalty and cohesiveness, which are major factors in achieving consensus. A second approach is to point out how collective and divergent views can be incorporated into a plan. This lets the goal of cooperation and development proceed without the guarded positions interrupting the consensus activity. Through looking at how divergent opinions can be included, the focus is on listing areas of agreement between ideas rather than dwelling on differences. This demonstrates that similarities are evident and that the goal of consensus is possible as more information is shared.

Managing Comments of and Reactions of Group Members

Managing comments and reactions of the group can create an atmosphere in which change is more likely. For most participants to "buy in" on consensus, a way must be provided for them to minimize the risks associated with change and vested ego involvement. Several communication skills help this process to occur, such as increasing understanding and reducing emotional barriers.

The first step to increasing understanding is to discover what the person means. Differences may not really be differences at all. A simple clarification of what a person means reduces misunderstanding and prevents disagreements from exploding.

A second step to increasing understanding is to check the commonality of evidence and reasoning of the individuals involved. In many cases, persons are using different premises or facts to substantiate a point of view, and this fosters the differences in opinions. When this discrepancy is corrected, understanding comes. On the other hand, on occasion even the evidence used is erroneous or incorrect, and going to the sources often clarifies this matter.

A third method of increasing understanding is to identify the basic value or objective that is influencing the opinion. Understanding is increased by discovering a more basic value that those who are disagreeing can accept. For example, a disagreement on the acceptance of late work may not be reconciled because of the ego investment of the student and teacher. If the discussion were to be turned to a more fundamental issue of fairness and justice to each member of the class, then it may be easier to agree about the issue. When issues do have a broader implication than the one producing the disagreement, setting the issue in a larger perspective promotes understanding.

Reducing emotional barriers is possible when you increase the self-esteem of group members. As self-esteem increases, it is possible to risk far more without fear, because the consequences are not interpreted as nearly so crushing. Making others feel good about who they are and what they are doing increases their self-esteem. Encouragement, such as "That sounds like a point we ought to consider," also reduces emotional barriers. Without being evaluative, this kind of statement reinforces the idea that a person has said something of importance. Other encouraging statements include "In light of what Bill has said, do you think we ought to modify our conclusions?", "John's suggestion makes me want to review the effects of what we've decided," and "Susan has pointed out a disadvantage from her point of view. How do you think it would affect the rest of you?"

Open questions often minimize emotional barriers that are associated with disagreement. Creating an atmosphere of inquiry promotes a more positive situation. Asking such questions as "What advantages does a plan like that offer?" or "How would that idea relate to the proposed changes?" encourages inquiry. Open-ended questions allow persons to respond pretty much as they would like to and protects their integrity at the same time.

Paraphrasing accomplishes a result similar to the open question. Understanding can be checked with paraphrasing and at the same time makes it possible to appear interested and non-challenging. Paraphrasing involves using such statements as "Would it be accurate to say . . ." or "In other words, are you indicating . . ." or "If I understood you correctly, you feel . . ."

A third approach to decreasing emotional barriers is to involve each member in the discussion. Every member of a group has a contribution to make and wants to feel that comments can be offered without having to force a way into the group. At times, involvement is encouraged by using such statements as "We haven't heard from the people at the side tables regarding . . ." or, if a group or person is silent, "We don't know how Jim feels about this" or "We haven't heard from those who have been around a long time."

Another way to decrease emotional barriers is to use summaries within the discussion. Many fail to realize that emotional reactions develop because group members are not clear about what has been said and where the group is going. Attention lags, interest drags, and the meeting sags. Summarizing helps by objectifying or highlighting agreement or disagreement. Objectifying is a means of taking a very emotional or loaded statement and restating it in an objective way so as to remove the emotion or make it more neutral. Summarize the statement made to allow others to react to your more neutral statement than to the original comment.

Another communication technique to help remove emotional barriers is to use feeling checks, such as "You seem to feel . . ." The focus of this check is on the feeling rather than on the content. Feeling checks help determine the emotions associated with the statements being made. Feeling reflections bring to the surface latent feelings that may underlie concerns and that can be dealt with when expressed clearly.

Essentially, the communication skills of the facilitator can help solicit understanding and seek to decrease the emotional barriers that make consensus more likely. Specific skills that facilitate consensus include discovering what the other person means; checking the commonality of evidence and reasoning; identifying more basic values; increasing the self-esteem of group members; using open-ended and paraphrasing questions; involving each member of the group in the discussion; using summaries to promote discussion; and providing emotional release through the use of reflections that keep the discussion moving.

Summary

Using group processes for needs analysis to gather information and determine the perceptions of individuals about the work they do has been described. Brainstorming and focus groups were shown to be effective methods for using interactive groups to generate ideas and document issues during needs analysis. The nominal group was described as a method to provide individuals a group structure to report needs and perceptions. Methods of getting consensus within an interactive group through increasing the skills of the facilitator were reported.

Activity: Use a Consensus Group Process

In a group, take the following exercise and act as a facilitator to achieve a sense of consensus.

Individual Training Needs Ranking Form

Instructions: Below are listed fifteen training needs identified by typical employees. Your task is to rank order them in terms of their importance to your personal needs. Place a 1 in front of the type of training that you feel to be your greatest need, and so on, to 15, your lowest training need.

_____ Coping with stress

_____ Maintaining interpersonal communication

_____ Writing memos and reports

_____ Inducting new employees

_____ Appraising employee performance

_____ Listening

_____ Planning

_____ Interviewing

_____ Training new employees

_____ Problem solving and decision making

_____ Developing self

_____ Supervising ethnic minorities

_____ Motivating employees

_____ Handling complaints and grievances

Now that each individual within the group has ranked his or her needs, have the group arrive at a consensus on the exact order of all fifteen items.

Instructions: This phase of the needs analysis is designed to discover the most important group needs. Your group is to reach consensus on rankings for each of the fifteen employee needs. This means that the final rankings for each of the needs must be agreed on by each group member before it becomes part of the group decision. Consensus may be difficult to achieve; therefore, not every item will meet with everyone's complete approval. Try, as a group, to make each ranking one with which all group members can at least partially agree. Use the suggestions on understanding others and minimizing emotional barriers.

References

Hindmarsh, T., and G. Mills. 1981. *Analysis of Communication.* Provo, Utah: BYU Press.

Pace, R. W. 1983. *Organizational Communication, Foundations for Human Resource Development.* Englewood Cliffs, N.J.: Prentice-Hall.

Pace, R. W., B. D. Peterson, and M. D. Burnett. 1979. *Techniques for Effective Communication.* Reading, Mass.: Addison-Wesley.

9. Methods of Documentation, Organizational Systems Analysis: Functional Approaches

A systems approach to analysis is concerned with the operations of the organization as a whole, rather than with individuals or groups that are part of the organization. A systems approach is global in design and intent. Measures of effectiveness, for example, examine the organization's ability to meet both internal and external demands. Effectiveness itself is defined not only in terms of indexes, such as production and profits, but also in terms of flexibility, adaptability, communication, coordination, and handling tension, strain, and conflict.

A systems approach has inherent in it special concerns about maintenance and survival of the organization. Survival and maintenance of the organization depends on how well the firm gets resources from its environment, uses those resources efficiently, and, in the process, meets the expectations of its stakeholders (any group or individual who can affect or is affected by the accomplishment of the organization's objectives).

Value

Methods to evaluate the system from a functional point of view vary and need to respond to a variety of organizational issues and concerns. This chapter will narrow the perspective of analysis to communication and the role it plays in the documentation phase of evaluating a system. The argument will be made that communication is a key variable in determining how efficient the organization is and where many of the discrepancies between what is desired and what is really happening occur.

Objectives

At the conclusion of this chapter, you will be able to do the following:

• Describe why communication is an essential focus for conducting a functional systems analysis.
• List the six steps for designing a functional organizational communication systems analysis.
• List the tools and methods for conducting a systems analysis when evaluating communication climate, information flow, and message content.
• Describe the eight factors of the organizational communication profile model, and justify why each is critical to understanding system problems and concerns.
• Given an instrument to measure communication climate, conduct and evaluate the results on an organization of which you are a member.

Rationale for Communication as a Focus of Systems Analysis

A functional analysis uses methods that measure and quantify the major variables and processes of an organization that affect the way in which it achieves both its internal and external goals. Mackenzie (1969), for example, identifies three continuous processes in organizations — planning, problem solving, and communicating — that affect the manner in which the organization operates and achieves its goals. A functional analysis would attempt to determine how well one or more of those processes is working.

In human resource and organization development, the major organizational processes are generally regarded as those such as planning, organizing, staffing, directing, and controlling, although Schein (1969) notes that communicating, group functioning, problem solving and decision making, leading, and competing and cooperating are the key human processes in organizations. Functional analysis could focus on one or all of these processes in order to determine how they affect the achievement or organization goals.

Organizations use human, physical, and technological resources to accomplish their goals. To use these resources, organization members must share information and make decisions. The process by which organization members interact, share, and cooperate is called communication. Although effective communication does not guarantee an efficiently operating organization, ineffective communication creates a condition that virtually precludes organizational efficiency.

Organizations, in fact, owe their very existence to communication. It is through communication that efforts are coordinated and resources are used to accomplish goals. Organizations are efficient to the extent that they achieve their goals, provide satisfaction for their members, and develop their capacity to survive in the future within the limitations of their resources. Communication is the central process that allows success to occur.

As an example of how one might conduct a functional analysis of an organizational system, we have selected the communication process as the focus. Regular analysis of the organizational communication system can provide information about potential problems before they become disruptive.

Three general categories of elements or variables have been analyzed most frequently (Goldhaber 1976; Richetto 1977; Dennis et al. 1978) from a functional point of view: (1) communication climate, (2) information flow, and (3) message content. Climate analyses have been concerned with employee perception, attitudes, feelings, and expectation about the organization and communication. Information flow analyses have focused on who-talks-to-whom and with what effect. Media usage, roles, patterns, load, and types of messages sent have been studied as part of understanding information flow. Message content analyses have generally sought to determine what happens to information as it is disseminated throughout an organization, resulting in data about distortion, information loss, and message fidelity (Pace and Hegstrom 1977; Pace 1983).

Designing A Functional Organizational Communication Systems Analysis

To conduct a functional analysis of organizational communication processes, it is necessary to identify aspects of the system that can be analyzed and to have instruments and procedures for conducting the analysis. At present, a broad array of instruments and tools is available for conducting a functional organizational communication analysis. Figure 9.1 summarizes the main features of organizational communication and itemizes some of the instruments and procedures used in making a functional analysis. The features are briefly defined and explained as the processes of designing analysis is described.

As an alternative to the use of individual instruments and procedures, consider administering the Organizational Communication Profile instrument to secure data on eight key features of communication in organizations. This is described later in the chapter.

Feature 1: Authority Structure

The first task in a functional systems analysis is to describe and portray the authority structure, duties, and responsibilities of the *communication units* in the organization. A communication unit is a person in a position.

Methods of Analysis

Organization charts help portray how positions are classified and distributed to create the organization.

Position descriptions describe how the functions are divided and delegated to individual units as duties, authority, and responsibilities.

Operating procedures structure the individual duties into work flow patterns.

Directives, instructions, and manuals of an organization represent the communication system designed to guide the way in which individuals carry out their duties.

Taken together, organization charts, position descriptions, operating procedures, and manuals of directives are a description of the structure and activity of an organization. They represent, however, a static picture of the organization that is embodied in

---

Figure 9.1   Designing a Functional Organizational Communication Systems Analysis

---

Step 1: Portray and describe the authority structure, duties, and responsibilities of "communication units" people in positions.
   a. Locate or create an organization chart, position descriptions, and operating procedures with accompanying manuals, directives, and instructions.
   b. Complete an equipment and documents inventory.
   c. Complete a Linear Responsibility Chart for the unit under analysis.

Step 2: Describe the flow of information and the technology to facilitate it.
   a. Make a diagram of the location of communication equipment and technology.
   b. Create a flow chart of paper production.
   c. Complete a log of mail procedures and processing.
   d. Complete a personal contact record form for select personnel.
   e. Conduct a network analysis.

Step 3: Measure message fidelity and distortion in information flow.
   a. Conduct a modified ECCO analysis focusing on the fidelity of messages using tests, unit analysis, or theme analysis.
   b. Look at communication load scores and locate sources of overload and underload in the system.

Step 4: Measure information adequacy as related to downward communication.
   a. Identify areas of key information and prepare an information adequacy test and administer to employees.
   b. Prepare and administer a Bateman-type information adequacy inventory.

Step 5: Measure communication satisfaction.
   a. Administer Downs and Hazen's Communication Satisfaction Questionnaire.
   b. Interview employees about their satisfaction with communication.

Step 6: Measure communication climate.
   a. Administer the Peterson-Pace Communication Climate Inventory.
   b. Administer Siegel and Turney's Survey of Organizational Climate.

---

massive written statements. Nevertheless, the basic authority structure, the duties, and the responsibilities assigned to people in positions may be described in these special written documents.

A functional analysis of organizational communication begins by creating a picture of the organization as represented by the structure, authority, duties, and responsibilities.

A *linear responsibility chart* is an alternative way of creating a picture of the authority structure of an organization (Larke 1954). *Factory* (March 1963) reported that the LRC is "being used in dozens of organizations to cut overhead costs, break bottlenecks, find training needs, spot responsibility gaps, even out work loads, uncover overlap and empire-building, clear up misunderstandings, weed out paper work not related to particular jobs, simplify control, and speed up decisions" (reprint, p. 3). In view of the vast array of potential problems revealed by the LRC, it can be a powerful tool for functional organizational communication analysis.

A linear responsibility chart is created by developing a matrix or grid with two axes. The horizontal axis (across the top) lists the positions in the unit being analyzed. The vertical axis (down the side) lists the functional responsibilities or work to be done. A system of symbols spells out who does what work, under whose supervision, and what kinds of relationships are involved. Figure 9.2 shows a completed LRC to illustrate the use of symbols for designating work procedures.

Number 1 means that the activity or function described is actually performed by the individual designated.

Number 2 means that the important aspects of planning, delegation, and control of the function described are handled daily, under the hour-by-hour direction of the individual designated.

Number 3 means that the individual indicated has specific responsibility over the subordinated who carries out the work.

Number 4 means that two or more individuals or groups must work cooperatively on the same or a similar activity and bring about a unified approach to the function; the person responsible for the coordination is indicated with a no. 4.

Number 5 means that the individual indicated is a specialist who must be approached for technical decisions affecting part of the overall problem or where delegation is extensive and only occasionally are decisions referred to more general supervision. The decision of the individual marked no. 5 must be followed.

Number 6 means that before a decision is made or an action taken, the individual indicated must be consulted. The individu-

---

Figure 9.2   Linear Responsibility Chart (Human Resource Training and Development Department)

Positions: 1 = Administrator; 2 = Assistant Administrator; 3 = Sales Training Specialist; 4 = Manufacturing Training Specialist; 5 = Clerical/Sec. Training Specialist; 6 = Management Development Specialist; 7 = Program Design Specialist; 8 = Materials, Equipment, and Facilities Coordinator

DUTIES	1	2	3	4	5	6	7	8
Prepares T & D philosophy and policies	1	6						
Prepares department budget	2	1	6	6	6	6	8	8
Develops programs for sec./clerical personnel	2	3			3	3	5	6
Arranges for materials, eqpt., and facilities		3						1
Edits written materials			4	4	4		1	
Conducts training	2		1	1	1			
Counsels employees on personal goals	1	4				1		
Produces audio-visual and video			2	2	2		4	
Schedules training programs	2	3	1	1	1	7		
Keeps records of financial transactions		2						
Develops course outlines, handouts, and exercises			6	6	6		1	
Evalutes training courses			2	2	2			

(Column header group: POSITIONS)

al's opinion must be heard, although his or her advice need not be followed.

Number 7 means that upon making a decision or taking an action, the individual indicated must be advised. The assumption is that knowledge of the action or decision will assist the person in carrying out his or her own responsibilities.

Number 8 means that there is no need to consult this person and that the person has no right of consultation, but it is normally done, likely to be done, or pertinent to do.

The LRC is completed by naming the function, program, set

of relationships, particular group, unit, organization to be analyzed. In the spaces across the top of the grid, the positions in the
unit to be analyzed are entered, arranged from higher to lower
levels or broadest to narrowest authority. Down the left side of
the grid, the items of work are listed, preferably, in some sequence. The grid is completed by assigning a number to each
block to indicate who does what, under whose supervision, and
in relationship with which others. The LRC should graphically
portray the entire unit being analyzed, including complex work
flows, involved procedures, and potentially confusing responsibilities. The LRC will be a factual source of information about organization structure, job descriptions, and procedures when
completed accurately.

Feature 2: Information Flow and Associated Technology

Information flow has to do with the way information is distributed
throughout an organization. The process of making information
available to organization members and securing information from
them is called the flow of information. Specific patterns of information flow evolve out of regular contacts and routine ways of
sending and receiving messages. Formal organizations exert control over the information flow process by designating authority
and work relations, assignment of offices, and the creation of special communication functions. How do we analyze the flow of
information?

Methods of Analysis

Documents and Equipment Inventory   This seems like a reasonable
place to begin since they represent some of the most visible and
conscious elements involved in information dissemination. In fact,
an inventory of documents and equipment as shown in Figure 9.3
might even precede the graphic portrayal of the authority structure since the documents inventoried may serve as sources of information for constructing the structure.

Paper Flow Diagram   The flow of information often begins with the
preparation of written materials. The following diagram (figure

Figure 9.3   Inventory of Documents and Equipment

ITEM	EXIST? YES	NO	FILE KEPT? YES	NO	LOCATION (SPECIFY)
Documents: Organization Charts					
Communication Policies					
Employee Handbook					
Manual of Procedures					
Company Magazine					
Company Newspaper					
Company Newsletter					
Labor Agreement					
Agenda for Meetings					
Minutes for Meetings					
Information of Meetings					
Routing Slips					
Correspondence					
Brochures					
Annual Report					
Employee Reviews					
News Releases					
Clippings					
Picture Record					
Bulletins					
Equipment	YES	NO	YES	NO	LOCATION (SPECIFY)
Telephones					
Dictating Units					
Duplicating Machines					

Figure 9.3   Inventory of Documents and Equipment (Continued)

ITEM	EXIST?		FILE KEPT?		LOCATION (SPECIFY)
	YES	NO	YES	NO	
Typewriters					
Postage Meters					
Collating Machine					
Bulletin Board					
Display Cases					
Microfilm/Microfiche					
Projectors					
Video Equipment					
Cameras					
Films					
Library					
Leaflet Racks					
Public Address System					

9.4) shows some typical trouble spots identified by a prominent manufacturer of duplicating equipment about how the flow of paperwork is handled in an office. A similar analysis of any office might identify problems in the flow of information.

Mail Log   One frequent source of difficulty in the flow of information in an organization is the processing of mail. A mail log form, as shown in figure 9.5, describes both incoming and outgoing mail in terms of the sender and the receiver of a piece of mail, the general content of the correspondence, the disposition and type of reply, and the time lapse between receipt and reply. The mail log is usually maintained by an individual assigned to sort and distribute the mail. Each item is logged in a central location as it is delivered to the organization and just prior to being picked up by the mail service.

Figure 9.4   Paper Flow Diagram

No, this isn't a game for time-study men. It's an exercise for top management. A walk around the office like you've never taken before.

Start where the mail comes in. Ever wonder why it's late to your desk? Or ripped? Or minus a return address? Is your mail opened by hand? 1

Ever get a copy of a report that has two pages 2's? Or, worse yet, none? Peek into the conference room. Chances are, you'll see hands gathering sheets of paper into sets. 2

Walk by your office. Secretary missing again? 3 She's probably been "volunteered" for another folding and inserting session. 4

Stop by the mailroom on your way home. Can your mailing equipment handle the billing that's got to get out tonight? 5 Do your hand-typed invoices look businesslike? Is every name and address correct? 6

Why take this walk? Simply this: since paper represents the written record of your business, your business can travel only as fast as the paper can flow in, through, and out of your office.

Figure 9.5   Mail Log

CHARACTERISTICS	LETTER NUMBER														
Type of Log (check one): _____ Incoming Mail _____ Outgoing Mail															
	1	2	3	4	5	6	7	8	9	10	11	12	13	14	15
From (incoming) To (outgoing)															
Client															
Supplier															
Government															
Other: _____															
To (incoming) From (outgoing)															
Manager															
Assistant Manager															
Supervisor 1															
Supervisor 2															
Other: _____															
Content															
Job-Related															
Personal															
Other: _____															
Disposition (incoming) Type Reply (outgoing)															
Personal Dictation															
Secretary Composed															
Form Letter															
Filed															
Referred: _____															
Other: _____															

Figure 9.5   Mail Log (Continued)

Type of Log (check one): _____ Incoming Mail _____ Outgoing Mail

CHARACTERISTICS	LETTER NUMBER														
	1	2	3	4	5	6	7	8	9	10	11	12	13	14	15
Time Lapse Between Receipt & Reply (outgoing)															
1 day															
2 days															
3 days															
4 days															
5 days															
6 days															
7 days or more															

Comments:

Person Making Log: _____ Date: _____

Page _____ of _____ pages

Personal Contact Record Form   Much of the information flow in an organization is accomplished through personal contacts. Two methods of recording contacts are used: (1) diary completed by the person who engages in the contact and (2) shadow, a person who follows an employee at a short distance and maintains the record but who checks periodically with the employee on the accuracy of the record. The shadow should be as unobtrusive as possible, but close enough to make an accurate record.

   A simple personal contact record form, as shown in figure 9.6, is divided into five parts: (1) direction of contact, (2) form of contact, (3) authority relationship of those involved in the contact, (4) content of the information, and (5) length of contact. This form

Figure 9.6 Personal Contact Record Form

CHARACTERISTIC	CONTACT NUMBER																	
	1	2	3	4	5	6	7	8	9	10	11	12	13	14	15	16	17	18
Direction																		
Self-initiated (1)																		
Approached (2)																		
Form																		
Telephone (intercom) (1)																		
Face-to-Face (pair) (2)																		
Group Meeting (3)																		
Memo or note (4)																		
Other: _____ (5)																		
Authority Relationship																		
Superior (1)																		
Subordinate (2)																		
Same Level (3)																		
Outside Organization (4)																		
Content																		
Job-Related (1)																		
Personal (2)																		
Other: _____ (3)																		
Length in Minutes																		
Under 3 (1)																		
3 to 15 (2)																		
15 to 30 (3)																		

Figure 9.6   Personal Contact Record Form (Continued)

CHARACTERISTIC	CONTACT NUMBER																	
	1	2	3	4	5	6	7	8	9	10	11	12	13	14	15	16	17	18
30 to 60 (4)																		
Over 60 (5)																		

Comments:

Recorder or Shadow: _____ Page __ of __ pages
Date: _____

records only personal contacts, since a separate record may be kept of formal written materials handled by the mails.

The form contains a record of all personal contacts made by the subject during a specified period of time — one hour, one day, one week. At the beginning of each day, a packet of forms is issued to the individual for use in recording all personal contacts except short personal greetings such as "hi," very simple, short requests, and telephone calls transferred to someone else. Otherwise, all face-to-face contacts, telephone calls, intercom conversations, meetings, teleconference calls, videophone calls, telegrams, memos, and short notes are recorded.

The record is completed by striking through the contact number following each personal contact in order to locate easily the column in which to make the record. Next, in the space opposite *Direction*, check a 1 or 2 to indicate whether you initiated the contact or were approached by someone else. Move to *Form* and check a number from 1 to 5 indicating whether the contact was by telephone, face-to-face, group meeting, informal note or memo, or other. Below that, in *Authority*, check a number from 1 to 4 indicating the authority relationship you have with the contact. If you attended a meeting, the relationship is with the person calling the meeting. For *Content*, decide whether the topics discussed were job related, personal, or other, and check the appropriate number.

Finally, under *Length,* check the correct number corresponding to the length of the contact.

ICA-Type Network Analysis Record Form   This form is used to gather data to show relationships among organization members in terms of the people from whom they get and to whom they give information. Figure 9.7 shows a sample form. It consists of spaces for subjects to recall and record the names of individuals they contact for each category of information and the general way the contact is made (telephone, face-to-face, written). The form and procedures allow the names and work locations of all organization members to be preprinted on the form; then each organization member simply scans the list of employees and checks off the names of people with whom he or she makes contact and completes the form. The recall method may result in fewer names being identified than may the roster method, but in large organizations the roster is impractical and may not be completed because of the size and time required to complete the form.

Instructions for completing the network analysis form asks each person to recall the names of those persons contacted during a specific period for each type of information. Each subject is asked to write the number of contacts that took place with each person identified for each form or medium of communication.

Figure 9.7   ICA Type Network Analysis Record Form

During to date date		WORK LOCA-TION	I received information directly related to doing my job from the following people:			I talked about matters not directly related to doing my job with the following people:		
			FACE TO FACE	TELE	WRIT-TEN	FACE TO FACE	TELE	WRIT-TEN
PERSONNEL								

The data are portrayed in diagrams that show the type and quality of relationship. The data for large organizations must be processed by computer. Richards (1974) developed a computer program that allowed contacts among as many as four thousand individuals to be analyzed. Although the process of analysis is somewhat complex and requires computer facilities, the technique seems to be highly reliable. Roberts and O'Reilly (1978) used network analysis in their study and concluded that "the results demonstrate that organizations can be described as complex, overlaid communication networks comprised of interlinked groups with individuals occupying different communication roles" (p. 288).

ECCO-Type Survey of Information Flow   ECCO is an acronym for Episodic Communication Channels in Organizations (Davis 1953). Information about the flow of real messages is gathered by means of a questionnaire given to employees at each level in the organization; preferably, all employees should receive questionnaires similar to the one illustrated in figure 9.8.

As employees arrive at work, they are handed a set of four or five envelopes in which questionnaires are enclosed. Each envelope has a time-of-day record on the outside indicating when it should be opened and the questionnaire completed. Upon completion, which should take no longer than three to four minutes, the questionnaires are returned to the envelopes and placed where they can be picked up by the analyst.

We have developed a set of guidelines for use in administering the survey:

1. Visit with employees when distributing and collecting questionnaires, but use as little of their time as possible.
2. Instruct the subjects on how to respond to the survey form prior to having them complete the first one, encouraging questions about the project and providing answers where possible.
3. Learn as many of the names of employees as possible and use them whenever given the opportunity, but make the point that each participant will be anonymous in the report of results.
4. Impress the employees with the value of their answers to the questions, making sure they realize that an "I don't know any of the information" answer is just as important as an "I know it all."

Figure 9.8   ECCO Analysis Questionnaire

Survey No. _____
               (Hour envelope opened)

Your Code No. _____

SURVEY OF INFORMATION FLOW (Confidential)

Prior to receiving this questionnaire, what did you know about the information in the box below?

Please check *one*: _____ I knew all about it.
                    _____ I knew something about it.
                    _____ I knew nothing about it.

   If your answer above was "I knew nothing about it," you have completed the questionnaire. Please return it to the envelope, seal the envelope, and leave it to be picked up. Thank you.

   If your answer above was "I knew all about it" or "I knew something about it," please complete the remainder of the questionnaire by providing the information requested.

1.   Please list the facts that you know about the information in the box:

      a. _____
      b. _____
      c. _____
      d. _____
      e. _____
      f. _____

2.   From *whom* did you first receive this information listed above?

      Place the source's code number on this line: _____
      (By using the code number, you maintain the anonymity of specific individuals.)

3.   By *what method* did you *first* receive the information listed above? Please check *only one* of the following: (See page 2 for rest of question)

WRITTEN OR VISUAL METHODS	TALKING OR SOUND METHODS
__ Memo or circular	__ Talking with one other person
__ Notice on bulletin board	in his or her presence

Figure 9.8   ECCO Analysis Questionnaire (Continued)

___ Personal letter
___ Booklet
___ Company newspaper
___ Company magazine
___ Local newspaper
___ Other, please explain
_____

___ Talking over the telephone
___ Talking and listening in a small group of two or more
___ Attending an organized group meeting or conference
___ Overhearing what someone else said
___ Listening to radio or television
___ Other, please explain
_____

4. Where were you when you first received the information listed above? Please check *only one* of the following:

    ___ At my desk or other location where I carry out my job duties.
    ___ Elsewhere in the room where I work.
    ___ Outside the room where I work, but still working.
    ___ Away from the office and building, but still working. (coffee break, etc.)
    ___ Away from the building, and not working (gone home after work, etc.).
    ___ Other. Please explain. _____

5. What was the approximate time that you received the information listed above? Please *write in* the day and hour. Day _____ Hour _____

6. Did you pass the information or any part of it to another employee? Please check *only one* of the following:

    ___No, I did not pass the information on.
    ___Yes, I did pass the information on.

7. If you answered yes to question 6, please list the code numbers of individuals to whom you told or sent the information. *Place the code numbers on the lines below:*

    1. _____   4. _____
    2. _____   5. _____
    3. _____   6. _____

Please check to see that you have answered all of the questions as accurately and completely as possible at this time. Please place the questionnaire in the envelope, seal, and place it to be picked up. Thank you for your cooperation.

5. If at all possible, arrange to pick up the envelopes as soon as the questionnaires have been completed.

6. Each questionnaire should have a space for a code number, which provides anonymity and confidentiality for employees. Codes may be created by having each person use the first initial of his or her last name and the last four digits of his or her home telephone number. A master list can be compiled and provided for each employee for purposes of identifying individuals from whom information was received and to whom it was given. Pick up the code sheets when you pick up the final envelopes.

7. Procedures for administering the survey form allow for information to be recognized at any time during the day or week when information tracing is being done. Therefore, it is important to avoid revealing the details of messages to employees in the first questionnaire. Some of the employees may not receive the information until the second or third survey envelopes. Thus, to avoid planting the information, the message must be phrased in a short and quite general manner, simply identifying the topic of the message. A message about changes in employee parking might appear in the box as Employee Parking Arrangements. The following suggestions about the preparation of messages may be helpful:

   a. Messages should be part of the regular, routine information program of the organization; they should consist of information that the management of the organization is planning to disseminate to employees regardless of the efforts to analyze the system.

   b. Messages should contain information that all members of the organization ought to receive. Since the objective of the tracing design is to chart the dissemination of information throughout the organization, a message appropriate to all members is preferable.

   c. Messages should be prepared in sufficient detail to provide enough to identify about ten factual bits of information; study the written statement to make certain that who, what, where, why, how, and when are included. Identify each of the bits of information precisely so they can be used to measure information loss, addition, substitution, change, and distortion.

Write true/false questions that can be included in the survey form to test how much employees know about the message. Employees can be asked to list the bits of information they know about the topic in the box, or they can answer the true/false questions as a test of what they know about the topic (see figures 9.8 and 9.9 for examples).

d. Messages should be initiated by a top management person in the unit being studied, and the message should be distributed in the usual manner. That is, if information is usually made available to organization members by a memo dictated by the manager, typed, and duplicated by a secretary, and mailed to department heads, that system should be used for the messages to be traced.

e. Alternative messages should be disseminated so that not even the manager and secretary will know which message is being traced. The first indication of which message is being followed occurs when the envelopes are opened during the first time period.

Flow Diagram   The flow of information can be portrayed by drawing a sociometric diagram consisting of circles representing employees with lines connecting employees who receive information from and tell information to one another. Figure 9.10 illustrates an information flow diagram.

Feature 3: Message Fidelity and Distortion

As information is disseminated in an organization, the content often is transformed by omissions, additions, and other changes (Guetzkow 1965), resulting in the distortion of information. Part of the analysis of organizational communication is determining whether and, if so, what kinds of distortions may be occurring during the information dissemination process.

Methods of Analysis

Listing Bits of Information   As was illustrated in the discussion of ECCO analysis above, employees can be asked to list the information they know when they complete the questionnaires. Later,

---

Figure 9.9   True/False Questions

Survey No. _____
                    (Hour envelope opened)

Your Code No. _____

SURVEY OF INFORMATION FLOW (Confidential)

1. Prior to receiving this questionnaire, what did you know about the infor-
    mation in the box below?

┌───┐
│   │
│   │
└───┘

Please check *one*: _____ I knew all about it.
                    _____ I knew something about it.
                    _____ I knew nothing about it.

   If your answer above was "I knew nothing about it," you have completed the questionnaire. Please return it to the envelope, seal the envelope, and leave it to be picked up. Thank you.
   If your answer above was "I knew all about it" or "I knew something
about it," please complete the remainder of the questionnaire by providing the information requested.

T. _____ F. _____ N.O.W. Accounts were pioneered in Massachusetts.
T. _____ F. _____ The organization is interested in processing N.O.W.
                    Accounts for Savings and Loans.
T. _____ F. _____ A N.O.W. Account is one set up especially for women.
T. _____ F. _____ N.O.W. Accounts were legal in many southern states
                    prior to this time.
T. _____ F. _____ Congress has set a 5% interest rate limit on N.O.W.
                    Accounts.
T. _____ F. _____ Both individuals and small businesses may use N.O.W.
                    Accounts.
T. _____ F. _____ Bank advertisements contribute to acceptance of
                    N.O.W. Accounts.
T. _____ F. _____ Federal Reserve System rules will not apply to N.O.W.
                    Accounts.
T. _____ F. _____ N.O.W. Accounts are clearly distinguishable from
                    checking accounts.
T. _____ F. _____ "N.O.W." stands for Negotiable Order of Withdrawal.

2. From *whom* did you first receive this information listed above?

Figure 9.9   True/False Questions (Continued)

Place the source's code number on this line:
(By using the code number, you maintain the anonymity of specific individuals.)

3. By *what method* did you *first* receive the information listed above? Please check *only one* of the following:

Figure 9.10   Hypothetical Information Flow Diagram

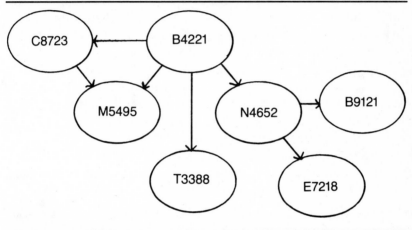

---

the list can be compared against a previously prepared list of information actually contained in the message.

Administer True/False Test   A short true/false test about bits of information in the original message can be constructed and administered to employees.

Administer Multiple Choice Test   Experts estimate that a good test writer, thoroughly familiar with the subject, ought to be able to write ten multiple choice test items in an eight-hour day, and that possibly two of the ten items will end up being good measures.

The other eight items will be good ideas, but they will be too difficult or too easy, or will not discriminate among test-takers.

A good test will not try to trick the test taker into selecting a wrong answer; neither will the choices make it easier for the taker to guess the correct answer. Thus test items should have all possible clues, tricky wording, and unnecessary information removed.

The characteristics of better multiple choice test items include the following: The stem or problem may be in the form of a question or an incomplete statement. The stem should be short and clear and present the problem. The alternatives should be arranged in descending order with respect to length from shortest to longest. The question-type stem should begin with a capital letter and end with a question mark. The responses should be grammatically correct, complete, and plausible as correct answers, without containing clues to the correct answer. The incomplete-statement-type stem should begin with a capital letter and have no punctuation at the end. The responses should begin with a small letter and end with a period. Each alternative should complete the stem, making a grammatically correct complete statement. Note the characteristics of acceptable multiple choice test items in the following examples:

Example 1: Which communication network role has the most power?
  a. A bridge
  b. A liaison
  c. An isolate
  d. A clique member

Example 2: An organization member who contacts few other members is called a(n)
  a. bridge
  b. liaison
  c. isolate
  d. clique member

Conduct an Information Unit Analysis   An IUA consists of comparing each word or series of words in a reproduced message with comparable words or phrases in the original message. Give one point for each information unit, even if they are slightly altered in tense or by substitution of synonyms. Score one-half point for each information unit that is significantly altered and yet retains the sense of the original. Give zero points for errors, distortions, and units of information with no correspondence to the original message. Sum the scores for each reproduction, and determine the amount of information reproduced accurately.

Conduct a Theme Analysis Theme analysis consists of making a list of themes in the original message, phrasing them as questions, and scoring one point for each theme present in a reproduction of the original message, regardless of the accuracy of the details (Pace, Peterson, and Boren 1975). An example of a theme question might be: Was anything about complaints of slow or overcrowded serving lines mentioned?

Feature 4: Information Adequacy

The adequacy of information that an employee receives from higher levels in the organization may be analyzed in two ways: (1) through an employee's estimate of the adequacy of the information or (2) through a test of what an employee actually knows about certain topics (Bateman 1979). Perceptual measures or estimates may be standardized, at least somewhat; however, tests must be developed individually for each organization (Stead 1983). Excerpts from Bateman's survey are included in figure 9.11.

ICA Survey

The survey instrument developed for the International Communication Association (ICA) Audit Project measures perceptions of

---

Figure 9.11   Bateman's Information Adequacy Survey

Among the following fringe benefits, policies, and practices, please indicate your understanding of the item by circling the appropriate number: 1 = no understanding; 2 = slight understanding; 3 = "average" understanding; 4 = good understanding; 5 = excellent understanding.

a. My health (hospital) insurance   1 2 3 4 5
b. My life insurance coverage   1 2 3 4 5

information adequacy by responses to two basic assertions: (1) "This is the amount of information I receive now," and (2) "This is the amount of information I want to receive."

If organization members indicate that the amount of information they receive about pay and benefits, for example, is about the same as the amount they want to receive, we can conclude that information is adequate, regardless of what organization members know about pay and benefits.

LTT Questionnaire

The questionnaire developed by Wiio (1976) to audit organizational communication also has measures of information adequacy. Organization members are asked to indicate answers to three questions:

1. "How much information do you get about the organization from . . . ?"
2. "How much information do you get about your own work from . . . ?"
3. "What kind of information do you get enough of . . . ?"

Feature 5: Communication Satisfaction

In contrast to information adequacy, communication satisfaction is concerned with how employees feel about the information they get and from whom they get it, regardless of the amount of information received.

Communication Satisfaction Questionnaire

Downs and Hazen (1977) have developed the most extensive measure of organizational communication satisfaction available. The four parts of the CS Questionnaire ask about employee satisfaction with (1) the amount or quality of information, (2) sources of information, and (3) communication activities, and (4) asks for estimates of productivity patterns. Figure 9.12 includes excerpts from Downs and Hazen's questionnaire.

Feature 6: Organizational Communication Climate

The communication climate of an organization consists of perceptions, attitudes, and expectations of organization members that

---

Figure 9.12 Downs and Hazen's Communication Satisfaction Questionnaire

---

Listed below are several kinds of information often associated with a person's job. Please indicate how satisfied you are with the *amount* and/or *quality* of each kind of information by circling the appropriate number at the right. (1 = low, 7 = high)

4. Information about my progress in my job	1	2	3	4	5	6	7
5. Personnel news	1	2	3	4	5	6	7
6. Information on company policies and goals	1	2	3	4	5	6	7

---

indicate to them that levels of trust, supportiveness, openness, candor, participative decision making, and concern for high performance goals exist in the organization.

Organizational Communication Climate Inventory

One of the most direct measures of organizational communication climate is Peterson and Pace's Communication Climate Inventory (Pace and Peterson 1979). The inventory consists of twelve items that measure six aspects of communication climate. Figure 9.13 includes an excerpt from the CCI.

Survey of Organizational Climate

The SOC was developed in the Office of Personnel Management as a "general diagnostic perception and attitude questionnaire for use in organizations with diverse functions and organizational structures" (p. 1). It measures six broad categories of characteristics, including (1) organizational communications, authority, trust, conflict, and change orientation; (2) supervisory; (3) group; (4) individual; (5) job; and (6)work outcomes. An excerpt from the survey is included in figure 9.14.

Consistent with our concept of analysis and its use, Siegel and Turney (1980) explain in *The Manager's Guide* to using the survey that it is "best viewed as a tool to be used by managers . . . to confirm his/her suspicions that 'something is wrong'; to add substance to those undefined perceptions" (p. 12).

Please respond to *all questions* as honestly and frankly as you possibly can.

In *no way* will your identity be associated with your responses nor will your responses be used in such a manner as to jeopardize you or your job.

Unless the wording of a particular item specifically indicates otherwise, respond in terms of your own impressions of the entire organization in which you work.

Indicate your response to each item by *circling just one of the five numbers* in the right-hand column. PLEASE DO NOT OMIT ANY ITEM! Use the following code to interpret the meaning of the numerical symbols.

5   Circle this number if, in your honest judgment, the item is a true description of conditions in the organization.

4   Circle if the item is more true than false as a description of conditions in the organization.

3   Circle if the time is about half true and half false as a description of conditions in the organization.

2   Circle if the item is more false than true as a description of conditions in the organization.

1   Circle if the item is a false description of conditions in the organization.

Please, do not attempt an intensive "word analysis" of the questions. And — of course — your responses should reflect your own judgments, not those of other people. There are no right or wrong answers.

Answer all questions in terms of your impression concerning your own organization! *You may now turn the page and begin.*

5   4   3   2   1   1. Personnel at all levels in the organization have a commitment to high performance goals (high productivity, high quality, low cost).

5   4   3   2   1   2. Superiors seem to have a great deal of confidence and trust in their subordinates.

5   4   3   2   1   3. Personnel at all levels in the organization are communicated to and consulted with concerning organizational policy relevant to their positions.

5   4   3   2   1   4. Subordinates seem to have a great deal of confidence and trust in their superiors.

5   4   3   2   1   5. Information received from subordinates is perceived by superiors as important enough to be acted upon until demonstrated otherwise.

5   4   3   2   1   6. All personnel receive information that enhances their abilities to coordinate their work with that of other personnel or departments, and that deals broadly with the company, its organization, leaders and plans.

5   4   3   2   1   7. A general atmosphere of candor and frankness seems to pervade relationships between personnel through all levels of the organization.

178

5 4 3 2 1   8. There are avenues of communication available for all personnel to consult with management levels above their own in decision making and goal setting process.

5 4 3 2 1   9. All personnel are able to say "what's on their minds" regardless of whether they are talking to superiors, subordinates or superiors.

5 4 3 2 1 10. Except for necessary security information, all personnel have relatively easy access to information that relates directly to their immediate jobs.

5 4 3 2 1 11. A high concern for the well-being of all personnel is as important to management as high performance goals.

5 4 3 2 1 12. Superiors at all levels in the organization listen continuously and with open minds to suggestions or reports of problems made by personnel at all subordinate levels in the organization.

Scoring and Analysis

1. *Trust Climate Score* — Sums numbers 2 and 4 on each inventory and divide by two. This is an individual score. To get a composite Trust Climate Score, sum all the inventories and divide total number of respondents.
2. *Participative Decision Making Climate Score* — Sum numbers 3 and 6 on each inventory and divide by two. This is an individual score. To get a composite Participative Decision Making Climate Score, sum all the inventories and divide by the total number of respondents.
3. *Supportive Climate Score* — Sum numbers 7 and 9 and divide by two. This is an individual score. To get a composite Supportive Climate Score, sum all the inventories and divide by the total number of respondents.
4. *Openness in Downward Communication Climate Score* — Sum numbers 8 and 10 and divide by two. This is an individual score. To get a composite Openness in Downward Communication Climate Score, sum all the inventories and divide by the total number of respondents.
5. *Listening in Upward Communication Climate Score* — Sum numbers 5 and 12 and divide by two. This is an individual score. To get a composite Listening in Upward Communication Climate Score, sum all the inventories and divide by the total number of respondents.
6. *Concern for High Performance Goals Climate Score* — Sum numbers 1 and 11 and divide by two. This is an individual score. To get a composite Concern for High Performance Goals Climate Score, sum all the inventories and divide by the total number of respondents.
7. *Composite Climate Score* — Sum the individual responses for the 12 items and divide by 12. This general average gives the Individual Climate Score (ICCS) for each respondent. For the Organization Composite Climate Score (OCCS), sum all the ICCC's and divide by the total number of respondents.

Figure 9.14   Survey of Organizational Climate

Most of the questions in this survey will ask you (1) how much you *agree* with things; (2) how *important* things are; and (3) how *often* things happen. Each of the questions is answered by circling a number.

	Strongly disagree	Disagree	Undecided	Agree	Strongly agree
For example: **How much do you *agree* or *disagree* with the following statements about your work group?**					
My group works well together.	1	2	3	4	⑤
In my group, everyone's opinion gets listened to.	1	2	3	④	5

In this example, Jane Doe was asked how much she agrees or disagrees with certain statements about her work group. She feels very strongly that her group works well together. However, she does not feel quite as strongly that everyone's opinion gets listened to, although she does agree that this occurs.

	Not important at all		Somewhat important		Very important
Some of the questions may look like this:					
How important is the respect you receive from the people you work with?	1	2	3	④	5

In this example, there are written descriptions above only some of the numbers. However, *any* of the 5 numbers can be used. Jane Doe feels that the respect she receives is more than "somewhat important" but not quite "very important." So she answered by circling 4.

Here are some, things that could happen to people when they do their jobs especially well. How likely is it that each of these things would happen to you if you performed your job especially well?

	Not at all likely		Somewhat likely		Very likely
75. How likely is it that you will be promoted or given a better job if you perform especially well?	1	2	3	4	5
76. How likely is it that your own hard work will lead to recognition as a good performer?	1	2	3	4	5
77. How likely is it that you will get a cash award or unscheduled pay increase if you perform your job especially well?	1	2	3	4	5

Communication Rules Analysis

Communication rules are the expectations of organization members that influence the way in which they interact in superior-subordinate dyads. Farace, Monge, and Russell (1977) indicate that the first step in a rules analysis is to identify each person's immediate supervisor and the supervisor's subordinates; hence, the "initial task is to generate a hierarchical list . . . of manager-subordinate relationships in which each person is clearly and unambiguously placed in the overall hierarchy" (p. 215).

The next step in the analysis is to define the communication rule topics. Although the rules may differ from situation to situation, questions covering thirteen different topics are typical (Johnson 1977). An excerpt from a usual rules questionnaire appears in figure 9.15.

A rules questionnaire often asks employees to indicate their level of satisfaction with the manner in which select relationships are managed. The questionnaire asks for an indication of the em-

---

Figure 9.15   Analysis of Communication Rules

Indicate your impressions of how you conduct "talk" with your supervisor. In the space on the right side, indicate your guess about how your supervisor would answer the question.

	MY PERCEPTION	SUPERVISOR WOULD PROBABLY SAY
3. When two people get together, one of them has to decide what they'll talk about. Generally, when you and your immediate supervisor talk, who usually decides on the topics to be discussed? a. He usually decides. b. I usually decide. c. It's split about evenly between us.	_____	_____
3a. How satisfied are you with this arrangement? a. I'd like more to say about what we talk about. b. I'm satisfied.	_____	_____

---

ployee's perceptions of the way in which communication rules are used, but it also asks for the employee's perceptions of how he or she thinks the superior (or subordinate) views those same rules.

With information from both parties about their own perceptions and how they think the other person feels about each of the rules, a measure of agreement and similarity of perception is secured. Questionnaire responses also provide an indication of how well one member of the dyad knows the view of the other. The degree to which the superior predicts what the subordinate actually says is a measure of how accurate the superior's views are of the overall communication relationship.

Critical Incidents

A critical incident is the report of an event that illustrates behaviors critical to the success or failure of a particular task. Critical incidents usually represent either very effective or very ineffective ways of doing things.

The critical communication incident approach involves having employees describe specific experiences involving communication with others in the organization that has been very effective or very ineffective in getting information across. An incident is acceptable if, in the employee's opinion, it relates to an important aspect of the job and describes behavior that is very effective or ineffective communication.

Each incident should represent a miniature case and report the specific behaviors and actions involved, be recent enough to be remembered easily, be reported by a person in a position to observe what happened, be consistent and clear, and be reasonably complete or self-contained.

The incidents are analyzed by identifying and underlining the statements that describe the critical behaviors. The critical elements are recorded in list form and studied for categories of problems and strengths. Descriptive titles are assigned to the categories. The procedures are similar to theme analysis mentioned earlier.

Summary

Six features of organizational communication have been identified along with select instruments, tools, and procedures for making an analysis of the features.

Recently, a few instruments have been developed that provide an overall look at organizational communication. Some general procedures have also been developed that help make the best use of time, resources,and instruments. We shall review some of those more comprehensive approaches.

Comprehensive Approach To Analyzing Organizational Communication

Procedures for conducting an organizational communication systems analysis have been described in some detail over the years (Goldhaber and Krivonos, 1977; Goldhaber and Rogers 1979). However, R. Wayne Pace and Brent D. Peterson, doing business as Organizational Associates, outlined specific procedures in the early 1970s for analyzing organizational communication that have been used extensively (Goldhaber 1979, 325; Goldhaber 1976, 382). Figure 9.16 summarizes the steps in the Pace-Peterson process and shows where instruments described above might be used to advantage.

To complement the procedures, they have also developed an Organizational Communication Profile instrument (Peterson and Pace 1986 — this is included in the Appendix) that gathers data on eight features of organizational communication and provides a comprehensive overview of the status of communication in an organization. Figure 9.17 portrays a model of the OCP variables and diagrams relationships among them. The eight key variables are listed as (1) organizational satisfaction, (2) communication climate, (3) information accessibility, (4) information load, (5) message fidelity, (6) information dispersion, (7) media quality, and (8) organizational culture.

The Organizational Communication Profile (OCP)* provides a way to survey organization members about such matters as where a person gets information, who receives the information, how available the information is, how accurate the information is, how much information someone gets, what the quality of the me-

---

*Information about availability of instruments, scoring, and normative data may be obtained by writing R. Wayne Pace or Brent D. Peterson, Department of Organizational Behavior, Brigham Young University, Provo, UT 84602.

Figure 9.16   Pace-Peterson Organizational Communication Systems Analysis

Step 1. *Feasibility Visit:* Analysts make organization on-site feasibility visit to determine whether doing the analysis is possible.

Step 2. *Initial Meeting:* Analysts meet with all unit personnel to preview philosophy, assumptions, expectations, and procedures associated with the analysis.

Step 3. *Administer Profile:* Administer the *Organizational Communication Profile* (Peterson-Pace) instrument to all personnel in the unit being studied to secure data on key features and variables.

Step 4. *In-depth Data on Variables:* Exploration of key features and variables of OCP using interviews, observations, and other procedures and instruments.

Step 5. *Complementary Units Data:* Gather data from complementary units, the public or community, and related groups concerning perceptions of organizational effectiveness and communication practices of organization members. Structured interviews and simple measuring instruments are used where appropriate.

Step 6. *Comparison of Data:* Compare organization profile data (step 3), in-depth data (step 4), and complementary units data (step 5) to locate points of similarity and difference.

Step 7. *Data Sharing Meeting:* Meeting with all unit personnel and select invited guests to review preliminary data on item-by-item basis to identify, examine, elaborate, and delete problem areas.

Step 8. *Interim Report:* Analysts write preliminary report and distributes it to all unit personnel and, if desired, to invited participants.

Step 9. *Form Task Groups:* Create and organize task groups consisting of unit personnel and, if desired, invited participants, for purpose of evaluating preliminary report.

Step 10. *Task Group Evaluations:* Task groups meet and review preliminary report in terms of personal meaning for them. Groups identify and enumerate problems and provide tentative alternative ways for taking corrective action. Task groups prepare their own reports.

Step 11. *General Meeting:* All task groups meet together to share their reports with one another. Select task members, usually elected by groups, assigned to merge group reports and prepare a single, unified document.

Step 12. *Analysts's Final Report:* Using their own preliminary report, the final report of task groups, and other data, analysts prepare final report and list of specific recommendations.

Step 13. *Final Report Meeting:* All unit personnel, invited guests, and analysts meet for purposes of having unit administrators and managers respond to report of task groups and analysts, and to discuss how to proceed after report.

Step 14. *Turnover Meeting:* Analysts meet with administrative staff to review procedures for organization members to assume full responsibility for continuing analysis and implementation of recommendations on long-range basis.

Figure 9.17   Model for Organizational Communication Profile

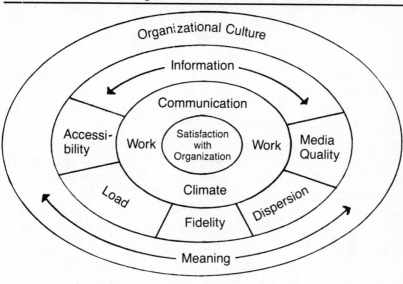

dia are by which the information is distributed, what the communication climate is, and what the culture of the organization is. The OCP is a written questionnaire that is relatively easy to administer and interpret which gives information about the overall functioning of the organization that may help confirm strengths and verify weaknesses.

Variables in OCP

Definitions of the eight variables measured by the OCP and a sample excerpt from the instrument itself are presented below.

1. Organizational Satisfaction

Perceptions of organization members about their work, supervision, pay and benefits, promotions, and co-workers in terms of how satisfied they are with them.

Work Satisfaction inventory items are 19, 20, 25, and 32 on the inventory are summed and divided by 4 to determine the individual score. To calculate a Work Satisfaction Score, sum all the inventory responses and divide by the total number of respondents.

Supervision Satisfaction items are 1, 9, 14, and 22. The items are summed and divided by 4 to determine the individual score. To calculate a Supervision Satisfaction Score, sum all the inventory responses and divide by the total number of respondents.

Pay and Benefits Satisfaction items are 3, 7, 16, and 17. The items are summed and divided by 4 to determine the individual score. To calculate a Pay and Benefit Satisfaction Score, sum all the inventory responses and divide by the total number of respondents.

Promotions Satisfaction items are 8, 13, 23, and 26. The items are summed and divided by 4 to determine the individual score. To calculate a Promotion Satisfaction Score, sum all the inventory responses and divide by the total number of respondents.

Co-workers Satisfaction items are 5, 11, 28, and 30. The items are summed and divided by 4 to determine the individual score. To calculate a Co-worker Satisfaction Score, sum all the inventory responses and divide by the total number of respondents.

2. Communication Climate

Perceptions of organization members about how the organization demonstrates that it trusts, supports, is open to, attends to, actively consults, and has a concern for high work standards of employees.

Trust items are 4 and 10. The items are summed and divided by 2 to determine the individual score. To calculate the organizational Trust Score, sum all the inventory responses and divide by the total number of respondents.

Participative decision making items are 6 and 21. The items are summed and divided by 2 to determine the individual score. To calculate the organizational Decision Making Score, sum all the inventory responses and divide by the total number of respondents.

Supportiveness items are 18 and 24. The items are summed and divided by 2 to determine the individual score. To calculate the organizational Supportiveness Score, sum all the inventory responses and divide by the total number of respondents.

Openness in downward communication items are 15 and 27. The items are summed and divided by 2 to determine the individual score. To calculate the organizational Openness in Downward

Communication score, sum all the inventory responses and divide by the total number of respondents.

Listening in upward communication items are 12 and 31. The items are summed and divided by 2 to determine the individual score. To calculate the organizational Listening. in Upward Communication Score, sum all the inventory responses and divide by the total number of respondents.

Concern for high performance goals items are 2 and 29. The items are summed and divided by 2 to determine the individual score. To calculate the organizational Concern for High Performance Goals Score, sum all the inventory responses and divide by the total number of respondents.

3. Media Quality

Perceptions of organization members of the extent to which publications, written directives, reports, and other media are viewed as appealing, appropriate, efficient, and reliable. To calculate the Media Quality score, sum numbers 33, 34,and 35 on each inventory and divide by 3. This is an individual score. To calculate the organizational Media Quality score, sum all the inventories and divide by the total number of respondents.

4. Information Accessibility

Perceptions of organization members of the extent to which information is available to them from a variety of sources in the organization. To calculate the Information Accessibility score, sum numbers 36–43 on each inventory and divide by 8. This is an individual score. To calculate the organizational Information Accessibility score, sum all the inventories and divide by the total number of respondents.

5. Information Dispersion

Perceptions of organization members of the extent to which a message is dispersed among organization members, or who knows something about a specific message. To calculate the Information Dispersion score, evaluate item 52 and determine who knew about the information and who did not. This score is simply the percentages of two responses to 52. To calculate the organizational

Information Dispersion score, divide by the total number of respondents.

6. *Information Load*

Perceptions of organization members of the extent to which they feel they receive more or less information than they can cope with or need to function effectively. To calculate the Information Load score, sum numbers 44–51 on each inventory and divide by 8. Then subtract this score from the Information Accessibility score. This will give an information underload score for the individual inventory. A minus (-) score indicates underload, and a plus (+) score indicates overload. To calculate the organizational Information load score, sum all the inventories and divide by the total number of respondents.

7. *Message Fidelity*

Perceptions of organization members of how many bits of information they know regarding a particular message in contrast to the actual bit of information in the message. The Message Fidelity score for each respondent is his or her answer to item 53. This gives the percentage of what he or she knew about the message. The organizational Message Fidelity score is calculated by summing all of the answers to item 53 and dividing by the total number of respondents. This score is reported as a percentage of what the respondents knew.

8. *Organizational Culture*

The image that organization members have of the total organization; the meaning that organization members have of their workplace. To calculate the Organizational Culture score, use only information collected from the timed test at the beginning of the profile. This is a Szalay Associative Group Analysis technique. It helps determine the cultural meanings that members have about their organization. It is calculated in the following manner: Words listed are given weighted scores by order of listing — the first listing receives the greatest weight (the weights for the first ten listings are 6, 5, 4, 3, 3, 3, 3, 2, 2, 1). The words and scores are then grouped into categories on the basis of similarity. These categories reflect the culture of the organization. Figure 9.18 is an example of this process:

Figure 9.18   Sample Data on Organizational Culture

In the box below, write the name of your organization. As you are timed for one minute, write all the words that come to your mind when you think of your organization. *Use only one word for each line.*

```
+-----------------------------------------------+
|                                               |
|              Pipsqueak Market                 |
|                                               |
+-----------------------------------------------+
```

WEIGHT	WORDS LISTED
6	1. Encouraging
5	2. Quality
4	3. Clean
3	4. Understanding
3	5. Good
3	6. Safe
3	7. Communicating
2	8. Service
1	9. Neat
1	10. Listening
1	11. Best
1	12. Secure
1	13. Helping
1	14. Growth
1	15. Caring

Thank you! You have completed this portion of this instrument. *Do not turn the page until given further instructions.*

The following word categories were selected from this sample data sheet.

RELATIONSHIPS		WORTH		ENVIRONMENT	
6	encouraging	5	quality	4	clean
3	understanding	3	good	3	safe
3	communicating	2	service	2	neat
1	listening	1	best	1	secure
1	helping	1	growth		
1	caring				

Figure 9.18   Sample Data on Organizational Culture (Continued)

To calculate the percentage of importance of each category, use the weights as follows:

Relationships:	sum the weights of each word	15
Worth:	sum the weights of each word	12
Environment:	sum the weights of each word	10
	Total the sums of all weights	37

Use the total to calculate the percentage of weights in each category.

Relationships:	15/37 = 41%
Worth:	12/37 = 32%
Environment:	10/37 = 27%

Data about organizational communication may serve as the basis of a wide variety of organizational interventions. As a survey instrument, the OCP is fully amenable to process consultation procedures that involve gathering and feeding information back to client groups.

Team building, intergroup interface sessions, third-party consultations, organizational mirroring, sociotechnical systems procedures, and contemporary problem-solving interventions can be used following OCP data gathering and analysis.

Specific interventions that focus on structural changes to influence information flow, to increase interaction and communication, and to confront and resolve differences all find their base in OCP data.

The OCP is grounded in communication theory and focuses on the central human processes in organizations. It provides data about perceptions and behaviors that affect nearly all other processes relevant to effective and efficient organizational functioning. Nevertheless, the OCP does not do everything, but it can reveal a great deal about organizational communication.

Summary

This chapter has examined ways to analyze an organizational communication system from two perspectives: (1) an interpretive approach using naturalistic methods and (2) a functional approach using empirical methods. Specific techniques, instruments, and procedures were discussed.

Activity

Make copies of the Communication Climate Inventory (figure 9.13) and administer it to ten individuals who are members of the same group or organization.

Following the instructions in the text, score the CCI and get both individual and composite climate scores for each variable and the group or organization.

Write a short paragraph describing the basic climate of the group or organization as revealed by the CCI scores.

References

Bateman, D. A. 1979. "Measuring Communication Effectiveness." Paper presented at the annual convention of the American Business Communication Association, December, Seattle, Washington.

Davis, K. 1953. "A Method of Studying Communication Patterns in Organizations." *Personnel Psychology* 6: 301–312.

Dennis, H. S., III, G. M. Goldhaber, and M. P. Yates. 1978. "Organizational Communication Theory and Research: An Overview of Research Methods." In *Communication Yearbook* 2 New Brunswick, N.J.: Transaction.

Downs, C. W., and M. D. Hazen. 1977. "A Factor Analytic Study of Communication Satisfaction." *Journal of Business Communication* 14: 63–73.

Farace, F. V., P. R. Monge, and H. M. Russell. 1977. *Communicating and Organization*. Reading, Mass.: Addison-Wesley.

Factory 121. March 1963. P. 88.

Funk, H. B., and R. C. Becker. 1952. "Measuring the Effectiveness of Industrial Communication." *Personnel* 29: 237–240.

Goldhaber, Gerald M. 1976. "The ICA Communication Audit: Rationale and Development." Paper presented at the Academy of Management Convention, Kansas City.

Goldhaber, G., and P. Krivonos. 1977. "The ICA Audit: Process, Status and Critique." *Journal of Business Communication* 15 (Fall): 41–56.

Goldhaber, G. M. 1979. *Organizational Communication*. Dubuque, Iowa: Wm. C.Brown.

Goldhaber, G., and D. Rogers. 1979. *Auditing Organizational Communication Systems: The ICA Communication Audit*. Dubuque, Iowa: Kendall/Hunt.

Greenbaum, H. H. 1974. "The Audit of Organizational Communication." *Academy of Management Journal* 17 (December): 739–754.

Guetzkow, H. 1965. "Communication in Organization." In *Handbook of Organizations*, edited by J. G. March. Chicago: Rand McNally, pp. 534–573.

Johnson, B. M. 1977. *Communication: The Process of Organizing*. Boston, Mass.: Allyn and Bacon.

Larke, A. G. 1954. "Linear Responsibility Chart — New Tool for Executive Control." *Dun's Review and Modern Industry* 64 (September).

"Linear Responsibility Charting." 1964. In *Organization Planning*. Rock Island, Ill.: U.S. Army Management Engineering Training Agency.

MacKenzie, Alex. 1969. "A Three-D Model of Management Processes." *Harvard Business Review* 47 (November–December): 80–87.

Pace, R. W. 1983. *Organizational Communication: Foundations for Human Resource Development*. Englewood Cliffs, N.J.: Prentice-Hall.

Pace, R. W., and Timothy G. Hegstrom. 1977. "Seriality in Human Communication Systems." Paper presented at the annual conference of the International Communication Association, Berlin.

Pace, R. W. and B. D. Peterson. 1979. "Measuring Organizational Communication Climate." Unpublished paper, Brigham Young University, Provo, Utah.

Pace, R. W., B. D. Peterson, and R. R. Boren. 1975. *Communication Experiments: A Manual for Conducting Experiments*. Belmont, Calif.: Wadsworth.

Pace, R. W. and H. W. Simons. 1963. "Preliminary Validation Report on the Purdue Basic Oral Communication Evaluation Form." *Personnel Psychology* 42 (April): 191–193.

Richards, W. D., Jr. 1974. "Network Analysis in Large Complex Systems: Techniques and Methods — Tools." Paper presented at the annual conference of the International Communication Association, Atlanta, Ga., April.

Richetto, Gary M. 1977. "Organizational Communication Theory and Research: An Overview." *Communication Yearbook I*. New Brunswick, N.J.: Transaction.

Roberts, K., and C. A. O'Reilly, III. 1978. "Organizations as Communication Structures: An Empirical Approach." *Human Communication Research* 4 (Summer): 283–293.

Schein, Edgar H. 1969. *Process Consultation: Its Role in Organization Development*. Reading, Mass.: Addison-Wesley.

Siegel, A. L., and J. R. Turney. 1980. *Manager's Guide to Using the Survey of Organizational Climate*. Washington, D.C.: Superintendent of Documents.

Stead, James A. 1983. "The Relationship of Information Adequacy/Confidence to Job Satisfaction Among Credit Union Employees." Unpublished M.A. thesis, Brigham Young University, Provo, Utah.

Wiio, O. A. 1976. "Organizational Communication: Interfacing Systems in Different Contingencies." Paper presented at the Annual Conference of the International Communication Association, April, Portland, Oregon.

10. Methods of Documentation, Organizational Systems Analysis: Interpretive Approaches*

Interpretive organizational systems analysis uses observational and intuitive methods to document the point of concern being evaluated. Rather than using substantial numerical methods, as reviewed in chapter 9, the reliance is centered on narratives, interviews, and observing others. The basic interpretive methods treated in this chapter include participant observation, account analysis, theme analysis, structural analysis, and in-depth interviews.

Value

Interpretive research and the approaches for doing it vary considerably. Strine and Pacanowsky (1985) remark, "Some pieces of interpretive research strongly resemble traditional 'org. comm.' studies complete with numbers. But others look like critical analyses of plays, filled with indented dialogue. Still others resemble new Journalism or fiction . . ." (p. 284). It is obvious that each interpretive method requires a different level of sophistication. Although this chapter may not prepare you to write a novel or engage in rhetorical criticism, it should provide the basic concepts that will enable you to do useful analyses. The aim is to discuss basic insights and procedures that should be mastered before one can become a successful analyst. The analytic concepts presented

---

are selected for illustrative purposes and should not be thought of as *the* only concepts to use.

Objectives

At the conclusion of the chapter, you will be able to do the following:

• List an example of artifacts, perspectives, values, and assumptions.
• Answer six questions that govern the procedures to use in interpretive analysis.
• Differentiate between examples that represent account, story, and metaphor analyses.
• Demonstrate, in a written exercise, the skill of using either account, story, or metaphor analysis to examine an issue of an organization of which you are a member.

General Considerations

In traditional analyses there is great reliance on instruments, such as inventories, attitude questionnaires, and structured interviews. The interpretive method of analysis relies heavily on the analyst as the "instrument," hence it is up to interpretive analysts to present a strong case for their findings. The analyst cannot rely on such statements as "My findings are valid because my questionnaire is valid and reliable." The outcome of an interpretive analysis rests on the shoulders of the analyst, who must convince those analyzed that their discoveries are helpful and insightful. The critical question is "Can the analyst 'discover' and 'interpret' significant organizational behaviors?"

What does the analyst look for? The search is for symbolic behavior that has organizational significance. What do the symbols allow organization members to see and do? How might they enable or constrain organizational activity? To quote Smircich (1985), "What are the words, ideas, and constructs that impel, legitimate, coordinate, and realize organized activity in specific settings? How do they accomplish the task? Whose interests are they serving?" (p. 67).

To help us answer these questions, let's look at the work of Lundberg (1985), who discusses four levels of organizational culture. These include (1) artifacts, (2) perspectives, (3) values, and (4) assumptions.

Artifacts

Artifacts can be verbal, behavioral, or physical. A verbal artifact could be a story. Behavioral artifacts include rituals and ceremonies. The visual (pictures, plaques, prints, clippings, and cartoons) and actual objects, such as golf clubs, pieces of sculpturing, or vases exhibited by members of an organization, are examples of physical artifacts.

Perspectives

Perspectives refer to the shared rules and norms of an organization.

Values

Values represent those ideas that organizational members use for judging situations, acts, and goals. They are the standards and ideals of the organization.

Assumptions

Assumptions are the tacit beliefs that organizational members hold. They are often implicit and so taken for granted that members execute them without consciously thinking about them. In that way, assumptions are the underpinnings of the first three levels. Further, Deal and Kennedy (1982) posit four key attributes of organizational cultures: (1) values, (2) heroes, (3) rites and rituals, and (4) cultural-communication networks.

Although Lundberg's and Deal and Kennedy's categories are helpful, it is important at this point to issue a caution. In our view the best cultural analysis takes place when the research focuses on *discovering* the symbolic behavior that "drives" organized activity. The idea is *not* to select the best system of cultural categories and then apply them. Finding indicators and displayers of organizational culture and then cataloging them does not tell much about the significance of such factors.

Each list of cultural components should be read as some potential categories that may emerge as important anchors of meaning. In one organization a particular component of culture may guide behavior, while in another it has little significance. Because culture is constructed by its members, it is unique; the researcher must discover that uniqueness. The analyst observes and records specific behaviors, develops themes out of those behaviors, and then assigns the theme to a category. A new category may have to be developed.

Interpretive research requires that the investigator be able to "see" taken-for-granted behavior and its significance. Taken-for-granted behavior is embedded in the everyday talk and routines. Sometimes, when organizational members have agreed to be observed, they say, "Well, you can observe us, but you will be disappointed because nothing ever happens here." To an outsider who is trying to fit in with an organization, however, a great deal is going on and much of it is unclear.

If you have seen the television show "The Waltons," then the following example will make sense. One family member, upon discovering that John Boy plans to become a writer and that he plans to write about the family, says, "I don't see how he can write about the family, we never do anything!" All of us are so accustomed to certain behaviors that we do not see them or how they have structured our world. When the behaviors are made visible and interpreted, one might be fascinated, amused, and even prepared for change.

Comedians (Bill Cosby and George Carlin, for example) have a special talent for taking the everyday language and routines that people take for granted and making them not only quite visible but also problematic. It is the capacity to make the unconscious conscious that must be developed by the interpretive analyst.

Another challenge is presented when one gathers data. Pacanowsky and O'Donnell-Trujillo (1982) stress that interpretive analysts must become very "familiar" with the organizational behavior that is being studied, but at the same time they must remain in a position to experience the behavior as "unfamiliar" so that it can be questioned and understood. As the researcher becomes more familiar with organizational routines, it becomes more difficult to see or question them. Students who are assigned a cultural analysis project often ask if they can do an interpretive study of an organization that employs them. The good news is that they are familiar with the organization, but the bad news is that they are familiar with the organization. When individuals examine their own workplace cultures, particular care must be taken to make organizational behaviors "strange." We will elaborate on this notion in the discussion of procedures.

What may appear to be mundane language or interaction can embody significant organizational processes and beliefs. For example, Roy (1960) describes and analyzes the interaction that takes place within a group of factory machine operators. His account of the "first awareness" of what was happening around him is important to the interpretive researcher. He states, "What I heard at first, before I started to listen, was a stream of disconnected bits of communication which did not make sense . . . What I saw at first, before I began to observe, was occasional flurries of horseplay so simple and unvarying in pattern and so childish in quality that they made no strong bid for attention" (p. 161). As he developed familiarity with the communication system, the interaction started to reveal structure. He discovered that there were "times" and "themes" that emerged out of the communication. The "breaks" during the day were labeled. There was coffee-time, peach-time, banana-time, fish-time, coke-time, and lunch-time. The themes were those of verbal interplay and included such items as "kidding themes." His interpretation contends that the times and themes were used as a source of job satisfaction and as a way of coping with monotony. There are certainly more implications, but the important point for the researcher is that what appears to be mundane has meaning, pattern, and significance.

If an analyst intends to make sense of an organizational culture, it is difficult, if not impossible, to specify what is being looked for except in a general way. There is a search for the "sense patterns" of the organizational membership that drive, legitimate, coordinate, and make possible their activity. The analyst must discover the "sensemaking" that is taking place and then describe its significance. The following is a set of procedures that represent *potential* methods and components:

Procedures

What culture is examined?   We suggested earlier that an organization is likely to have several cultures. In view of this an analyst
will have to set some boundaries at the outset, even if they are
arbitrary. Size of the organization may dictate this. Cultural analysis requires time, and in this regard it is not an inexpensive process. The actual study may alter the boundaries selected at the
outset. Even small organizations may contain several cultures that
may become apparent in the course of study.

What is the focus of study?   Our discussion of culture indicated that
there are several ways that workplace culture can be examined.
The origins, manifestations, outcomes, and management of cultures can be studied. Our focus has been on obtaining an "understanding" of organizational culture. This approach has the
advantage of presenting a more comprehensive picture of the organization and tends to focus on significance that is generated by
members of the organization.

What constitutes data?   Talk is the primary data of cultural analysis.
It is in the talk that cultures are brought to life and acted out, or
as Pacanowsky and O'Donnell-Trujillo (1983) would suggest, organizational reality is brought into being. In traditional studies,
data usually consist of numbers, whereas the data in interpretive
studies are organizational "messages." These messages may be
selected from communicative interactions, organizational documents, organizational outputs, and physical artifacts. Language
plays a dominant role in analyzing interaction, but nonverbal aspects should not be discounted. Ideally, interactions should be
videotaped so that nonverbal cues can be included in the analysis. However, even a description of nonverbal behavior can aid
the reader in understanding the interaction. The analysis of
documents can give insight into the "official" version of an
organization.

The congruence or divergence between document statements
and actual behavior may add an interesting dimension to cultural
analysis. Bantz (1983) suggests that organizational messages that
are products of the organization as well as those that serve "image

building" for the organization can be analyzed by examining how they are discussed and reconstructed by organizational members, and studying the way in which the output (report) is used by the members to construct meanings and expectations of the organization. Physical artifacts of the organization also "send messages" about the culture of that organization. Furniture, art, space, and design are artifacts that convey meaning and feeling in an organization. They are a type of data.

How are the data gathered?   The two major means of gathering data are participant observation and interviewing. Participant observation means that the researcher observes and interviews organizational members about the observations and what they might mean. The observer gets "involved" with the meanings of organization members who are observed. Interviews are used to clarify observations. Pacanowsky and O'Donnell-Trujillo (1982) point out that "what is required then are details — detailed observations of organizational members 'in action' and detailed interviews (formal or informal) of organizational members accounting for their actions . . ." (p. 127). If a rich description and plausible presentation of an organizational culture is to take place, then detailed data are necessary. Enough time must be spent to become very familiar with the organization. Depending on the situation, the researcher takes notes, makes tape recordings, takes pictures, and collects documents and other outputs. Field notes are extremely important for illustrating communicative exchanges. Getting down or recording exactly what was said is a real challenge. If the researcher is going to capture the nuances of organizational communication, however, precise and accurate records are important.

How are data generated?   The discovery of sensemaking processes necessitates the use of techniques that illuminate taken-for-granted behavior. In this regard, data are generated or "brought to light." People engage in everyday routines without thinking about them, and they hold "tacit knowledge" or understandings that they never verbalize. How are taken-for-granted behavior and tacit knowledge revealed so that the analyst can see how people are making sense of their behaviors?

Pacanowsky and O'Donnell-Trujillo (1982) suggest that analysts should constantly ask organizational members "Why?" when referring to particular behaviors or statements. This sort of digging can produce accounts that reveal sensemaking. It must be remembered that "why" questions are used to determine *how* organizational members are making sense. Nevertheless, "why" people are really doing or saying something is *not* the issue. Louis (1985) suggests that the researcher can get at tacit knowledge by looking for (or provoking) conditions under which such knowledge becomes accessible. Conditions that allow for getting at tacit knowledge include disruptions or crises, because the "normal" is disturbed and brought to light. Individuals who experience contrast (multiple roles) can often provide descriptions of tacit knowledge held by various groups. The investigator might probe (or provoke) by asking a group to produce an image of itself or discuss what epitomizes that group. Another technique is to focus on a "critical incident" and then ask the group to reflect on its meaning.

How are data interpreted? The analyst must have sufficient data, be able to "see" how organizational members are experiencing, discover patterns of sensemaking, and finally interpret the significance of the sensemaking. In the final analysis the researcher is responsible for the interpretation made. The thorough analyst will seek out supplemental inputs and perspectives, however. This enables greater scrutiny of data and permits an investigator to state the type of bias that may be in a final report. Louis (1981, 1985) discusses levels of interpretation in a research process. She suggests that they include (1) the member's interpretations, (2) negotiated interpretations between member and analyst, (3) the analyst's interpretations, (4) negotiated interpretations between two analysts, (5) validation of a analyst's interpretations between two researchers, (5) validation of a analyst's interpretations by an organizational member, and (6) critical interpretations of the analyst. The appropriateness of these levels is dependent on the particular study and researcher. What is important is the notion of various perspectives so that different nuances of the organizational culture do not elude the investigator.

   To this point we have stressed the basic considerations and procedures for analyzing organizational culture from an *emergent* perspective. That is, the researcher discovers the culture as it is being "performed," "accomplished," or "enacted." After the researcher determines what is important to the culture in terms of "driving" it, labels may be attached to particular constructs or labels may be created for those constructs.

Preconceptualized Approach

Although we favor the emergent approach, there are other ways to conduct interpretive analyses. One such approach, a "preconceptualized" one described by Bantz (1987), lays out what is important in advance on the assumption that the items examined will give significant insights into organizational culture. Bantz states that "the Organizational Communication Culture [OCC] approach entails a methodology that (1) gathers messages; (2) analyzes the messages for four major elements — vocabulary, themes, architecture, and temporality; (3) analyzes the symbolic forms in the messages — metaphors, fantasy themes, and stories; (4) infers patterns of organizational meanings from the elements, symbolic forms, and the messages themselves; (5) infers patterns of expectations from the elements, symbolic forms, meanings, and the messages themselves; and (6) weaves these patterns of meanings and expectations into a tapestry of the Organizational Communication Culture . . ." (p. 6).

Researchers who adopt a preconceived approach tend to analyze messages in terms of symbolic forms. Three such symbolic forms that have been found useful in organizational study include (1) account analysis, (2) story analysis, and (3) metaphor analysis. These forms tell about organizational cultures, although it must be stressed that they do not tell all.

Account Analysis

Account analysis involves asking people to provide explanations for their behavior. An "account" is a statement used by people whenever one of their actions is challenged (Scott and Lyman 1968). In other words, people usually give accounts when they are asked to justify their actions; givers of accounts provide explanations that they perceive as socially acceptable. For example, if you were asked why your term paper was late, you would no doubt try to present verbal justifications that you thought were socially (culturally) acceptable. This tells how you make sense of the culture and what you think is important. Getting at "legitimate" behavior in the organization tells us a great deal about organizational constraints. When an individual accounts for a particular behavior, more is involved than reason-giving. The verbalization is an act that has a number of implications. Account analysis has been used to illustrate organizational identification (Cheney 1983), the link between organizational decision making and identification (Tompkins and Cheney 1983), the reconstruction of an event's context (Buttny, 1985), account acceptability in the organizational setting (Buckholdt and Gubrium 1983), and identification of organizational culture (Faules and Drecksel 1986). Accounts can be obtained by observation of naturally occurring interaction by interviewing and by administering a questionnaire. Account analysis can help the "change agent" discover what justifications members *think* are operative in the organization. Knowledge of accounts may also help managers realize that different cultural contexts require different managerial strategies.

Story Analysis

Story analysis examines organizational narrations or stories. The story is a form of organizational symbolism that "members use to reveal or make comprehendible the unconscious feelings, images, and values that are inherent in that organization" (Dandridge, Mitroff, and Joyce 1980, 77). Stories are used to give meaning to critical events. There are different types of stories and story analysis. Some of these include *myths* (Sykes 1970), *legends* (Brunvard, 1980), *sagas* (Borman 1972, 1983), and *master symbols*. Stories are used for sensemaking. Members use stories to determine what organizational events and activities mean. You have probably been involved in an organization where stories have been used to socialize new members (Brown 1985), convey policy, make a particular point, or epitomize what the organization is "all about" or illustrate what really counts "around here."

Stories are potent anchors of meaning. Martin (1982) suggests that the story is an effective tool for communicating a policy in that it is more memorable and believable than other symbolic forms. Wilkins (1978) found that the number and type of stories told may be related to the level of employee commitment. The content of stories, who tells them, and how they are told can give insight into significant organizational behaviors. How does the researcher obtain stories? Mitroff and Kilmann (1975) suggest that "stories are like dreams. Most of us have to be trained not only to recognize them, but also to appreciate their significance. For this reason, it is almost impossible to get at the stories that govern organizations directly. Like dreams they have to be gotten at indirectly" (pp. 19–20). Of course, it would be ideal to observe stories as they occur in everyday interaction. This may require an excessive amount of time, however.

Observation may provide data, but the analyst must rely primarily on the interview. Faules (1982) used story analysis to examine performance appraisal. "The interview strategy was to (1) get respondents to talk about what organizational members talk about in reference to performance appraisal, (2) get respondents to focus on stories about performance appraisal, and (3) get respondents to develop those stories with as much detail as possible. A typical sequence of questions would include: What do people talk about when they are discussing performance appraisal? What are the major concerns? What are the favorable and unfavorable factors in the appraisal system? Can you give me an incident that would illustrate that factor? Describe the incident in as much detail as you can. How often are such incidents discussed? Are there other incidents that you have seen or heard about? Describe those for me" (pp. 153–154). Stories should be looked upon as creations. In the creating and re-creating process, organizational members are revealing the sensemaking of that organization. In view of this, members can be asked to create stories that embody the practices, aspirations, and climate of an organization. Stories can be analyzed by looking for dominant themes and patterns of thought.

Metaphor Analysis

We have already recognized the metaphor in our discussions as being a potent device in the construction of reality. The metaphor is certainly a way of thinking that is used so often that its impact operates at a low level of awareness. What is important is the way that metaphors shape thinking. As the reader has already discovered, the metaphors used to describe an organization can limit and direct what it is possible to think about. For example, if organizations are thought of as "garbage cans" (Cohen, March, and Olsen 1972) rather than "machines," a variety of behaviors can be considered. In addition, it must be remembered that from a subjective position, "rather than a person perceiving a world and then giving it an interpretation or meaning, perception is of an already meaningful (interpreted) world" (Koch and Deetz 1981, 2). Metaphors, then, are the organizational world and operate as an inherent part of the thinking and behavior of members.

Metaphors are gathered by observing and recording members' talk. In addition to naturally occurring exchanges, the analyst can interview, set up group sessions, or ask members to write on topics that have the potential to generate metaphors. Organizational documents may also provide useful data. Metaphors are analyzed by looking for patterns and dominant themes.

Some Final Comments

In our discussion of cultural analysis we pointed out that this type of study may tell *too much*. It is highly descriptive, and individuals may be identified by the specific language they use. This raises the issue of how cultural analysis should be conducted and how it should be presented. Even when presented in nonevaluative terms, such research can be threatening. Should an organization's culture be put on public display? This question raises more arguments than we can possibly deal with here. However, we would like to specify some of the conditions that lead to responsible analysis. The confidentiality of participants should be protected. Participants should be informed that they have the right to refuse observation or questioning. Final reports should be available to participants. The participant-observer process depends on trust, and the researcher should think very carefully about the impact of what is finally written. If someone is gracious enough to allow the researcher to enter a private world, there is a responsibility to avoid destroying that world for the sake of a "good story."

Reports of cultural analysis should take advantage of the nature of this type of research. Write for effect! If interpretive analysis adds the dimension of "feeling," then the writer should not be tied to the format of a technical report. Much of this will depend on the audience and its expectations. However, such reports ought to contain "thick description." This means dialogue and description that provokes imagery. The "display" might take the form of dialogue, debate, a diary, novel, or short story. There are different "ways of knowing," and these ways can be portrayed in a variety of formats.

Activity

Write a story about "how you get something done" in an organization of which you are a member. Have two other members of the group also complete this activity.

In writing the story, identify hypothetical characters, use narrative and dialogue to reveal thoughts and feelings, and describe actions and behavior in detail.

Collect the three stories and analyze them for dominant themes and patterns of thought and action. Write a short paragraph explaining what the stories revealed about "how to get something done" in that organization.

References

Bantz, C. R. 1981. "Interpreting Organizational Cultures: A Proposed Procedure, Criteria for Evaluation, and Consideration of Research Methods." Paper presented at the ICA-SCA summer conference on Interpretive Approaches to the Study of Organizational Communication, Alta, Utah.

————. 1983. "Naturalistic Research Traditions." In *Communication and Organizations: An Interpretive Approach,* edited by L. L. Putman and M. E. Pacanowsky. Beverly Hills, Calif.: Sage.

————. 1987. "Understanding Organizations: Analyzing Organizational Communication Cultures." Paper presented at the University of Utah summer conference on Interpretive Approaches to the Study of Organizational Communication, Alta, Utah.

Borman, E. G. 1972. "Fantasy and Rhetorical Vision: The Rhetorical Criticism of Social Reality." *Quarterly Journal of Speech* 58: 396–407.

————. 1983. "Symbolic Convergence: Organizational Communication and Culture." In *Communication and Interpretive Approach: An Interpretive Approach,* edited by L. L. Putman and M. E. Pacanowsky. Beverly Hills, Calif.: Sage.

Brown, M. H. 1985. "That Reminds Me of a Story: Speech Action in Organizational Socialization." *Western Journal of Speech Communication* 49 (Winter): 27–42.

Brunvard, J. H. 1980. "Heard About the Solid Cement Cadillac or the Nude in the Camper?" *Psychology Today,* 14: 50–62.

Buckholdt, D. R. and J. F. Gubrium. 1983. "Practicing Accountability in Human Service Institutions." *Urban Life* 12: 249–268.

Buttny, R. 1985. "Accounts as a Reconstruction of an Event's Context." *Communication Monographs* 52 (March): 57–75.

Cheney, G. 1983. "On the Various and Changing Meanings of Organizational Membership: A Field Study of Organizational Identification." *Communication Monographs* 50 (December): 342–362.

Cohen, M. D, J. G. March, and J. P. Olsen. 1972. "A Garbage Can Model of Organizational Choice." *Administrative Science Quarterly* 17: 1–25.

Dandridge, T., I. Mitroff, and W. Joyce. 1980. "Organizational Choice." *Administrative Science Quarterly* 17: 77–82.

Deal, T. E. and A. A. Kennedy. 1982. *Corporate Cultures: The Rites and Rituals of Corporate Life.* Reading, Mass.: Addison-Wesley.

Faules, D. F., 1982. "The Use of Multi-Methods in the Organizational Setting." *Western Journal of Speech Communication* 46 (Spring): 150–161.

Faules, D. F., and L. G. Drecksel. 1986. "Organizational Cultures Reflected in a Comparison of Work Justifications Across Work Groups." Paper presented at the University of Utah summer conference on Interpretive Approaches to the Study of Organizational Communication, Alta, Utah.

Koch, S., and S. Deetz. 1981. "Metaphor Analysis of Social Reality in Organizations." Paper presented at the ICA-SCA summer conference on Interpretive Approaches to the Study of Organizational Communication, Alta, Utah.

Louis, M. R. 1981. "A Cultural Perspective on Organizations: The Need for and Consequences of Viewing Organizations as Culture-Bearing Milieux." *Human Systems Management* 2: 246–258.

———. 1985. "An Investigator's Guide to Workplace Culture." In *Organizational Culture,* edited by P. J. Frost et al. Beverly Hills, Calif.: Sage.

Lundberg, C. C. 1985. "On the Feasibility of Cultural Intervention in Organizations." In *Organizational Culture,* edited by P. J. Frost et al. Beverly Hills, Calif.: Sage.

Martin, J. 1982. "Stories and Scripts in Organizational Settings." In *Cognitive Social Psychology,* edited by A. Hastorf and I. Isen. New York: Elsevier-North Holland.

Mitroff, I. I., and R. H. Kilmann. 1975. "Stories Managers Tell: A New Tool for Organizational Problem Solving." *Management Review* 64: 19–20.

Pacanowsky, M. E., and N. O'Donnell-Trujillo. 1982. "Communication and Organizational Cultures." *Western Journal of Speech Communication* 46 (Spring): 115–130.

———. 1983. "Organizational Communication as Cultural Performance." *Communication Monographs* 50 (June): 126–147.

Roy, D. 1960. "Man and Time: Job Satisfaction and Informal Interaction." *Human Organization* 18: 158–168.

Scott, M. B. and S. M. Lyman. 1968. "Accounts." *American Sociological Review* 33: 46–62.

Smircich, L. 1985. "Is the Concept of Culture a Paradigm for Understanding Organizations and Ourselves?" In *Organizational Culture,* edited by P. J. Frost et.al. Beverly Hills, Calif.: Sage.

Strine, J. S., and M. E. Pacanowsky. 1985. "How to Read Interpretive Accounts of Organizational Life: Narrative Bosses of Textural Authority." *Southern Speech Communication Journal* 50 (Spring): 283–297.

Sykes, A. J. 1970. "Myths in Communication." *Journal of Communication* 20: 17–31.

Tompkins, P. K. and G. Cheney. 1983. "Account Analysis of Organizations: Decision Making and Identification." In *Communication and Organizations: An Interpretive Approach,* edited by L. L. Putnam and M. E. Paconowsky. Beverly Hills, Calif.: Sage.

Wilkins, A. 1978. "Organizational Stories as an Expression of Management Philosophy: Implications for Social Control in Organizations." Unpublished doctoral dissertation, Stanford University, Stanford, California.

11. Stage 3: Stating Preferences

The third stage in analysis involves the development of a set of guidelines, principles, or notions that serve as a statement of preferences against which to compare the documented situation described in stage 2 in chapter 3 and during the past seven chapters. The purpose of the guidelines is to help locate differences between a situation in which there are no problems (a more or less ideal situation) and the situation being analyzed.

The preferred situation helps direct the analyst's thinking about what kind of performance, behavior, attitude, skill, or practice ought to be expected in the situation being analyzed. Preferences are usually found in five different places:

1. Job and position descriptions
2. Performance standards and statements
3. Organization policies
4. Excellent practices in other organizations
5. Theories of organization and behavior

This chapter will describe the philosophy and methods associated with the development of guidelines for recognizing the most relevant preferred situation.

Value

One of the most difficult tasks for an analyst is to determine when an actual problem exists. Although we think of a problem as the difference between what we have and what we want, the concept of "what we want" varies among members of an organization. Managers who have responsibility for living within a budget tend to believe that even if some difference does exist, the difference is not one that justifies doing anything about the situation. The difference is not large enough or important enough or relevant enough to make a difference in the organization. Even if the difference were reduced, the consequence would not be significant enough to justify the investment.

Both managers and analysts suffer from an inability to distinguish clearly between situations that deviate from some preferred position and situations that do not deviate. The difficulty often lies in not having a clearly specified description of what is preferred. Many things may be preferred. Something that is preferred now may change in a few minutes. The preferred situation may depend on how much it costs to maintain the preference. For example, how much would you prefer to spend on a night out? The answer may depend on what you mean by a night out, or how much you have to spend, or what you might get as a result of the night out, or what you think might develop in the future as a consequence of the night out, or how you feel about nights out in general. In other words, how much you spend on a night out depends on many other things.

This chapter is designed to explain what is meant by a preference, where they come from, how they are expressed, how to recognize a preference in an organization, and how preferences can be used to establish the existence of a problem.

Chapter Organization

This chapter fills out the concept of "preference" as used in the third stage in the process of analysis. Preference is defined, where preferences come from is discussed, how people and organizations state preferences is examined, how to recognize a preference in the context of an organization is explained, and how preferences can be used to establish the existence of a problem is reviewed.

Objectives

At the conclusion of this chapter, you will be able to do the following:

- Explain what is meant by a "preference."
- Describe five sources of preferences in an organizational setting.
- Recognize how preferences are expressed and state one or more preferences derived from each of the five sources.
- Identify preferences that exist in the organization with which you are associated or in an organization with which you are familiar.
- Outline a plan for using preferences to establish the existence of a problem in an organization.

The Meaning of "Preference" in Analysis

A problem, as we have discussed earlier, consists of some difference between what we want and what we have. The idea of a want is tied directly to some sense of our lack. When a person "wants," the implication is that the person recognizes some lack or scarcity or shortage of something. If you want money, you appear to have a shortage or are lacking in money some way. If you want love, you see yourself, at least, as being short of or having less love than what you expect to have. Thus what we want has to do with making up the shortage.

How do we tell when we have enough? When would your shortage of money be made up? When would you no longer expect to have more love? At what point would you be satisfied and no longer have a want? How does anyone or any organization tell when they have enough? The answer lies in your preferences.

To prefer something is to give it greater value or liking. A preference is your indication of what you value or like most in this instance. A statement of preferences represents a list of the results that we like or value and place in higher priority over similar results. Kaufman (1979) provides a convenient category system for thinking about results and preferences. He suggests that we have both organizational goals (outputs) and societal goals (outcomes) (p. 27). Outputs or organization goals represent results within the organization, such as yearly profit, stockholder vote of confidence, and money for continuation of operations. These are the goals to be achieved through the processes or ways in which we manage the resources of the organization. Societal outcomes or goals are represented by results that are external to the organization, such as more people surviving and contributing to society, reduced air pollution, reduced fatalities, improved quality of life, and fewer welfare recipients.

A statement of organizational preferences might be the same as a list of the outputs or organization goals of the company. In that case, stating preferences is simply stating company goals. In most cases, company officers are seeking to implement processes that achieve or exceed their goals for the company. In nearly every instance, however, preferences are part of choices made concerning which resources will be used to create the products of the company that go into accomplishing the goals of the company.

The goals of the company represent preferences in terms of outcomes; the way in which the production is organized reveals a preference; the people, equipment, financial resources, and time allocated to a particular process indicate or are based on preferences. A job description, performance standards, and organization policies all represent statements of preferences for the way in which jobs should be done.

What is wanted in an organization in contrast to what the organization has is reflected in the statement of preferences. An analyst will not be able to determine whether a problem exists without having a clear concept of what is preferred in the organization. On the other hand, organizations that fail to have a clear statement of goals (and objectives, or the results to be achieved by the ways in which their resources are used) for what is to be achieved by units of the organization, as well as the organization as a whole, will have a difficult time determining whether they have problems.

An analysis may very well highlight the desirability of stating organization preferences in order to determine whether problems exist. As Kaufman (1979) also indicates, "If we are now achieving certain results, and we want another result, then we *must* be precise in describing the gap or measurable discrepancy between current and desired outcomes" (p. 37). And, of course, we cannot determine what the gap is if we do not have clearly stated outcomes or preferences.

Stating Outcomes and Preferences Clearly

The statement of preferences is often prefaced with the terms *precise* or *clear*. Precision and clarity come from writing and talking about things in ways that are measurable. In our case here, we are writing about the goals of the company and/or the goals of a unit of the company, and/or about the goals of a specific individual within a unit. In human resource development, we are usually more interested in the goals of people than we are the goals of nonpeople elements of the organization. Thus we are looking for statements about the goals of people that can be measured. The more precise the measurement, the more accurate it will be.

The statement of preferences develops a "normative prescription" (Lawrence and Lorsch 1969, 19) indicating what kinds of behaviors and organizational functioning are preferred.
The prescriptions usually tell what outcomes or results are to be achieved, along with a precise, measurable, recognizable indication of how you will tell when the result has been achieved. The prescription or statement of preference should reveal the conditions under which its achievement will be measured and who will do the measuring.

The statement of organization and individual goals is often related to what is happening now. Preferences, on the other hand, usually represent what you want to achieve in the future, even though the future may be tomorrow. Thus we usually have two lists of goals, results, or outcomes:

1. A list of results or outcomes that represent what is happening now; this list comes from stage two in the analytical process and through the steps for documenting a concern.
2. A list of results or outcomes that represent the desired results or outcomes; this is the list about which we are talking now. This list of outcomes or results indicates our preferences, the kinds of results and outcomes the organization or individuals should be achieving.

Sources of Preferences

Preferences in the work environment tend to come from four different sources: (1) job and position descriptions, including performance standards; (2) organization policies; (3) excellent practices of other organizations; and (4) theories of organization and behavior. Let us look at each of these sources.

Job and Position Descriptions

We shall examine descriptions of positions as the focus of this section, and consider job descriptions and position descriptions as essentially the same. Position descriptions are the formal statements that provide information about jobs. A good description gives those evaluating the job a clear picture of why that job exists and what is supposed to be accomplished by the job. A description (job or position) indicates the responsibilities of the person holding the position or assigned to do the job. Position descriptions come out of the work done as part of designing the job; thus, if the job is designed to be completed efficiently, and the tasks involved in doing the job are described accurately, we shall have a picture of the things a person is to do in order to perform effectively.

A well-written position description specifies the broad function to be achieved as well as the primary responsibilities of the position, the measures of accountability, and the expected standard or level of performance at which the tasks should be performed. Each description represents a statement of the preferred way of doing the job. With a job or position description in hand, you should be able to identify what is considered to be the preferred way to complete the job.

Position descriptions of two different entry-level jobs may illustrate how the descriptions provide information for determining whether problems exist.

Job Title: Secretary I

Duties include the following:

1. Takes and transcribes dictation accurately and in a timely way.
2. Types correspondence, memos, reports, and forms in a timely manner.

3. Attends meetings and takes and transcribes minutes accurately.
4. Answers the telephone and takes messages efficiently.
5. Sorts and distributes mail accurately.
6. Performs other tasks as directed.

Job Title: Computer Control Clerk

Duties include the following:

1. Schedules jobs (registration, class schedule, adds and drops, accounts payable, and budget) to be run on a weekly calendar (5 percent of the time).
2. Sets up data for submission to the computer (25 percent).
3. Verifies data that have been set up for submission to the computer (5 percent).
4. Makes adjustments in job setup as jobs are changed (10 percent).
5. Does terminal entries and keypunch work (25 percent).
6. Submits jobs to the computer (5 percent).
7. Checks the computer output on each job run (5 percent).
8. Resolves errors in the processing of data (5 percent).
9. Arranges for binding and delivery of reports (5 percent).
10. Does secretarial and general office work, such as filing, typing, and ordering supplies (10 percent).

In most cases, the standards of performance are somewhat implicit in the actual duties, such as with the computer clerk arranging for binding and delivery of reports. If arrangements are made for binding and delivery of the reports in a timely manner, the measure of accountability is the actual action taken. In the case of the secretary, more specificity may be necessary to determine whether the duties are being performed, since the duties do not indicate *how* accurately work is to be done. How many errors are allowable?

Nevertheless, the position descriptions indicate what is to be done and when the performance is generally acceptable (Batten 1981, 87–110) . Deviations from the descriptions generally constitute grounds for declaring the existence of a problem.

Management and supervisory position descriptions are more difficult to describe and hence often more difficult to use clearly in determining whether problems exist. The description of the manager of public relations, for example, may read something like the following:

Job Title: Director of Public Relations

Duties include the following:

1. Meets on a weekly basis with the Vice President of Administration and discusses projects, news, promotional items, and matters consistent with the master plan.
2. Holds weekly staff meetings to discuss current projects and news concerns and to make assignments.
3. Generates public relations projects in the areas of public affairs, electronic media, performance scheduling, and related areas.
4. Chairs the community relations committee.
5. Meets regularly with the press to keep channels open for generating news.
6. Supervises photographers and makes periodic assignments.
7. Maintains current staff biographical information and photos.
8. Supervises any and all other projects that affect the relationship of the company with its internal and external communities in general image building.

If the person holding the position is not doing the job as described, which could be documented using procedures for a task analysis or a performance analysis, a deficiency or discrepancy would be documented, and a problem could be declared because the current performance was not comparable to the preferred way of doing the job.

As you can see, there is a close connection between analytical procedures and decisions about how a job should be done. If the position and job descriptions are current, differences between the descriptions and the way in which the work is being done should represent problem areas. Without the position descriptions, which are also the statement of preferences, it would not be possible to determine whether a problem exists.

Organization Policies

Most organizations have a statement of policies that govern a wide variety of activities to be done in the organization, including guidelines for compensation, benefits, safety, equipment maintenance, market selection, expansion, and growth. Policies provide general but definite guidelines for all employees in carrying out their assignments. Policies give direction to and provide standards for making decisions. Policies standardize ways of thinking about and doing things in the organization. Policies provide for the uniform treatment of problems and people (Pace 1983).

Policies are statements by which the effectiveness of the organization can be judged. Deviations from policy should lead to less efficient (less effective and more costly) performance. The policies of an organization are clear sources of information about what types of actions and thinking are preferred in the organization. A study of policies should yield a list of guidelines for determining preferred ways of behaving in the organization.

Policies consist of general statements, "understandings" if they are not stated, that tell what kinds of actions should be taken in a given circumstance. A policy statement of Pacesetter Seminars, on the issue of discrimination in hiring, might read as follows:

> Pacesetter Seminars shall provide employment, training, compensation, promotion, and other conditions of employment without regard to race, color, religion, national origin, sex, or age, except where age or sex are essential, bona fide requirements for conducting seminars.

The policy is *not* a position description, but a statement that could be applied to any position. It provides information for evaluating how well the organization is doing with regard to hiring and other personnel practices. Where actions are not compatible with policy provisions, it is likely that a problem exists.

Policies should reflect the goals of the organization and translate the plans and objectives into statements that guide the thinking of managers and other employees. Policies should emerge out of the basic philosophy of the organization and make a declaration that indicates what the organization is about and what it values.

Excellent Practices of Other Organizations

As the front flap of the cover of Peters and Waterman's popular book *In Search of Excellence* (1982) says, "What can we learn from our best managed companies . . . ?" A flyer came across my desk the other day in which the author explained that he "came to value knowing what my counterparts in other organizations were trying and what was working." Horton (1986) reports in his book *What Works for Me* about the practices of chief executive officers of sixteen organizations in the United States. Finally, Mills's book *The New Competitors* (1985) is fully illustrated with examples of the practices of "new generation" managers and how they handle personnel matters.

Although these are only a few of the publications on the market that have caught our interest recently, the one characteristic they have in common is that they contain reports on the best or at least excellent practices of individuals and companies. The things that people do well help set the standards for their competitors. Our best practices indicate what others should be able to do. The possibilities in our lives are illustrated by the great performances of people like us. If we can discover what excellent companies are doing, then we can set that standard for ourselves and, it is hoped, narrow the gap between our average or mediocre performances and those excellent practices of others.

If you want to know whether or not you have a problem, look at how well someone similar to yourself is doing the kinds of things you are doing. If you want to know what the real standards are for expected performance, look at what others are doing. The difference between excellent company practices and our own company practices is the definition of a problem, unless you want to be left further behind, or unless you do not care how the company performs. Few people or companies can totally ignore the best of others. They signal what our preferences ought to be.

Plunkett and Hale (1982) refer to the process of using excellent practices as finding "comparative data" (p. 20). They suggest that you can locate a problem by comparing a situation that seems to be working well with a situation that is suspect. The difference between the two situations is the basis of a problem.

Theories of Organization and Behavior

The familiar concept of theory as a systematic statement of underlying principles that have been verified to some degree is the way in which we shall think about this topic. The deeper meaning suggests that a theory is an idea or mental plan of a way to do something. Thus, a theory, as we shall think of it, may be a mental plan for how to do something based on principles that are grounded in some reality.

Although excellent practices in a company may represent a type of theory, we tend to find actual statements of principles that support mental ways of doing things. Some argue that theories cannot be counted on to give very good directions for doing things, but others explain that nothing is as practical as a good theory. We shall assume that "good" theories provide the standards and guidelines for excellent practices.

Where do we find theories? The most common place to dig out theories is in a textbook. Professors frequently write books to describe systematically the state of current theories. Professors may appear to have less concern about actual practices than employees of an organization, because they feel they are writing about principles that provide ideal standards and guidelines to guide actual practices. Organization and company practices should, if the theories are accurate, attempt to approximate the ideal described by the theory. A powerful axiom suggests that practice should approximate theory, rather than the other way around.

Sometimes a theory can be deduced from a set of practices. That happens when you see the commonalities among several good practices that can be expressed in the form of a principle. The principle explains why the practices were good ones. If you follow the principle, theory argues, your next practice should be a good one also. If the principle is tested occasionally and found to be fairly predictive, the assumption is that we have a fledgling theory on our hands. A good theory is something that should be valuable and, from a professor's point of view, publishable.

Using Preferences to Identify Problems

If a problem is the difference between what you want and what you have, the key task at this stage in the analytical process is to take the information about what is preferred and compare it against what was actually documented as happening. In organizations, it is possible to look at problems at several different levels.

For example, the most common model of organizational processes includes the following:

Level 1: Individual Personality, Attitude, and Style
Level 2: Interpersonal Relations, Patterns, and Influence
Level 3: Group Formation, Development, and Maintenance
Level 4: Intergroup Processes, Dynamics, and Culture

People issues, such as goal setting, decision making, power, conflict, and stress, are most apparent at the intergroup level, although aspects of each of the major issues associated with the intergroup level find expression at the earlier levels (Hellriegel, Slocum, and Woodman 1986, vii–xiii). Each level has a set of criteria or guidelines that express what appears to be the preferred ways in which the processes should be handled.

Task issues, such as individual job performance, also find their expression at each level. At level 1, the issue is how well an individual handles his or her job. At level 2, the issue is how well individuals work together to get jobs done. At level 3, the issue is how well teams function. And at level 4, the issue is how well the institution or company functions as a network of interacting groups.

Often, task issues are associated with functional activities in the organization, such as operations, finance, marketing, personnel, and development. In any case, the analyst is looking for guidelines that reveal how and how well things should be done.

Once the preferred way of doing things is identified, it can be compared against how the company, group, or individual is actually performing. Differences may be considered problems. For individuals working in human resource development, the guidelines, preferences, and principles that reflect best practices serve as the basis for the design of training programs. The best practices of management are translated into supervisory, middle management, and executive development programs. The best practices in functional and technical areas serve as the basis for training in each of those areas. If you want to solve problems, identify where members of the organization should be and create training and development programs to lead them there.

Summary

This chapter has defined the concept of preferences, identified the basic sources of preferences, and reviewed how preferences are used to identify problems. Human resource and organization development staff must constantly search for practices and theory that can serve as standards for quality performance in an organization. Comparing current performance with the preferred ways of doing things provides for the identification of problems, but the preferential guidelines also serve as the basis for creating training and development programs to solve the problems.

Activity

Select a key person in an organization of which you are a member. Make an appointment to meet with the person for thirty minutes. Use the following questions in conducting the interview with this individual. Find out about his or her preferences regarding the organization.

Interview Schedule

1. What functions or activities in the organization are you personally responsible for carrying out?
2. Which of these functions or activities is operating at the least efficient level?
3. If this least efficient unit were operating at peak performance, what would it be like? (Probe: How would it differ from the present? What would a somewhat ideal unit be like?)
4. Would there be any cost savings to the organization by having this least efficient unit operating at peak performance?

After the interview, take your notes and write a clear statement of preference for the least efficient unit.

References

Batten, Joe. 1981. *Expectations and Possibilities*. Reading, Mass.: Addison-Wesley.

Hellriegel, Don, John W. Slocum, and Richard W. Woodman. *Organizational Behavior*, 4th Edition. St. Paul, Minn.: West.

Horton, Thomas R. 1986. *"What Works for Me."* New York: Random House.

Kaufman, Roger. 1979. *Identifying and Solving Problems: A Systems Approach,* 2d edition. San Diego, Calif.: University Associates.

Lawrence, Paul R., and Jay W. Lorsch. 1969. *Developing Organizations: Diagnosis and Action.* Reading, Mass.: Addison-Wesley.

Mills, D. Quinn. 1985. *The New Competitors.* New York: Wiley.

Pace, R. Wayne. 1983.*Organizational Communication.* Englewood Cliffs, N.J.: Prentice-Hall.

Peters, Thomas J. and Robert H. Waterman, Jr. 1982. *In Search of Excellence.* New York: Harper & Row.

Plunkett, Lonre C., and Guy A. Hale. 1982. *The Proactive Manager.* New York: Wiley.

12. Stage 4: Comparing Preferences with Documentation

In its simplest form, the point of comparison consists of determining the difference between what you have and what you want. The point of comparison attempts to reveal whether the documented concerns represent activities in the organization that deviate from guidelines and preferences. The point of comparison attempts to answer two key questions:

1. Are there differences between what is happening and what ought to be happening?
2. Are the differences important enough to do something about?

If both the documentation and the guidelines and preferences are clear, the differences may be easy to recognize and to declare as definitely detrimental to the organization. In other instances, the existence of differences may be more subtle and difficult to relate to objective data.

Value

Many of our efforts in analysis are stymied at this point. Managers may recognize and accept the documentation of concerns and the guidelines and preferences, but they may disagree about the extent to which the differences actually represent important deviations from the guidelines. If key people fail to recognize or accept the fact that the differences make a difference to the organization, little support will be given to proposals to remove the deficiencies or to prevent minor deficiencies from becoming larger ones. Thus the point of comparison may need to be developed very carefully, with the best tools and methods available.

Chapter Organization

This chapter will describe ways to make comparisons and portray them using charts, diagrams, and other visuals. The essential details of analogies, metaphors, and deduction will be described as tools for making comparisons. In direct language, the theory of explanation in terms of consequences and effects will be discussed. Since the point of comparison depends on demonstrating that the differences make a difference to the organization, the central thrust of comparison is showing the seriousness of consequences and what consequences certain differences make to an organization.

Objectives

After studying this chapter, you should be able to do the following:

- Explain what is meant by "making a comparison" between what you have and what you want.
- List several methods for making comparisons and describe the procedures associated with each one.
- Distinguish between a difference with little consequence and a difference of significant impact.

Theory of Comparisons

All analysis involves comparisons. That is, we must find similarities and differences in a situation to determine whether they will produce comparable results. A comparison involves placing one set of characteristics on top of another set and identifying the attributes that the sets have in common. Comparison also involves the weighing of parallel features to determine or arrive at relative values. Such terms as *pretty* and *beautiful* express a concept of comparison. If something is called ugly, it compares unfavorably with something that is called beautiful. In other words, the ugly element shares very little in common with the beautiful one.

Comparison is part and parcel of our language and way of thinking about things. Through comparison we are able to recognize when two situations share something in common. We assume that if the two situations have certain elements in common, similar consequences will occur. If negative and detrimental consequences occur in one situation and it is similar to another, we anticipate the same negative, detrimental consequences in the second situation.

In the theory of metaphor, it is generally held that metaphors must be created; that is, a metaphor is based on the premise that there are similarities between two situations but they are not readily apparent. To discover the similarities, it is necessary to impose the characteristics of one situation on the other and to show or demonstrate the similarities. An analogy that did not exist before has now been forced to occur (Gerhart and Russell 1984, 109–119).

Analysis functions on a metaphoric level, yielding data and conclusions that often transcend usual ways of seeing similarities and differences between situations. Comparisons provide information that may alter our view of one or the other or both situations involved in the comparison. For example, suppose you have information that a truck is stuck at an underpass with a load that will not pass under it. What should you do about the situation? With what does it compare? Rather, what is the metaphor that can be created to deal with this situation?

You can look at other situations that seem to have a number of characteristics in common with this one. The metaphor involves trying to put a larger object into a smaller space.

What comes to mind? Usually, the idea of making the larger object smaller or making the smaller space larger springs to the forefront. The first act may be to unload part of the truck so that it can proceed through the underpass. A second task might be to raise the underpass opening so that the loaded truck could pass under it without touching. But the metaphor involves more than that.

The task is not to duplicate, like an analogy or a literal comparison, but to see to the heart of the similarity. It is most obvious to look at the top of the load where it touches the underpass and consider that place the problem. However, the metaphor, as stated, suggests that we should take the unorthodox approach to looking at the whole situation and consider ways of compressing the entire conveyance so that it could fit into the smaller space. The little boy who thought of letting some air out of the tires on the truck appears to have been viewing the situation in a way consistent with the more comprehensive metaphor.

Hyman and Anderson (1965) suggest that we may fail to recognize a problem because we start our search "by looking at the wrong elements" (p. 53). In the case of the stuck truck, our attention is directed toward the top of the truck, since that appears to be where the difficulty arose; hence the problem is defined in terms of the "top-of-the-truck" set, but the solution actually is found by defining the problem in terms of a bottom-of-the-truck set.

The question is "Where is the right place to look for a definition of a problem?" The answer is, as yet, unknown. We are looking for the elements that are keeping us from accomplishing our goal or becoming like our vision. At this stage in the process of analysis, we usually have large amounts of information, usually more than we can process. Add to that the puzzle that we do not know in advance what to look at or what information will most likely reveal the critical problem.

Since we are looking for places where the information we have deviates from what would be expected in a splendidly functioning organization, the most appropriate strategy is to hold the image of the preferred way of functioning in our minds while we "run over the elements of the problem in rapid succession several times, until a pattern emerges which emcompasses all [the] elements simultaneously" (p. 54). In other words, we should avoid focusing on specific elements, which will eventually be necessary to recognize the problem, prematurely or too early. We need to get a view of the entire situation so that we can visualize how it compares with the preferred situation before exploring the details.

A second suggestion offered by Hyman and Anderson (1965), for helping us to recognize more clearly problem areas or deviations from preferred situations, is to hold off deciding what the problem is immediately but proceed gradually to refine and define the problem area. They discovered from research on problem solving that people who offered early definitions of a problem had more difficulty recognizing a more accurate definition later than those who held off and offered only very tentative ones early on. They conclude that "more evidence is required to overcome an incorrect hypothesis than to establish a correct one" (p. 55).

A third suggestion for making comparisons and recognizing problems is to "keep the mind loose by activating a variety of possibilities" (p. 56). The recognition of a problem is made difficult by the way in which the data and elements are arranged. Some familiar deviations from preferred situations are masked by unfamiliar arrangements. It may be a good idea to vary the order and location of the information so as to reorder what is known, which may reveal problems that were obscured otherwise.

A fourth suggestion offered by Hyman and Anderson is to avoid persisting too long in one direction. "If you are getting nowhere on a problem, abandon your approach and try to find a new difficulty as a basis for solving the problem," they explain (p. 57). The idea is to locate a difficulty (tentative problem area), and try it out to see if it is a true deviation. If it doesn't work, drop it and look for an entirely different difficulty.

A final, fifth suggestion is to critically evaluate your own ideas but positively and constructively evaluate the ideas of others (p. 59). Research on this precept suggests that individuals who had positive attitudes toward what others were doing tended to have better final ideas.

Hyman and Anderson suggest, also, that these ideas can be summarized into two general precepts (p. 62):

1. "Look before you leap."
2. "After you have leaped, if you find yourself bogged down, find out what you are doing and then do something else."

Problem recognition is a perplexing task that requires very thoughtful review of information that may be inadequate but very detailed. The ability to compare an overall situation as described by sketchy information with some preferred situation held in a person's mind is extraordinary.

Methods of Making and Displaying Comparisons

To compare implies a process for putting two phenomena together in order to identify points of resemblance or likeness. In some instances, actual physical objects may be placed side-by-side so that an inventory of characteristics or critical points of likeness can be identified. A list of features can be made to see how well the objects resemble one another. In other cases, two objects may be scanned visually for elements that they have in common and that constitute critical points of resemblance. Where the two lists *differ* represents a potential problem area. The critical skill here is the ability to discriminate between characteristics that are similar and different.

Classifying by Concept

A concept represents a selection of characteristics so as to re-create a mental picture of the object or situation being analyzed, resulting in a comparison of the concept of the object or situation rather than the individual characteristics. For example, how do you recognize when an employee has excessive stress or burnout? The task is to compare the employee's total behavior against a concept or mental image of an employee who behaves without stress or burnout. Listing the individual behaviors of both stressed and nonstressed employees in an effort to locate the similarities and differences may be less productive than taking the employee's behaviors as a whole and comparing the total pattern against a mental image of a nonstressed employee.

What the employee does, what the employee says, what vocal cues the employee provides, and how the employee moves and reacts may reveal a pattern that compares in concept with an employee under excessive stress. The total pattern of behavior appears to be going in the direction of burnout, although individual behaviors and characteristics might not provide adequate evidence of a problem.

Determining Rule Violations

This method is often slightly more complex to apply, but it is achieved by comparison on the basis of how well the person, behavior, or situation conforms to or violates a principle or set of principles. Determining rule violations is complicated by the fact that in many organizations, the rules or principles for how a person or situation should function are not stated. This leaves the analyst in the position of making and justifying a decision about a deficiency on the basis of indirect rules or principles or theory rather than on the basis of explicit principles.

The first step in determining rule violations is to state the principle involved in the most concrete and logical form possible. Even the most naive manager or executive will be impelled or at least intrigued by an analysis that proceeds from clearly stated principles. In the instance of burnout, for example, the rules that allow you to tell the difference between an employee who has burnout and one who does not have burnout might involve the following:

1. People with burnout feel fatigued rather than energetic more often than others.
2. People with burnout work harder and accomplish less than others.
3. People with burnout forget more appointments, deadlines, and possessions than others.
4. People with burnout seem more cynical and disenchanted than others.
5. People with burnout are more irritable, short-tempered, and disappointed in those around them than others.

Of course, other principles could be stated as well, but these five may suggest the rule violation concept of making comparisons. The question becomes "How often are the rules violated or adhered to?" Since these principles were phrased in terms of the problem, the analyst would, naturally, attempt to determine whether the data indicated that an employee or a group of employees behaved in ways consistent with principles of burnout. If so, the analyst should conclude that a problem exists.

Creating Hypotheses

Quite frequently, not even the principles or rules for acceptable and unacceptable ways of behaving are fully known, making them somewhat difficult to state directly and clearly. Such a circumstance, however, is somewhat commonplace among those who work in scientific endeavors. The scientific method relies to a great extent on the creation of hypothetical principles or rules that have some degree of plausibility for being the rules that actually govern the best ways of doing things, even though they are not openly acknowledged as such.

Problem identification, using hypothetical principles or hypotheses, involves looking at the data and projecting a rule that might explain the difference between effective and less effective functioning in that situation. Hypotheses are the basic mechanism of thinking creatively. To be creative, you need to visualize what could happen or what you think ought to be happening and articulate or phrase your projections as principles or rule. At that point, you can compare the creative rules with your data. Differences should be tentatively considered as problems.

Significant Versus Insignificant Differences

A difference between what we want and what is happening at the time is called a problem. We recognize problems by the way in which our information shows differences between how people in the organization and the organizational processes function and how we would like to have them function. We have reviewed ways to help discover differences; now we plan to look at ways to tell when the differences make a difference to the organization.

"The organization" is usually represented by *managers*. Thus an analyst must find ways to show managers that the problem areas are sufficiently important that something needs to be done about them. The most likely criterion or requirement for importance has to do with productivity and profits. Is the problem keeping the company from making and selling more products and from receiving a higher rate of return on its investments? The question to be answered is "Does a little burnout or stress really affect our productivity and profits?"

The effects are often somewhat subtle and difficult to connect directly to problems. If we reduced the person's stress, would productivity and profits increase? Unfortunately, organizations are so complicated, with so many connections to nonpeople influences, such as inflation, employment patterns, distribution methods such as trucking and railroads, and availability to resources, that a simple causal relationship is often impossible to make. Results are often achieved by the efforts of hundreds of people, making the work of one person dependent on many, many others. Nevertheless, the motivation of one person may deeply affect the work of lots of others. The failure of one person may deal a deep blow to and even block the completion of work by a large number of other people.

In reality, problems are sufficiently important to do something about when they affect the work (and hence the productivity and profitability) of many others in the organization. Another measure of problem importance is its affect on sales of products. A problem becomes important when it contributes to a decline in the size of the market.

A concern, as developed in chapter 2, focuses primarily on the well-being of employees; a problem, on the other hand, tends to focus more on the verifiable effects of concerns on company productivity and profitability. There should be a connection between the two. Concerns trigger an interest in analysis; problems are the result of analysis.

The principle that guides most thinking on the issues of what is important and how important it is may be phrased this way: "If managers think it is important, it is important." Several sages in the field have observed that "nothing happens until managers buy into the process." Problem importance can probably be judged by how directly the deficiency affects or is going to affect a manager.

Rather than be concerned only with demonstrating some direct effect on productivity, profitability, and managers themselves, which results essentially in crisis problem solving, great analysts work with long-range, strategic plans to anticipate problems. Preventive maintenance keeps problems from emerging and reduces the likelihood that productivity and profitability will be affected directly, and helps managers keep from having a troublesome problem develop.

Some problems are deemed critical when they show that some employees are doing better than others. That is, when wide differences between top performers and bottom performers are apparent, the costs of keeping the bottom performers may be interpreted as an important deficiency.

Last, problems may be considered of sufficient importance to do something about when customers and clients report that the organization and its employees are not doing well. That means that an analyst may often need to look outside the organization for evidence of significance. Customer complaints and observations make lasting impressions on managers who are cost conscious, because they know where the money comes from. The "rubber hits the road" with the customer and his or her money.

Summary

We have attempted to answer three questions in this chapter:

1. What does it mean to make a comparison to identify a problem?
2. What are some ways to make comparisons?
3. How do you tell when you have an important problem?

Four suggestions for managing comparisons to recognize and specify problems were discussed. Finally, several criteria that might be used to recognize the importance of problems were offered.

Activity

Identify a situation in which attendance is important (coming to class, going to the movies, meeting a friend, participating in a discussion group, being on time for work).

Situation: _____

Write a rule concerning attendance in that situation. When should the person arrive? What sort of tolerances are there on this time frame? Can the person be late? If so, how late without being penalized?

Observe actual attendance patterns and identify violations or deviations from the rule.

Write a short paragraph explaining what the deviations are and how important they seemed to be in that situation. Determine whether the deviations are important enough to do something about. In short, explain if the differences between the preference and the actual pattern of arriving has a cost that warrants taking action to correct the situation.

References

Gerhart, Mary, and Allan Melvin Russell. 1984. *Metaphoric Process*, Fort Worth, Tex.: Texas Christian University Press.

Hyman, Ray, and Barry Anderson. 1965. "Solving Problems." *Science and Technology* (September): 36–41.

13. Stage 5: Defining a Problem

The fifth stage in the process of analysis is to determine what types of problems exist in the organization. Human resource development specialists and scholars generally agree that three fundamental kinds of problems can be identified:

1. Deficiencies in employee knowledge, attitude, and skill — referred to often as *performance* problems.
2. Deficiencies in the way people are managed in the organization, referred to generally as *management* problems.
3. Deficiencies in the design of the organization, especially in terms of its mission, distribution of responsibilities, and assignment of authority — referred to most of the time as *organization* problems.

Performance problems are solved, corrected, or minimized through the use of human resource training methods. Performance problems stem from the inability of an employee to do his or her job well or up to standard because he or she does not have the knowledge, attitude, or skills necessary to do the job. Performance problems are based in training needs.

Management problems are solved, corrected, or minimized by implementing new ways to manage employees. In terms of working hard and producing well with minimal levels of error or scrap, management problems often involve lack of motivation on the part of employees. Management problems are often solved by new methods of motivation. Management problems involve the development of special skills in managers. Although managers acquire knowledge, skills, and attitudes in ways similar to other employees, we usually consider management problems to be solved through the methods of management development.

Organization problems are often resolved by making structural changes in the company. That is, organization problems are solved by changing the way the organization is arranged and how the work is done. The way the work is done is a reference to what many call the "technology" of the workplace or organization. Sometimes the technology of work involves pieces of equipment, other times it involves only the way in which a person does something. Both the procedures used by a person and the equipment associated with getting the work done are referred to in the term *technology*. Organization problems are most often resolved through the methods of organization development.

Value

The importance of recognizing and classifying different types of problems revealed by the analytical procedures described in this book is highlighted by a key principle of problem solving: the definition of a problem usually implies the methods by which the problem can be solved. Much confusion has been created by the inaccurate or inappropriate definition and classification of problems. If a problem is defined as a deficiency in knowledge, the most appropriate solution is one that provides or overcomes the deficiency in knowledge. If a problem is defined as a lack of motivation or energy, the best solution is one that overcomes the lack of energy and motivation. To apply a knowledge remedy to a motivation problem would be counterproductive and inefficient.

You will be a more competent and useful human resource development professional if you can recognize and classify problems accurately. Once the problem is clear, we can select more appropriately the most effective ways to attack the problem.

Chapter Organization

This chapter discusses how deficiencies and problems are classified and what types of human resource training, management development, and organization development methods are associated with making changes in the problem areas. Although this chapter summarizes what methods are appropriate to use in each area, the theory and techniques that are associated with the methods are discussed in other books.

Objectives

After studying the materials in this chapter, you should be able to do the following:

- Define and characterize two types of problems or needs identified through the processes of analysis:
  - a. human resource training needs
  - b. organization development needs
- Identify and describe several methods for making changes associated with each type of need.

Types of Problems or Needs

Training is designed to reduce the gap between actual employee performance and what is desired by changing the behavior of people. This is accomplished by helping the individual acquire knowledge, attitudes, and skills needed to perform as expected. Changing individual behavior is the objective of human resource training.

Performance problems can occur within any group or level in the organization: line, staff, skilled workers, unskilled workers, professionals, paraprofessionals, supervisors, middle managers, upper managers, and executives. In all functional areas, such as manufacturing, sales and marketing, finance and accounting, personnel, public relations and corporate communications, engineering, computers and information systems, as well as purchasing, safety, planning, and administration, training may be an important and powerful approach to reducing performance problems.

Training tends to focus on three variables of performance: (1) the skills to perform a job, (2) the knowledge essential to understanding how to perform a job, and (3) the attitudes associated with vigorous and sustained work. Activities involved in helping individuals acquire knowledge, attitudes, and skills are known as training programs. Training can occur in a wide variety of settings, including classrooms, on-the-job, auditoriums, and hallways. Training can be formal or informal; it can be structured or unstructured. Training can deal with any subject matter, any attitude, and any skill. As long as the objective of change is individual skill, knowledge, or attitude, the methods of training are appropriate.

Efficiency in training is achieved by designing the skill, attitude, and knowledge acquisition sessions so that they are consistent with basic principles of understanding, appreciation, and development. Five theoretical frameworks underlie nearly all work done in training: (1) rational, (2) behavioral, (3) experiential,(4) role/positional, and (5) achievement/motivational.

Rational Training   Rational training theory posits that people decide to behave as a result of the beliefs they hold about things. Thus training programs bring about change in a person's performance by changing the beliefs he or she holds.

Behavioral Training   Behavioral training theory is based on the assumption that people behave as a result of the consequences they experience while living in the world. Thus training programs bring about change in a person's performance by structuring the consequences relevant to that aspect of a person's behavior that is to be changed.

Experiential Training   Experiential training theory argues that people behave as a result of their perceptions of their own experiences and what they mean. Thus training programs bring about change in a person's performance by providing experiences that can be evaluated and interpreted and serve as the basis for behaving.

Role/Positional Training   Role/positional training theory is grounded in the premise that people behave as a function of the expectations of others. Thus training programs provide opportunities for those with whom a person works to discover mutual expectations and negotiate different demands so that they can behave in ways beneficial to all concerned.

Achievement/Motivational Training   Achievement/motivational training theory assumes that people behave as a result of aspirations
they hold. Thus achievement/motivational training programs help
the individual identify his or her aspirations, translate them into
goals, and intensify interest in achieving the new goals.

Each theoretical perspective has associated with it a set of
methods, procedures, and techniques that serve to implement the
philosophy. Theorists of each perspective make claims and have
evidence to suggest that the associated methods can be highly effective. Thus the selection of a particular training approach should
be made on the basis of which approach will deal most effectively
with the gap in performance and produce the kind of change you
need to close it. Sometimes behavioral methods are best; sometimes achievement/motivational methods are best. A solid ac-
quaintance with the theoretical bases of training methods and
techniques can help you make an educated decision about how to
proceed to create the most efficient ways of reducing gaps in
performance.

The primary strategies of HRD include technologies such as
workbooks and manuals, seminars, media-based programs, experiential and participative exercises, programmed instruction,
behavioral reinforcement, counseling sessions, and on-the-job
training.

The skills of HRD include the design and creation of workbooks and manuals, the development of media products, administering training program details, managing the human resource
development function in an organization, facilitating groups, writing, instructing, marketing programs, counseling, assisting individuals to apply what they have acquired on the job, developing
theoretical perspectives, planning and goal setting, evaluating
programs, and, especially, serving as an analyst.

Management Development

The literature on management development (Pace and Mills 1987)
clearly suggests that human resource development methods and
strategies are most amenable to achieving the goals of management development. Huse (1980) provides a definition of manage-

ment development that parallels a basic definition of HRD: management development is "any planned effort to improve current or future manager performance by imparting information, conditioning attitudes, or increasing skills" (p. 105).

In distinguishing between management development and other ways (primarily organization development) to accomplish organization change, House explains that change can be produced by replacing poor performers, by imposing controls such as budgets, restrictive procedures, or close supervision, by the realignment of position responsibilities and the reorganization of individual job assignments, and by outright coercion.

The essential difference between management development and organization development is that the HRD methods used require "a change of attitude and understanding," which are not necessary in the methods of organization development. The development of management skills involves both conceptual learning and behavioral practice. Whetton and Cameron (1984) argue that "training programs that do not provide a broad conceptual understanding of skill topics and instead emphasize rote behavior modeling overlook the need for flexible application" (p. 3). Nevertheless, they concur that management development can be achieved with an HRD program that combines conceptual learning with behavioral practice, since both are necessary for effective skill development.

Organization Development Needs

An alternative approach to human resource training that is designed to bring about change to improve productivity and profitability in organizations is called Organization Development, or OD. HRD (Human Resource Development) and (OD) have evolved from different concerns and scholarly pursuits. HRD focuses on changing the individual; OD focuses on changing the organizational system.

Jamieson, Kallick and Kur (Nadler 1984) explain that "practitioners in each area have concentrated on their own theoretical bases and practical issues with little concern for the role of other professionals who contribute to similar results" (p. 29.3). But now is the time for reflection on how and where HRD and OD can contribute to mutually beneficial efforts. We would argue that the study of analysis is an ideal place to begin serious explorations of mutuality.

Organization development is designed to reduce gaps between organization functioning and productivity and profitability. OD uses systemwide interventions to affect organization processes, such as planning, organizing, staffing, directing, controlling, communicating, problem solving and decision making, leading, competing and cooperating, and group functioning, as well as resource acquisition and disbursement, budgeting, and even accounting. French, Bell, and Zawacki (1983) explain that OD is a "process of planned system change that attempts to make organizations (viewed as social-technical systems) better able to attain their short and long-term objectives. This is achieved by teaching the organization members to manage their organization processes and culture more effectively" (p. 7).

Some pessimism about OD has emerged among scholars in the field suggesting that the ideology of OD runs counter to the bureaucratic functioning of most organizations, resulting in an inability of organization members to make changes. Schein and Griener (1977) comment that OD works best in an "organic" system rather than a functional one, which is characterized by open communication, interdependence among groups, considerable trust, joint problem solving, and employees who take risks.

On the other hand, bureaucracies tend not to be very organic, making OD interventions difficult to use. In addition, bureaucracies are not amenable to becoming organic systems; although the goals of OD are to bring about more open communication, trust, risk taking, and joint problem solving, for OD interventions to work one needs to have an organization that already embodies the goals of OD.

In view of this dilemma in the OD field, Schein and Greiner conclude that OD practitioners should use OD interventions to improve or refine the operations of bureaucratic organizations, rather than to attempt to bring about significant changes in the system. Working within the confines of the environment and technological and organizational realities of the bureaucracy, OD practitioners should work on ways to cure the "behavioral diseases" of bureaucracies by attacking the "behavioral symptoms" with appropriate OD interventions.

OD interventions, in contrast to human resource training, are activities that intervene in the work life of groups of organization members. Human and social processes are the main targets, but organizational processes such as planning, authority, and decision making are also important. OD interventions also bring about structural changes, such as providing for different duties, responsibilities, and policies.

The most common interventions involve groups and include such techniques as team building (both within groups and between groups), fishbowling, conflict resolution meetings, role analysis and negotiation, process consultation, T- or sensitivity groups, and quality circles. Huse (1980) compiled a list of OD strategies and techniques that indicates the comprehensive nature of OD interventions.

Strategies for providing information include such techniques as client-centered counseling, laboratory training, management by objectives, management seminars, managerial grid, merger laboratory, motivation training, survey feedback, and third-party consultation.

Strategies for developing new work designs and organizational structures include decentralization, differentiation/integration, flow of work, job enrichment, leadership-situation engineering, operations research, Scanlan Plan, sociotechnical fit, and structural change.

Other strategies often used include career and life planning, organizational mirroring, confrontation meetings, coaching, role analysis, and strategic planning.

Thus we can see that problems that call for changes in individual attitudes, knowledge, and skills are classified as human resource training deficiencies or gaps, and are changed using the methods, strategies, and techniques of HRD. On the other hand, problems that call for changes in the structure and processes of the technical and social systems of the organization are classified as organization development deficiencies or gaps, and are changed using the methods, strategies, and techniques of OD.

Summary

This chapter has differentiated between human resource training and management development problems and organization development problems in order to reveal how types of problems are identified and characterized. HRD and OD have been distinguished from one another on the basis of goals (individual versus systems change) and methods (training versus interventions). Strategies of HRD and OD were described and examples cited.

Activity

Using the data from the practice activities in chapters 6, 7, and 9, distinguish between human resource training, management development deficiencies, and organization development deficiencies by categorizing problems identified as either training needs or organization needs.

References

Burke, W. Warner. 1980. "Organization Development and Bureaucracy in the 1980's." *Journal of Applied Behavioral Science,* 423–437.

French, Wendell L., Cecil H. Bell, Jr., and Robert A. Zawacki (eds.). 1983. *Organization Development: Theory, Practice, and Research,* Plano, Tex.: Business Publications, revised edition.

Huse, Edgar F. 1980. *Organization Development and Change,* 2d edition. St. Paul, Minn.: West.

Nadler, Leonard (ed.). 1984. *The Handbook of Human Resource Development.* New York: Wiley.

Pace, R. Wayne, and Gordon E. Mills. 1987. *Bibliography of Management Development Literature.* Alexandria, Va.: American Society for Training and Development.

Schein, V. E., and L. E. Greiner. 1977. "Can Organization Development Be Fine Tuned to Bureaucracies?" *Organizational Dynamics,* 48–61.

Whetten, David A., and Kim S. Cameron. 1984. *Developing Management Skills.* Glenview, Ill.: Scott, Foresman.

14. Letting Others Know

The process of analysis is not complete until the results are made available to others, especially the key decision makers in the organization. The primary vehicle for letting others know what has been accomplished in an analysis is the report. Three different types of reports are often used: (1) the formal report, (2) the memorandum report, and (3) the letter report. We shall focus on the formal report, since it assumes that we are dealing with a highly complex topic that may require greater length, a less informed reader who may require more explicit statements and greater clarity, and an important use of the report that requires more formality. This chapter will focus on two aspects of presenting the report: 1) the formal written report, and 2) the formal oral presentation.

Value

Developing the written and oral presentations occurs simultaneously because the information for both is essentially the same. What differs is how the information is packaged and displayed to the client. These differences will be outlined in this chapter. The written report is important and must be well prepared. Don't be tempted, however, to not expend significant time in preparing for the oral presentation, because this is where the entire effort of analysis is introduced to the key stakeholders within the organization. In a figurative sense, this is where the rubber first meets the road, and an excellent written effort can be short-changed if proper care is not taken to prepare and deliver the information effectively.

Chapter Organization

Preparing the written report should include three sections: (1) prefatory parts, (2) text parts, and (3) supplemental parts. Developing and presenting the oral presentation requires an additional six activities: (1) writing an executive summary, (2) preparing display materials for the presentation, (3) scheduling and preparing the facility for presentation, (4) preparing and making a forceful delivery, (5) conducting the question and discussion section, and (6) writing a memo formalizing proposed activities.

Objectives

At the conclusion of this chapter, you should be able to do the following:

- Correctly prepare the prefatory parts of a written report.
- Use the proper form and style for writing the text of a report.
- Properly include all supplemental parts of a written report.
- List what should be included in the two-page executive summary.
- Given your own project, correctly display an executive summary by properly including all the key elements.
- Correctly prepare display materials to present the information using the appropriate rules of thumb and guidelines for media preparation.
- Correctly list the five characteristics to make a forceful delivery of an oral presentation and display them in the formal presentation made.
- Correctly list the suggestions to follow in listening to and answering questions in the discussion following the formal presentation and display them following the oral presentation.
- Write an effective memorandum on the results of the presentation by listing the decisions that were made and presenting the plan of action that will follow.

The Written Report

Three parts of the report will be discussed: (1) prefatory parts, (2) text, and (3) supplemental parts.

Prefatory Parts

Prefatory parts contain information that identifies the report and provides preliminary comments about the report itself. The six prefatory parts are as follows:

1. *Title Cover:* This contains only the complete formal title of the report, completely capitalized and centered on the page.
2. *Title Page:* This page follows the cover and contains four pieces of information:
    a. The title, which is a repetition of the cover, but located at the top of the page
    b. The author's name and title
    c. The individual or group for whom the report was prepared
    d. The location and date where the report was prepared
3. *Letter of Transmittal:* This letter explains that the report is being transmitted from the author to the reader, some background comments, and a few comments about the content for emphasis of importance.
4. *Table of Contents:* This provides an outline of the report and serves as a convenient locator for specific sections. List the various sections of the report and the page on which each begins. The table of contents should consist of the topic headings and subheadings of the report.
5. *Table of Illustrations:* This conveys a list of illustrations, tables, figures, and other graphic aids and the pages on which they are located.
6. *Abstract:* This is a brief, condensed version of the entire report, highlighting the most important points.

Text

1. *Introduction:* This section provides the general framework of the report, much like introducing one person to another. It tells the reader something about the nature of the subject and of the report itself. Information about the conditions under

which the report was prepared, the author's philosophy and approach, and why the report is important may be presented.

2. *Purpose:* This is a statement of the precise reason why the analysis was completed and what the report is meant to accomplish.

3. *Scope:* This section explains the extent of coverage of the analysis and any limitations of the analytical process and procedures.

4. *Sources of Information:* This section provides information about where the information came from, including who was involved in the analysis and what kinds of information are being presented.

5. *Methods of Information Collection:* This section enumerates, identifies, and otherwise describes the methods of analysis used. The reader should be able to judge whether the data are valid.

6. *Location of Analysis:* This part explains where the analysis was conducted, and may explain the actual physical locations and work setting in which data were collected.

7. *Limitations:* There are some instances in which a report was prepared under time, money, resources, accessibility of data, confidentiality, and methods constraints. Whenever such constraints exist and materially affect the quality of a report, they should be stated.

8. *Definition of Terms:* When technical terms cannot be avoided, they should be clearly defined for the reader.

9. *Background:* Since most reports are prepared in response to some concern, they are just one step in a chain of events. It is helpful for the reader to have some idea what the events are. A scenario orients the reader and provides cues necessary to understanding and responding to the report.

10. *Preview:* This is a summary of the organization and details of the entire report to help the reader anticipate what is coming.

11. *Findings and Interpretations:* This is the heart of the report in which all information and data pertinent to your analysis are presented. This is the largest section of the report and contains several sections.

12. *Summary, Conclusions, and Recommendations:* This section provides the reader with a brief recap of the report, synthesizing

and reviewing the major points. It clearly states the inferences drawn from the actual information presented and enumerates the recommendations.

Supplemental Parts

1. *Bibliography:* This is a formal listing of the sources, including books, articles, and other reports, consulted in preparation of the report.
2. *Appendix:* This section is used to present data that support the findings, including mathematical analyses, raw data from questionnaires, and copies of instruments.
3. *Index:* This is an alphabetical listing of the major subjects and names discussed in the report accompanied by their page location. An index is used only in the most formal and lengthy reports.

Now that you have completed the written report that is to be submitted to the client or to management, the second half of this chapter will focus on how to give an oral presentation of your report most effectively.

The Oral Presentation

The written report prepared according to the information in the first half of this chapter has all the data needed to put the oral presentation together. The written report detailed the entire process of establishing the concern, documenting it through analysis, and comparing the concern to guidelines. Procedures, methods, results, and conclusions are represented in that document. The oral presentation takes that extended document and makes it live in a highly energized, short, and systematic meeting with key executives.

Executive Summary

The executive summary (ES) is a two-page report that briefly highlights the findings, reports trends, makes recommendations, and summarizes conclusions. The ES is similar to the abstract prepared in the written report described earlier. An executive should be able to read the ES within five minutes and be able to see the presentation and engage in meaningful discussion and questioning when the presentation has concluded. Outlined below are elements that should be included in this ES.

Point of Concern   The first statement in the ES lists the point of concern and states the objectives for the analysis that was done; in short, this was the purpose of the analysis.

Methods Used in Analysis   List the method(s) used to gather information and the numbers of employees involved. The executive can go to the written report for more details if necessary.

Findings   Briefly and succinctly report what was found. This can be taken from the written report.

Trends   Trends are summary statements of what the findings mean and are developed by interpreting the results. For example, if the findings stated that "turnover is highly correlated to commuting distance, additional travel time in bad weather, and the distance lived from the worker's extended family," the trend or probability statement indicates that "the potential for turnover is more likely when increases are evident in commuting distances, additional travel time in bad weather, and the distance lived from the worker's extended family."

Conclusions and Recommendations   Summarize the trends and list alternatives for the key executives to ponder.

The ES should be limited to two pages and becomes the heart of the oral presentation. The oral report reviews these issues and prepares the groundwork for the discussion that follows.

Display Materials

The oral presentation usually needs media support to make it effective. Note the word *support;* use the media to reinforce and help clarify the report. The oral report focuses on the executive summary, and the media support enhances the points to be made.

Visual aids and overhead projectors frequently are used to support the oral presentation. Brief guidelines for using both mediums are offered.

Visual Aids   Five requirements of good visuals are suggested to support the oral presentation. Good visuals should (1) serve a need and have a definite purpose, (2) support the oral presentation or play a subordinate role, (3) be easily visible to all, (4) have a professional appearance and be simple and direct, and (5) be practical (Wilcox 1967).

Overhead Transparencies   The five requirements above apply to transparencies. In addition, eleven rules of thumb are suggested to guide preparation (Mills 1987):

1. Place only one idea on an overhead.
2. Do not exceed six words per line.
3. Do not exceed six lines per overhead.
4. Use the dimension, either horizontal or vertical, that will display the information best.
5. Letters should not be less that one-quarter inch high; half-inch or larger ones tend to work best.
6. Color adds interest. When multiple colors are used, use complementary colors for best results.
7. Simplify ideas; complex figures are hard to read.
8. Use one word or short phrase to represent an idea, rather than complete sentences. The overhead is to support the written text in the audience's hand, rather than to duplicate it. When selecting a word or words, use the verb and nouns.
9. When displaying data, use pie charts, histograms, bar charts, and lines rather than numbers. Using color to differentiate information is helpful. Again, keep the displays simple and let the text material add the detail.
10. Computer-generated overheads using a plotter are effective. Again, keep the displays simple.
11. The size of the material displayed should fit within a 7 × 9-inch frame.

   Practice using both the visuals and overhead prior to the oral delivery to eliminate distractions. Know how to use the on-off switch and operate the focus mechanism of the overhead projector.

Facilities

Know where the presentation is to be made so that plans for placing equipment and visuals, distributing information, and seating arrangement can be made. Schedule the room for the appropriate date. Arrive early on the day of presentation to arrange the room as desired.

Oral Delivery

The content issues for the oral presentation are included in the ES. The oral report provides the necessary background, rationale, insights, perspectives, and suggestions to make the executive summary meaningful.

Present the materials in a memorable way by immediately gaining the audiences attention and creating credibility for the ideas; use both verbal and nonverbal behaviors to convince the audience that the material to be presented is important to them. Develop in the audience a need to listen and become involved in what is displayed. The material presented documents a point of concern that the organization has, and this will generate interest; build on this fact and increase interest by noting consequences that may be associated with the concern. Increased credibility will come as professionalism is displayed, the rigorous efforts of documentation are outlined, and questions are answered thoughtfully and meaningfully in the discussion. Good, animated delivery of the presentation will be important.

Five key features should characterize the delivery: (1) confident behavior, (2) sense of urgency, (3) sense of clarity, (4) keen sense of directness, and (5) animated and expressive vocal and physical behavior (Pace, Peterson, and Burnett 1979).

Confident Behavior   Thorough preparation — knowing the facts, details, methods, trends, and recommendations, and being conversant in the organization, its policies, goals, products, and concerns — is a tremendous confidence builder. The statement "If you are prepared, you will not fear" has merit. To appear confident, keep a bold front, even in the face of inconsequential errors. Remember, the fear and trembling felt is much more apparent in the mind of the presenter than it is to the members of the audience. The serenity developed from within because of meaningful preparation will be important and do much to calm the nerves during the delivery. Practice is important, because just as muscles are strengthened through exercise, so good delivery is developed through practice of oral communication skills.

Sense of Urgency   The importance of the message to the audience must be communicated. The quiet intensity of the voice and genuine enthusiasm for the ideas presented will display this urgency. Building the excitement and importance of the message in the audience comes first from developing the enthusiasm within. The presenter must have this excitement in order to transfer it to the audience.

Sense of Clarity   Understanding what is to be communicated is the first step to stating the message forcefully. Clearly knowing the information not only develops confidence but allows the presenter to speak with directness, create excellent examples, focus on important issues, and respond directly to questions. When what is to be said is clear, it is said with greater clarity. In addition, include the proper emotions in the voice, and if the concept is solemn or sacred, portray that mood.

Keen Sense of Directness   Direct eye contact increases the influence of the presenter with the audience. Look each member of the audience right in the eye; talk to all of them in turn; be friendly and look friendly; forget yourself and concentrate on getting your ideas across to them.

Animated and Expressive Vocal and Physical Behavior   Add variety to vocal patterns to avoid being monotonous. Give emphasis to important ideas, but avoid painful or unpleasant extremes in force, loudness, and explosiveness. Generate variety by drawing out meaning of passages. Be physically active by gesturing and punctuating points, dramatizing meanings, and making natural and spontaneous gestures.

Practice the five features of forceful delivery outlined above. Practice standing, walking, gesturing, and moving with confidence. Speak with urgency. Exaggerate the sound of your voice so that it appears quietly intense. Test out a variety of ways of speaking to communicate genuine enthusiasm. Practice uttering words and phrases that communicate the full meaning embodied in them. Speak words and phrases that represent ideas, concerns, and goals clearly. Look each member of the audience in the eyes and speak directly to him or her. Videotape the practice activities and evaluate them.

Leading the Question and Discussion Section

The question and discussion section of an oral presentation allows the executives or audience to respond and probe by asking questions and discussing the findings as they relate to the point of concern. In some cases the analyst serves as a moderator of this activity; in others he or she acts as a consultant and responds to issues as they are presented. Some basic guidelines on facilitating a discussion are presented here (Wilcox 1967):

1. Listen to questions, and make sure the questioner speaks up so the question is understood clearly.
2. Listen to the entire question before proceeding to answer it. If two or three questions are included, answer each one individually rather than collectively.
3. Ask for clarification, if necessary, and restate the question in its essence to make sure it is understood. If necessary, restate it in simpler terms.
4. In answering the question, avoid feeling defensive, and adapt the answer to the apparent purpose of the questioner, such as seeking clarification, sharing information, or objecting.
5. Organize the answer so that it will be both explicit and understood, and use appropriate delivery principles.

Writing a Memo to Review the Meeting

Some action items usually remain after the meeting which need to be completed at a future date. Document the items yet remaining in a memo or letter to summarize what has happened and what is yet to occur. The memo is particularly helpful if interventions are proposed. Include in the memo or letter your appreciation for their involvement; list the events completed; state action items that were suggested and the proposed time lines for follow-up to occur; describe what yet needs to occur; and specify what resources are needed to continue.

This communication is usually helpful for all concerned. If there are questions or differences in view of roles or resources to be committed to complete the tasks associated with the interventions, this letter provides the basis for the clarification.

Summary

The written report is your way of presenting all the details of your analysis. The oral presentation is your approach to getting your client or management excited about your analysis. An effectively written report and a motivating oral presentation are like the wrapping paper of a package — make them worthy of the analysis effort that has been expended.

The written report is used to help develop the oral presentation. Begin by writing the executive summary, which summarizes for those involved the objective of the analysis, methods used, findings and trends, recommendations, and conclusions. Guidelines on how to display and use visual aids or overheads in the oral presentation were listed; rules of thumb on how to create and use them in the presentation were shown.

Five suggestions were given to help prepare a forceful delivery and practice effectively prior to the oral presentation. Suggestions for involvement in the question and discussion session were included. The memo that should follow the meeting was reviewed, with suggestions on its structure and value. The memo clarifies what items still require action and details the resources needed to move to the next phase of intervention.

References

Mills, G. E. 1987. *Media in Human Resource Development*. Provo, Utah: BYU Press.

Pace, R. W., B. D. Peterson, and M. D. Burnett. 1979. *Techniques for Effective Communication*. Reading, Mass.: Addison-Wesley.

Wilcox, R. P. 1967. *Oral Reporting in Business and Industry*. Englewood Cliffs, N.J.: Prentice-Hall.

BIBLIOGRAPHY

Alreck, P. L., and R. B. Settle. *The Survey Research Handbook*. Homewood, Ill.: Irwin, 1985.

Anderson, H. P. "The Corporate History Department: The Wells Fargo Model." *The Public Historian* (1981): 25–30.

Bantz, C. R. "Interpreting Organizational Cultures: A Proposed Procedure, Criteria for Evaluation, and Consideration of Research Methods." Paper presented at the ICA-SCA summer conference on Interpretive Approaches to the Study of Organizational Communication, Alta, Utah, 1981.

———. "Naturalistic Research Traditions." In *Communication and Organizations: An Interpretive Approach*, edited by L. L. Putman and M. E. Pacanowsky. Beverly Hills, Calif.: Sage, 1983.

———. "Understanding Organizations: Analyzing Organizational Communication Cultures." Paper presented at the University of Utah summer conference on Interpretive Approaches to the Study of Organizational Communication, Alta, Utah, 1987.

Bateman, D. A. "Measuring Communication Effectiveness." Paper presented at the annual convention of the American Business Communication Association, Seattle, December 1979.

Batten, Joe. *Expectations and Possibilities*. Reading, Mass.: Addison-Wesley, 1981.

Bellman, G. "Surveying Your Supervisory Training Needs." *Training and Development Journal* 29 (February 1975): 25–33.

Borman, E. G. "Symbolic Convergence: Organizational Communication and Culture." In *Communication and Interpretive Approach: An Interpretive Approach*, edited by L. L. Putman and M. E. Pacanowsky. Beverly Hills, Calif.: Sage, 1983.

———. "Fantasy and Rhetorical Vision: The Rhetorical Criticism of Social Reality." *Quarterly Journal of Speech* 58 (1972): 396–407.

Bostrom, Alan, and Bruce Stegner. *CRISP, Crunch Software Interactive Statistical Package*. San Francisco, Calif.: 1986.

Brown, M. H. "That Reminds Me of a Story: Speech Action in Organizational Socialization." *Western Journal of Speech Communication* 49 (Winter 1985): 27–42.

Brunvard, J. H. "Heard About the Solid Cement Cadillac or the Nude in the Camper?" *Psychology Today* 14 (1980): 50–62.

Buckholdt, D. R., and J. F. Gubrium. "Practicing Accountability in Human Service Institutions." *Urban Life* 12 (1983): 249–268.

Buening, C. R., II. *Communicating on the Job, a Practical Guide for Supervisors.* Reading, Mass.: Addison-Wesley, 1974.

Burke, W. Warner. "Organization Development and Bureaucracy in the 1980's." *Journal of Applied Behavioral Science* (1980): 423–437.

Buttny, R. "Accounts as a Reconstruction of an Event's Context." *Communication Monographs* 52 (March 1985): 57–75.

Cheney, G. "On the Various and Changing Meanings of Organizational Membership: A Field Study of Organizational Identification." *Communication Monographs* 50 (December 1983): 342–362.

Cherrington, D. J. *Personnel Management, The Management of Human Resources.* Dubuque, Iowa: Brown, 1987.

Cohen, M. D., J. G. March, and J. P. Olsen, "A Garbage Can Model of Organizational Choice." *Administrative Science Quarterly* 17 (1972): 1–25.

Cummings, L., and D. Schwab. *Performance in Organizations, Determinants and Appraisal.* Glenview, Ill.: Scott, Foresman, 1973.

Dandridge, T., I. Mitroff, and W. Joyce. "Organizational Choice." *Adminstrative Science Quarterly* 17 (1980): 77–82.

Davies, I. *Competency Based Learning: Technology, Management Design.* New York: McGraw-Hill, 1973.

Davis, K. "A Method of Studying Communication Patterns in Organizations." *Personnel Psychology* 6 (1953): 301–312.

Deal, T. E., and A. A. Kennedy. *Corporate Cultures: The Rites and Rituals of Corporate Life.* Reading, Mass.: Addison-Wesley, 1982.

Dennis, H. S., III, G. M. Goldhaber, and M. P. Yates. "Organizational Communication Theory and Research: An Overview of Research Methods." *Communication Yearbook* 2. New Brunswick, N.J.: Transaction Books, 1978.

Deterline, W. A. *Instructional Technology Workshop.* Palo Alto, Calif.: Programmed Teaching, 1968.

Downs, C. W., and M. D. Hazen. "A Factor Analytic Study of Communication Satisfaction." *Journal of Business Communication* 14 (1977): 63–73.

Emery, F. E. *Rutures We Are In.* Leiden: Martinus Nijhoff, 1976.

———. *Report on the Hunsfoss Project.* London: Tavistock Documents Series, 1964.

Factory 121, (March 1963): 88.

Farace, F. V., P. R. Monge, and H. M. Russell. *Communicating and Organization.* Reading, Mass.: Addison-Wesley, 1977.

Faules, D. F. "The Use of Multi-Methods in the Organizational Setting." *Western Journal of Speech Communication* 46 (Spring 1982): 150–161.

Faules, D. F., and L. G. Drecksel. "Organizational Cultures Reflected in a Comparison of Work Justifications Across Work Groups." Paper presented at the University of Utah summer conference on Interpretive Approaches to the Study of Organizational Communication, Alta, Utah, 1986.

Flanagan, John C. "The Critical Incident Technique." *Psychological Bulletin* 51, (1954): 327–358.

Fogi, L., C. L. Hulin, and M. R. Blood. "Development of First-Level Behavioral Job Criteria." *Journal of Applied Psychology* 55, (1971): 3–8.

French, Wendell L., Cecil H. Bell, Jr., and Robert A. Zawacki (eds.). *Organization Development: Theory, Practice, and Research*. Plano, Tex.: Business Publications, revised edition, 1983.

Funk, H. B, and R. C. Becker. "Measuring the Effectiveness of Industrial Communication." *Personnel* 29 (1952): 237–240.

Gerhart, Mary, and Allan Melvin Russell. *Metaphoric Process*. Fort Worth, Tex.: Texas Christian University Press, 1984.

Gilbert, T. *Human Competence, Engineering Worthy Performance*. New York: McGraw-Hill, 1978.

Gilbreth, Frank B. and Ernestine G. Carey. *Cheaper by the Dozen*. 1948. Reprint. New York: Bantam, 1984.

Goldhaber, Gerald M. "The ICA Communication Audit: Rationale and Development." Paper presented at the Academy of Management Convention, Kansas City, 1976.

———. *Organizational Communication*. Dubuque, Iowa: Wm. C. Brown, 1979.

Goldhaber, G., and P. Krivonos. "The ICA Audit: Process, Status and Critique." *Journal of Business Communication* 15 (Fall 1977): 41–56.

Goldhaber, G., and D. Rogers. *Auditing Organizational Communication Systems: The ICA Communication Audit*. Dubuque, Iowa: Kendall/Hunt, 1979.

Goyer, R. S., W. C. Redding, and J. T. Rickey. *Interviewing Principles and Techniques*. Dubuque, Iowa: Brown, 1968.

Greenbaum, H. H. "The Audit of Organizational Communication." *Academy of Management Journal* 17 (December 1974): 739–754.

Griffin, R. W. *Task Design an Integrative Approach*. Glenview, Ill.: Scott, Foresman, 1978.

Guetzkow, H. "Communication in Organization." In *Handbook of Organizations*, edited by J. G. March. Chicago: Rand McNally, 1965.

Harless, J. H. *An Ounce of Analysis*, McLean, Va.: Harless Performance Guide, 1974.

Hawes, Leonard C. *Pragmatics of Analoguing*. Reading, Mass.: Addison-Wesley, 1975.

Hellriegel, Don, John W. Slocum, and Richard W. Woodman. *Organizational Behavior*, 4th edition. St. Paul, Minn.: West, 1986.

Hertzberg, F., B. Mausner, and B. Snyderman. *The Motivation to Work*, New York: Wiley, 1959.

Hindmarsh, T., and G. Mills. *Analysis of Communication*, Provo, Utah: BYU Press, 1981.

Horton, Thomas R. *What Works for Me*. New York: Random House, 1986.

Hovland, C. I. *Human Learning and Retention*. In *Handbook of Experimental Psychology*, edited by S. S. Stevens. New York: Wiley, 1951.

Huse, Edgar F. *Organization Development and Change*, 2d edition. St. Paul, Minn.: West, 1980.

Hyman, Ray, and Barry Anderson. "Solving Problems." *Science and Technology* (September 1965): 36–41.

Johnson, B. M. *Communication: The Process of Organizing,* Boston, Mass.: Allyn and Bacon, 1977.

Kaufman, Roger. *Identifying and Solving Problems: A Systems Approach,* 2d edition. San Diego, Calif.: University Associates, 1979.

Kerlinger, F. N. *Foundations of Behavior Research.* New York: Holt, Rinehart & Winston, 1983.

Kirchner, W. K., and M. D. Dunnette. "Identifying the Critical Factors in Successful Salesmanship." *Personnel* 34 (1957): 54–59.

Koch, S. and S. Deetz. "Metaphor Analysis of Social Reality in Organizations." Paper presented at the ICA-SCA summer conference on Interpretive Approaches to the Study of Organizational Communication, Alta, Utah, 1981.

Larke, A. G. "Linear Responsibility Chart — New Tool for Executive Control." *Dun's Review and Modern Industry* 64 (September 1954).

Lawrence, Paul R., and Jay W. Lorsch. *Developing Organizations: Diagnosis and Action.* Reading, Mass.: Addison-Wesley, 1969.

Leedy, P. D. *Practical Research, Planning and Design.* New York: Macmillan, 1983.

Louis, M. R. "A Cultural Perspective on Organizations: The Need For and Consequences of Viewing Organizations as Culture-Bearing Milieux." *Human Systems Management* 2 (1981): 246–258.

———. "An Investigator's Guide to Workplace Culture." In *Organizational Culture,* edited by P. J. Frost. et al. Beverly Hills, Calif.: Sage, 1985.

Lundberg, C. C., "On the Feasibility of Cultural Intervention in Organizations." In *Organizational Culture,* edited by P. J. Frost. et al. Beverly Hills, Calif.: Sage, 1985.

MacKenzie, Alex. "A Three-D Model of Management Processes." *Harvard Business Review* 47 (November–December 1969): 80–87.

Mallory, W. J. "Technical Skills." In *Training and Development Handbook,* 3d edition, edited by R. L. Craig. New York: McGraw-Hill, 1987.

Martin, J. "Stories and Scripts in Organizational Settings." In *Cognitive Social Psychology,* edited by A. Hastorf, and I. Isen. New York: Elsevier-North Holland, 1982.

Merrill, P. F. "Task Analysis: An Information Processing Approach." *NSPI Journal,* vol. XV, no. 2 (1976): 7–11.

Mills, D. Quinn. *The New Competitors.* New York: Wiley, 1985.

Mills, G. E. *Media in Human Resource Development.* Provo, Utah: BYU Press, 1987.

Mitroff, I. I., and R. H. Kilmann. "Stories Managers Tell: A New Tool for Organizational Problem Solving." *Management Review* 64 (1975): 19–20.

Nadler, Leonard (ed.). *The Handbook of Human Resource Development.* New York: Wiley, 1984.

Orne, M. "On the Social Psychology of the Psychological Experiment: With

Particular Reference to Demand Characteristics and Their Implications." *American Psychologist* 17 (1962): 776–783.

Pacanowsky, M. E., and N. O'Donnell-Trujillo. "Communication and Organizational Cultures." *Western Journal of Speech Communication* 46 (Spring 1982): 115–130.

————. "Organizational Communication as Cultural Performance." *Communication Monographs* 50 (June 1983): 126–147.

Pace, R. W. *Organizational Communication, Foundations for Human Resource Development.* Englewood Cliffs, N.J.: Prentice-Hall, 1983.

Pace, R. W. and Timothy G. Hegstrom. "Seriality in Human Communication Systems." Paper presented at the annual conference of the International Communication Association, Berlin, 1977.

Pace, R. Wayne, and Gordon E. Mills. *Bibliography of Management Development Literature.* Alexandria, Va.: American Society for Training and Development, 1987.

Pace, R. W. and B. D. Peterson. "Measuring Organizational Communication Climate." Unpublished paper, Brigham Young University, Provo, Utah, 1979.

Pace, R. W. and H. W. Simons. "Preliminary Validation Report on the Purdue Basic Oral Communication Evaluation Form." *Personnel Psychology* 42 (April 1963): 191–193.

Pace, R. W., B. D. Peterson, and R. R. Boren. *Communication Experiments: A Manual for Conducting Experiments.* Belmont, Calif.: Wadsworth, 1975.

Pace, R. W., B. D. Peterson, and M. D. Burnett. *Techniques for Effective Communication.* Reading, Mass.: Addison-Wesley, 1979.

Patton, Bobby R., and Kim Griffin. *Problem-Solving Group Interaction.* New York: Harper & Row, 1973.

Peters, Thomas J., and Robert H. Waterman, Jr. *In Search of Excellence.* New York: Harper & Row, 1982.

Plunkett, Lonre C., and Guy A. Hale. *The Proactive Manager.* New York: Wiley, 1982.

Richards, W. D., Jr. "Network Analysis in Large Complex Systems: Techniques and Methods — Tools." Paper presented at the annual conference of the International Communication Association, April 1974.

Richetto, Gary M. "Organizational Communication Theory and Research: An Overview." *Communication Yearbook I.* New Brunswick, N.J.: Transaction Books, 1977.

Roberts, K. and C. A. O'Reilly, III. "Organizations as Communication Structures: An Empirical Approach." *Human Communication Research* 4 (Summer 1978): 283–293.

Roethlisberger, F. J. *The Exclusive Phenomena.* Cambridge, Mass.: Harvard University Press, 1977.

Roy, D. "Man and Time: Job Satisfaction and Informal Interaction." *Human Organization* 18 (1960): 158–168.

SAS User's Guide: Statistics. Version 5 Edition. Cary, N.C.: SAS Institute, 1985.

Saxe, John Godfrey. "The Parable of the Blind Men and the Elephant." In *Communications: The Transfer of Meaning*, by Don Fabun. Beverly Hills, Calif.: Glencoe Press, 1968, pp. 12–14.

Schein, Edgar H. *Process Consultation: Its Role in Organization Development.* Menlo Park, Calif.: Addison-Wesley, 1969.

Schein, V. E., and L. E. Greiner. "Can Organization Development Be Fine Tuned to Bureaucracies?" *Organizational Dynamics* 5, (Winter 1977): 48–61.

Scott, M. B., and S. M. Lyman. "Accounts." *American Sociological Review* 33 (1968): 46–62.

Siegel, A. L., and J. R. Turney. *Manager's Guide to Using the Survey of Organizational Climate.* Washington, D.C.: Superintendent of Documents, November 1980.

Skinner, B. F. *Science and Human Behavior.* New York: Macmillan, 1953.

———. *About Behaviorism.* New York: Knopf, 1974.

Smircich, L. "Is the Concept of Culture a Paradigm For Understanding Organizations and Ourselves?" In *Organizational Culture*, edited by P. J. Frost. Beverly Hills, Calif.: Sage, 1985.

Smith, G. D., and L. E. Steadman. "The Value of Corporate History." *Harvard Business Review* 59 (November/December 1981), 69–76.

SPSS X User's Guide. New York: McGraw-Hill, 1983.

Stead, James A. "The Relationship of Information Adequacy/Confidence to Job Satisfaction Among Credit Union Employees." Unpublished M.A. thesis, Brigham Young University, Provo, Utah. 1983.

Stewart, C. J., and W. B. Cash, Jr. *Interviewing, Principles and Practices.* Dubuque, Iowa: Brown, 1985.

Strine, J. S., and M. E. Pacanowsky. "How to Read Interpretive Accounts of Organizational Life: Narrative Bosses of Textural Authority." *The Southern Speech Communication Journal* 50 (Spring 1985): 283–297.

Sykes, A. J. "Myths in Communication." *Journal of Communication* 20 (1970): 17–31.

Tolle, E. R., and W. I. Murray. "Forced-Choice: An Improvement in Teacher Rating." *Journal of Educational Research* 51 (1958): 680–685.

Tompkins, P. K., and G. Cheney. "Account Analysis of Organizations: Decision Making and Identification." In *Communication and Organizations, An Interpretive Approach*, edited by L. L. Putnam and M. Pacanowsky. Beverly Hills, Calif.: Sage, 1983.

Whetten, David A., and Kim S. Cameron. *Developing Management Skills.* Glenview, Ill.: Scott, Foresman, 1984.

Wiio, O. A. "Organizational Communication: Interfacing Systems in Different Contingencies." Paper presented at the annual conference of the International Communication Association, Portland, Oregon, April 1976.

Wilcox, R. P. *Oral Reporting in Business and Industry.* Englewood Cliffs, N.J.: Prentice-Hall, 1967.

Wilkins, A. "Organizational Stories as an Expression of Management Philosophy: Implications for Social Control in Organizations." Unpublished doctoral dissertation, Stanford University, Stanford, California, 1978.

Word Perfect, Version 4.2 Edition. Orem, Utah: Word Perfect Corporation, 1987.

Zemke, R., and T. Kraminger. "Linear Responsibility Charting." In *Organization Planning*. Rock Island, Ill.: U.S. Army Management Engineering Training Agency, 1964.

———. *Figuring Things Out: A Trainer's Guide to Needs and Task Analysis*. Reading, Mass.: Addison-Wesley, 1982.

———. "Prefatory Note." *Business Periodicals Index* 29 (1987).

APPENDIX

ORGANIZATIONAL COMMUNICATION PROFILE

BRENT D. PETERSON AND R. WAYNE PACE

ORGANIZATIONAL ASSOCIATES P.O. BOX 7270, UNIVERSITY STATION, PROVO, UTAH 84602

THE *ORGANIZATIONAL COMMUNICATION PROFILE (OCP)* IN-STRUMENT IS AN APPROACH FOR SURVEYING ORGANIZATION MEMBER ATTITUDES, PERCEPTIONS, EXPECTATIONS, AND SATIS-FACTIONS SO AS TO PROVIDE INFORMATION ABOUT COM-MUNICATION AND THE CLIMATE OF THE ORGANIZATION FROM THE POINT OF VIEW OF ORGANIZATION MEMBERS.

THE *OCP* FOCUSES ON SUCH ORGANIZATIONAL COMMUNICA-TION CONCERNS AS: COMMUNICATION CLIMATE, ORGANIZA-TIONAL SATISFACTION, MEDIA QUALITY, INFORMATION ACCES-SIBILITY, INFORMATION LOAD, ORGANIZATION CULTURE, IN-FORMATION DISPERSION, AND MESSAGE FIDELITY.

BEFORE BEGINNING THE QUESTIONNAIRE WAIT FOR SPECIAL INSTRUCTIONS FROM THE FACILITATORS. THANK YOU FOR YOUR WILLINGNESS TO PARTICIPATE!

In the box below write the name of your organization. As you are timed for one minute, write all the words that come to your mind when you think of your organization. *Use only one word on each line.*

```
┌─────────────────────────────────────┐
│                                     │
│                                     │
│                                     │
│                                     │
└─────────────────────────────────────┘
```

1. _____

2. _____

3. _____

4. _____

5. _____

6. _____

7. _____

8. _____

9. _____

10. _____

11. _____

12. _____

13. _____

14. _____

15. _____

Thank you! You have completed this portion of the instrument. **Do not turn the page until given further instructions.**

Please respond to all questions as honestly and frankly as you possibly can!

Unless the wording of a particular item specifically indicates otherwise, respond in terms of your own impressions of this organization.

Indicate your response to each item by circling a number. PLEASE ANSWER EACH ITEM! Use the following instructions to interpret the meaning of the numerical symbols:

1 — Fill in this blank if the item is a false description of conditions in the organization.

2 — Fill in this blank if the item is more false than true as a description of conditions in the organization.

3 — Fill in this blank if the item is about half true and half false as a description of conditions in the organization.

4 — Fill in this blank if the item is more true than false as a description of conditions in the organization.

5 — Fill in this blank, if in your judgment, the item is a true description of conditions in the organization.

PLEASE, DO NOT ATTEMPT TO INTENSIVELY ANALYZE EACH QUESTION, AND — OF COURSE — YOUR RESPONSES SHOULD REFLECT YOUR OWN JUDGMENTS, NOT THOSE OF OTHER PEOPLE. THERE ARE NO RIGHT OR WRONG ANSWERS.

You may now begin. Thank you and good luck!

	False				True

1. Your supervisor disciplines with tact and does   1   2   3   4   5
   not try to embarrass you publicly.

2. Personnel at all levels in the organization   1   2   3   4   5
   demonstrate a commitment to high perfor-
   mance goals (high productivity, high quality,
   low cost).

3. This organization provides adequate pension   1   2   3   4   5
   plans and other special benefits.

4. Supervisors seem to have a great deal of con-   1   2   3   4   5
   fidence and trust in their subordinates.

5. Your co-workers generally do quality work.   1   2   3   4   5

6. Personnel at all levels in the organization are   1   2   3   4   5
   communicated to and consulted with con-
   cerning organizational policy relevant to their
   positions.

7. Your organization's policy concerning vaca-   1   2   3   4   5
   tions is fair.

8. Your organization has no dead-end jobs —   1   2   3   4   5
   everyone has a chance to be promoted.

9. Your supervisor congratulates you when you   1   2   3   4   5
   do good work.

10. Subordinates seem to have a great deal of   1   2   3   4   5
    confidence and trust in their supervisors.

11. Your co-workers are good people and enjoy-   1   2   3   4   5
    able to be around.

12. Information received from subordinates is   1   2   3   4   5
    perceived by supervisors as important
    enough to be acted upon until demonstrated
    otherwise.

	False				True

13. Your organization has a good system for evaluating your performance.　　1　2　3　4　5

14. Your supervisor lets you know where you stand.　　1　2　3　4　5

15. All personnel receive information that enhances their abilities to coordinate their work within the organization.　　1　2　3　4　5

16. Your organization pays you well for the work you do.　　1　2　3　4　5

17. Your organization provides adequate coffee and rest breaks.　　1　2　3　4　5

18. A general atmosphere of candor and frankness seems to pervade relationships between personnel through all levels of the organization.　　1　2　3　4　5

19. Your working conditions are as good as your organization could possibly provide.　　1　2　3　4　5

20. Your organization provides you with every opportunity to gain a sense of accomplishment in your work.　　1　2　3　4　5

21. There are avenues of communication available for all personnel to consult with management levels above their own.　　1　2　3　4　5

22. Your organization provides you with plenty of freedom to work on your own and not be closely supervised.　　1　2　3　4　5

23. Your chance for promotion is excellent if you do your best work.　　1　2　3　4　5

24. All personnel are able to say "what's on their minds" regardless of whether they are talking to subordinates or supervisors.　　1　2　3　4　5

	False				True

25. Your organization provides you with every opportunity to turn out quality work.

    1 2 3 4 5

26. Your organization promotes qualified individuals on a regular basis.

    1 2 3 4 5

27. Except for necessary security information, all personnel have relatively easy access to information that relates directly to their immediate jobs.

    1 2 3 4 5

28. Your co-workers get along well with one another.

    1 2 3 4 5

29. A high concern for the well-being of all personnel is as important to management as high performance goals.

    1 2 3 4 5

30. Your fellow workers are supportive of one another and do their best to help one another.

    1 2 3 4 5

31. Supervisors at all levels in the company listen continuously and with open minds to suggestions or reports of problems made by personnel at all subordinate levels in the organization.

    1 2 3 4 5

32. Your work is interesting and it provides you with a challenge.

    1 2 3 4 5

33. The communications sent out by the company help you identify with and feel a vital part of the company.

    1 2 3 4 5

34. Company publications are interesting and helpful.

    1 2 3 4 5

35. Written directives and reports from the company are clear and concise.

    1 2 3 4 5

Instructions for Questions 36 through 51.

You receive information from various sources within the organization. For each source listed below, circle the number that best indicates the amount of information you are now receiving from that source.

This is the amount of
information I receive
now

Source of Information	Very Little	Little	Some	Great	Very Great
36. Your immediate supervisor	1	2	3	4	5
37. Co-workers/colleagues in your own unit	1	2	3	4	5
38. The "grapevine"	1	2	3	4	5
39. The manager of your immediate supervisor	1	2	3	4	5
40. Top management (executive management team)	1	2	3	4	5
41. Subordinates (if applicable)	1	2	3	4	5
42. Written communications (newsletters, memos, etc.)	1	2	3	4	5
43. Electronic communications (mail, video, telephone, etc.)	1	2	3	4	5

Now, circle the number that best indicates the amount of information you want to receive from that source.

This is the amount of information I want to receive

Source of Information	Very Little	Little	Some	Great	Very Great
44. Your immediate supervisor	1	2	3	4	5
45. Co-workers/colleagues in your own unit	1	2	3	4	5
46. The "grapevine"	1	2	3	4	5
47. The manager of your immediate supervisor	1	2	3	4	5
48. Top management (executive management team)	1	2	3	4	5
49. Subordinates (if applicable)	1	2	3	4	5
50. Written communications (newsletters, memos, etc.)	1	2	3	4	5
51. Electronic communications (mail, video, telephone, etc.)	1	2	3	4	5

Prior to receiving this questionnaire, what did you know about the information in the box below?

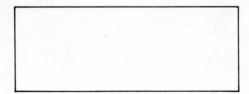

52. Please check one: 1. _____ I knew nothing about it

                          2. _____ I knew something about it

If your answer to item 52 was "I knew nothing about it," you have completed this portion of the questionnaire. Proceed to question number 60.

If your answer to item 52 was "I knew something about it," then read the following message and circle the number following item 53 closest to the approximate number of information items you knew prior to reading the message.

MESSAGE

53.	1	2	3	4	5
	0-2	3-4	5-6	7-8	9-10

By what method did you receive the information in the message? Circle True (T) if you received the information by the method indicated. Circle False (F) if you did not.

54. T   F   Memo

55. T   F   Notice on bulletin board

56. T   F   Personal letter

57. T   F   Immediate supervisor

58. T   F   Talking over the telephone

59. T   F   Attending an organized group meeting or
                           conference

60. Now if you would like, in the space provided below, state how
     you really feel about your organization. (Use 25 words or less.)

YOU ARE FINISHED!
THANK YOU VERY MUCH!

AUTHOR INDEX

SUBJECT INDEX